Waterford Whispers News

NEWSAGEDDON

Gill Books

Gill Books
Hume Avenue
Park West
Dublin 12
www.gillbooks.ie

Gill Books is an imprint of M.H. Gill & Co.

978 07171 7950 3

Copy-edited by Jennifer Armstrong
Proofread by Ruth Mahony
Designed by seagulls.net
Illustrations by Rory Thompson
Printed by BZ Graf, Poland

Waterford Whispers News is a satirical newspaper and comedy website published
by Waterford Whispers News. Waterford Whispers News uses invented names in
all the stories in this book, except in cases when public figures are being satirised.
Any other use of real names is accidental and coincidental.

For permission to reproduce photographs, the author and publisher gratefully
acknowledge the following:

© Alamy: 8, 26, 35B, 146, 156; © Getty Images: 12T, 89; © iStock: 5, 8, 11, 12B,
13, 17, 19, 20, 21, 24, 27, 29, 30, 31, 33, 34, 35T, 36, 37, 38, 39, 40, 41, 42, 43, 44,
45, 46, 49, 50, 51, 53, 56, 61, 62, 67, 69, 70, 74, 77, 78, 79, 80, 85, 87, 90, 98, 99,
102B, 103, 104, 105T, 106B, 107, 108, 109, 110, 111, 112, 113, 115, 116, 117T, 117B,
118, 119T, 120, 121, 122, 123, 124, 125, 126, 127, 128, 129, 130, 131, 132, 133, 135,
136, 137, 138, 140, 141, 142, 147, 148, 149, 151, 155, 157, 158, 162, 167, 169; ©
Shutterstock: 5, 7, 23, 28, 50, 63, 64, 68, 70, 71, 73, 81, 84, 86, 89, 93, 95, 96, 102T,
105B, 106T, 119B, 139, 144, 150, 152, 154, 156, 160, 165, 166.

The author and publisher have made every effort to trace all copyright holders,
but if any have been inadvertently overlooked we would be pleased to make the
necessary arrangement at the first opportunity.

This book is typeset in Georgia.

The paper used in this book comes from the wood pulp of managed forests. For
every tree felled, at least one tree is planted, thereby renewing natural resources.

A CIP catalogue record for this book is available from the British Library.

5 4 3 2 1

I would like to thank my co-writers Karl Moylan and Gerry McBride for all their hard work, and also our cartoonist Rory Thompson for his beautiful artwork and book cover. Thanks to Alan McCabe on drums. Ally Grace on bass. And a big massive huge thank you to our readers for sharing our content online and making us laugh uncontrollably at yer brilliant comments. Love, peace and respect, y'all.

About the Author

Colm Williamson created *Waterford Whispers News* in 2009 when he was unemployed. Though it began as a hobby, with Colm sharing stories with family and friends, his unique brand of topical, distinctly Irish satire quickly attracted thousands of fans. Now, *Waterford Whispers News* has over 570,000 Facebook followers, and an average of two million page views on the website every month. Colm runs *Waterford Whispers News* from his home town of Tramore in Co. Waterford.

CONTENTS

How to own, operate and read this book

Due to some obscure EU health and safety law (thank you, EU bastards) all books must now include a health and safety guide outlining the proper procedures when it comes to owning, operating and reading a book.

If you do almost all your reading on your phone, i.e. perusing the text above and below memes, *Waterford Whispers News* (*WWN*) understands that coming into possession of a book may be a troubling and confusing experience for you. The following advice will help you.

CAREFUL! Each page in this book could be used as a deadly weapon in the right AND wrong hands. The edges of pages are notoriously sharp and can result in things called 'paper cuts'. If a paper cut was to slit one of your body's main arteries you could bleed out in seconds. This outcome would invite embarrassment onto your family, who would be forced to deny that you died in such idiotic circumstances and to offer some far less shameful explanation, such as you tried to hump the family dog and then joined Fianna Fáil.

CAREFUL! When turning the pages of this book, please ensure you are seated in a chair in an upright position with both feet planted firmly on the ground. If you are currently in a car or on a boat, train or plane, we must advise against attempting to operate this book.

CAREFUL! Intense and repeated swiping or scrolling motions will not work. Books are different from smartphones. We won't tell you again.

CAREFUL! This book contains words that have been assembled in a certain order to form sentences, which may in turn cause smiling, scowling, laughter, tears or diarrhoea. *WWN* is not liable for any damage caused to your underwear, or your couch if you are a particularly aggressive sharter.

CAREFUL! Attempts to tag your friends or family in the pages of this book will prove futile. Instead, try shouting at the person directly, and encourage them to use their eyes to look at the page of interest. You can even point at it directly with your finger. Alternatively, you can read a passage aloud to someone. Due to Liam Neeson being a stingy, money-grabbing bastard, he was unable to narrate the audio book for free. However, our legal team inform us that there is nothing to stop you imitating his voice when reading this book.

If you still don't feel confident and ready to proceed to the remaining pages, read back over the instructions above and take a deep breath. You'll be fine.

'You're fucking welcome,' Europe tells Ireland after €13bn Apple tax ruling

EUROPEAN Commissioner for Competition Margrethe Vestager, who investigated Apple's European tax affairs, has insisted that the vast majority of the company's €13 billion in unpaid tax is due to Ireland, telling the Oireachtas Finance Committee, 'You're fucking welcome.'

Vestager told the hearing it would be up to Ireland as a member state to 'stop dragging its heels and to grow a pair of fucking balls' when dealing with multinationals.

Clearly exasperated, she asked, 'You mad cunts were broke nine years ago, begging for money you were, and now you're turning your nose up at €13 billion, why?'

Met with silence and several shrugs from the Oireachtas Finance Committee, Vestager proceeded to write out the amount on a piece of paper, before aggressively holding it up and shouting, 'See all those zeros? It's enough to get every citizen in this country pissed for three days.'

Finally getting a reaction, one committee member asked exactly how many pints per citizen would the tax-back amount to, and if she could also include 'fags' and 'rollie tobacco' in the equation.

'Seriously, what in the actual fuck is wrong with you?' she replied, gathering up her things in disgust, before concluding. 'You people need to get your priorities straight. It's like you don't want the money or something. Just take it and don't spend it on silly things.'

The EU Commission originally decided to investigate Apple after the multinational told the US Senate it had a 'Paddy tax arrangement' with Ireland, with an inquiry later finding that Apple paid just €50 tax on every €1 million of profit accrued.

BREXIT LATEST

Government's Brexit plan consists of lighting a candle in nearest church

ALLAYING any fears the Irish public may have had about the country's preparedness for the various potential pitfalls relating to Britain's exit from the EU, the government has committed to finding the nearest church to light a candle in.

'We have nothing to fear but fear itself and the possibility that the country will be economically obliterated by the Brits pressing self-destruct,' Taoiseach Enda Kenny told the Dáil yesterday, while appearing to soil himself.

'To anyone worried about Ireland, may I just say, we'll be grand,' the Taoiseach said as he proudly showed the chamber the match he would use to light the candle in the church, which is yet to be picked out. Seeking to reassure the public further, he added, 'We haven't ruled out lighting two candles.'

To ensure the government's plan could be enacted in a forthright, frugal and time-saving manner, a committee comprising 10 TDs will be set up in the coming weeks to decide on the church to light a candle in. Once the venue has been determined, opposition parties are expected to demand an inquiry into what took the committee so long, further delaying the lighting of the candle. The process is expected to cost the taxpayer €40 million.

'I don't know if anyone else has thrown their hat in the ring yet, but I'd love to be the one to light the candle,' Leo Varadkar revealed to reporters outside Leinster House, who were seen running away from the Fine Gael TD.

News that the government has decided to take decisive action on the issue of Brexit has been welcomed by members of the public.

'It's reassuring that in response to Theresa May's vague shite-talk, we Irish have been able to match Britain on that front, maybe even eclipse them in the whole we've-no-fucking-clue-what-we're-doing department,' shared relieved Waterford man Colm Ganney.

EDUCATION NEWS

'We're still the bestest at learning good' – Irish universities hit back at fall in rankings

IRISH third-level institutions have responded to the news of their continued slide down the QS World University Rankings with a passionate defence of their institutions.

Despite consistently pleading with the government to invest more funding in a sector ravaged by cuts, many leading educators remained defiant and countered the latest rankings.

'Ireland good. Education good. Ireland education good,' explained one leading university figure.

'Lots of cuts. Bad government. No more lots of staff, now lots more students try learn,' read another statement from a senior member of Trinity College, Dublin, written in crayons.

The government has said it will carefully consider the pleas to invest in the future education of Ireland's young adults before rejecting such requests.

One university to buck the downward trend is NUI Galway. It has since reassured everyone that the university will remain humble about the news and refuses to lord it over the other universities from here until the end of time like many would have expected it to.

'I've always been an admirer of Donald Trump' – Taoiseach

TAOISEACH Enda Kenny congratulated US President-elect Donald Trump, after he beat Democratic opponent Hillary Clinton in a dramatic election count result this morning.

Mr Kenny said the people of the United States have made a very clear choice and that he always knew Trump would win the presidency, stating he looks forward to meeting him soon.

'I've always been an admirer of Donald Trump,' Kenny opened up, scratching his nose. 'He's such a lovely man and a deserving president. I was rooting for him from the very beginning of this campaign, and I hope to meet him and his beautiful wife very soon.'

However, sources in Leinster House confirmed that an emergency government meeting was called early this morning in a bid to decide who should go to the US for St Patrick's Day 2017.

'The Taoiseach requested a box of straws and a scissors,' one insider said. 'I think Leo Varadkar picked the short straw and may be the one who has to meet Mr Trump with a bowl of shamrock in the White House next year.'

Asked if he regretted his comments about Trump being 'racist and sexist' earlier this year, Kenny claimed he was only messing at the time and just poking fun at the future president of the United States.

'Donald will know I was only blaggarding with him,' Kenny stated. 'We're always messing and joking like that in politics. I look forward to playing a round of golf with him at his place in County Clare, but I'm more concerned about making the Irish recovery great again.'

Did you know?

A worrying 0.0001% of the Irish population remain unaware of the 1916 Rising.

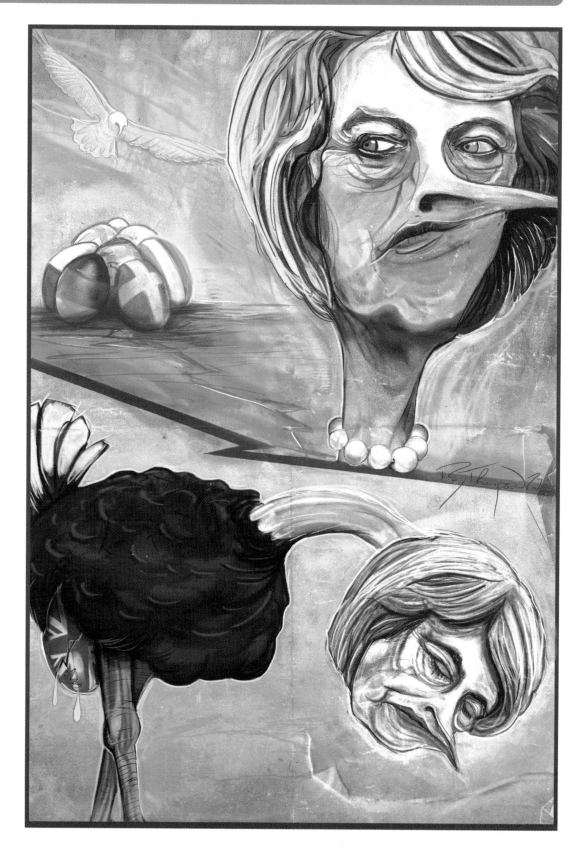

BREXIT LATEST

'Good fucking riddance': EU welcomes May speech

THE European Union has welcomed today's speech by Theresa May, stating it was happy the British prime minister had finally got her finger out.

President of the European Commission Jean-Claude Juncker congratulated Mrs May for her lengthy speech, which outlined 12 priorities for negotiations with the EU and confirmed her government's intention to leave the European single market.

'To be honest, I wasn't really listening to it, I'm just happy Britain has started making shapes,' Juncker stated. 'Good fucking riddance to them.'

The long-awaited speech was the highlight of Britain's news today, with every other EU member nation looking on in jest at the country's own self-importance and inability to care about any other nation – only themselves.

Leading EU figures denied they were jealous or apprehensive at Britain's ability to form new trade agreements with leading economic powers such as China and the US, adding that bitterness just wasn't a factor going forward.

'You'd swear they came up with the idea of a European Union, the way they're spouting on,' Juncker later commented. 'They didn't even use our currency, and were always moaning like spoiled little shits. I'll give her silly plans a read later in the year, whenever I get time. For the moment, I've got a union to run.'

The media's sharp focus on May's address and the possible ramifications for negotiations with the EU is expected to end once Donald Trump tweets about his dislike of 'animals with long, untrustworthy necks'.

COYBIG! Ireland voted sixth best tax haven in the world

IRISH eyes were indeed smiling at the weekend, following the news that this little country is now the sixth best place in the world for corporations to set up shop and pay fuck-all tax while doing so.

'COYBIG' (an acronym for 'Come On You Boys in Green') trended on Twitter following the release of a survey by Oxfam that listed the countries with the best track record for corporate tax chicanery. Ireland came just behind Switzerland, Singapore, Cayman Islands, Netherlands and Bermuda.

'The name on the survey is "worst" tax havens ... but surely if we're in the top 10 that makes it the *best* tax havens, no?' argued one delighted man spotted running up and down O'Connell Street with a tricolour bearing the words 'You'll never beat the Irish' draped over his shoulders.

'Either way, it just goes to show how Ireland is the fucking best little country in the world. There's nothing we can't do: rugby, soccer, boxing, UFC, letting huge multinational corporations ride us rotten ... we're just the best.'

Although the mood of the nation was upbeat, several members of government have admitted that they had hoped to be placed higher than sixth on the list. In a bid to top next year's poll, they are already putting in place a series of sweeteners and loopholes to allow companies to pay even less tax.

'Fuck back to Malta and stop annoying us,' High Court tells O'Brien

BUSINESSMAN Denis O'Brien has been told by the High Court to 'fuck back to Malta' after losing his action over statements made in the Dáil about his banking affairs, WWN can confirm.

Ms Justice Ursula Rafferty today dismissed the businessman's action, stating that Dáil utterances are protected from judicial condemnation and court interference, and telling O'Brien to stop annoying the court every time his feelings get hurt.

'Denis, we could name a courtroom after you at this stage,' Justice Rafferty began, referring to the dozens of litigation cases brought forward by the Maltese citizen. 'I feel it's time to just give it to you straight, Denny, cause it doesn't seem to be registering in that thick skull of yours. Please, fuck back to Malta for yourself and stop annoying us.'

Her comments were greeted with ecstatic applause from the hoard of attending press, barristers and lawyers.

'I think I can speak for everyone here when I say that we're absolutely sick of the fucking sight of you, trying to defend "your good name",' she continued, using

air quotes and rolling her eyes. 'Seriously, are you not getting it yet? There's no defending that shit anymore. How about you stop suing people if you're so precious about how you're being perceived by them? Best thing you could do now is fly back to your little tax haven and ignore what people say about you back in Ireland. Go on, off with you now,' she shooed.

With that, the packed courtroom stood up and cheered as the disgraced O'Brien sheepishly left the courtroom, with Justice Rafferty demanding, 'And take your slimy legal team with you!'

Central Bank donated to Irish Museum of Fuck-Ups

A generous anonymous donor has gifted the Central Bank building to the Irish Museum of Fuck-Ups after meeting the €60 million plus valuation placed on the Temple Bar premises.

'Disastrous changes to financial regulation in the early 2000s, spearheaded by then Taoiseach Bertie Ahern, followed by the subsequent collapse of Irish banks, makes the soon-to-be-former location of the

Central Bank the ideal exhibit for any fuck-up museum,' the anonymous donor wrote in a letter to the museum.

'I have no idea where we'll put it, we ran out of room ages ago,' Martin Cally, Head Curator of the Irish Museum of Fuck-Ups, told WWN.

'Suppose if we take the redress scheme for the survivors of the Magdalene Laundries off the wall and put it by the tribunal

of inquiry into the Kerry Babies case, it might just fit,' a visibly overworked Cally added, surveying some of the 2,450 rooms in the museum.

Cally and his team exhibited the €2.65 million in rent the Central Bank pays to a US property vulture fund that in turn pays no tax in Ireland as a part of a fuck-up retrospective earlier this year.

'Fuck it, we'll just have to build a whole new wing for the Central Bank,' Cally concluded, pulling clumps of his hair from his head. 'This museum just keeps on expanding.'

Empty Dáil session on Tuam babies probably not symbolic of anything

THE public has been told not to read anything into the fact that Minister for Children Katherine Zappone delivered remarks on the Commission of Investigation's discovery of human remains in Tuam to an empty Dáil this morning. Experts were quick to confirm that it was not symbolic of an insidious malaise that periodically sets into Irish society, thus creating the perfect circumstances for scandals to excel and flourish.

Those knowledgeable on political discourse and Irish history admitted that while there was a temptation to see this morning's discussion as symbolic of a sometimes malignant apathy at the heart of Irish society, it simply isn't true.

'The leader of the opposition isn't there because he's at some talk on Brexit, but who knows where the government is? However, it would be wrong to suggest that an empty Dáil is like some metaphorical emptiness and apathy we all possess once speeches are made, fists are shaken and the cameras turn away,' explained Ireland expert John Gobbin.

'Now, I know you might be thinking that the fact no one turned up to talk about it sure says a lot about Ireland, but you'd be very wrong,' added Gobbin. 'It was just an average day in the Dáil and in no way a visual representation of our collective failure as a nation and a society. That's just the sort of talk from people who want us to feel guilty about everything that happens that our society is in some way complicit in.'

The small collection of TDs amongst the empty seats of a chamber that in recent years heard testimony of how shocked everyone was by child abuse carried out by Catholic priests, once again filled the room with orations that sounded suitably shocked and heartbroken; however, it would be inappropriate to suggest it is symbolic in any way.

'Ah come off it, TDs' jobs aren't only about turning up to the Dáil to be seen, they're in Oireachtas committee meetings most of the day. What, do you want the country to drop what it's doing and prioritise getting to the bottom of the horrors carried out in mother and baby homes across the country? Eh, heard of a little thing called the recovery? It doesn't keep itself going, you know. We've got to get our priorities straight, we can't do both,' added someone you wouldn't want to be friends with.

Denis O'Brien announces bid for Irish presidency

MEDIA mogul and multibillionaire Denis O'Brien has today announced his bid for the Irish presidency.

Following in the footsteps of American businessman and peer Donald Trump, O'Brien stated he will begin campaigning early next year in what is expected to be the hottest Irish presidential election since the foundation of the state.

'I'm really looking forward to making Ireland okay again,' he said, wearing a baseball hat with the same phrasing. 'I'm going to build a wall around my financial affairs – made from solicitors. Believe me, this wall will be impervious to public scrutiny. It will be great. Okay?'

The Taoiseach was the first to offer his support to the Cork man, who currently resides in Malta because it's nice and warm there (and for no other reason), stating O'Brien will be a perfect contender to represent Ireland's current climate.

'He's a lovely man, Denis, and he will make a great president if elected,' the Taoiseach said with his mouth. 'Sure, he's basically representing the country already with his large stake in the Irish media. It would only make sense that someone with such an influence would put himself forward for such a position.'

O'Brien has said that his first act in office will be to abolish the current government and centralise power to the office of the president. While there has been no confirmation on other measures, it is believed he would also cancel bank holiday weekends.

'DO you know why we pulled you over there?' asked the people of Ireland, addressing a very sheepish and uncomfortable-looking garda force early this morning at a checkpoint.

Very aware of the fact that there was a multitude of reasons as to why they were being questioned, but not wanting to give too much away, the approximately 12,000 or so gardaí risked a timid 'Brake light?' answer, before they were asked to move to the safety of the hard shoulder and step out of their vehicle.

'We're kind of against it, time-wise this morning,' stuttered every guard in Ireland, from Commissioner Nóirín O'Sullivan right down to rank-and-file traffic cops. 'If you want to just stick a fine in the post there, or get us to

Entire Garda Síochána force told to pull into the side of the road there

call into the station tomorrow, but we have to …'

The gardaí, sweating now, were hushed by a single raised hand from the people of Ireland, and told again, in a sterner tone this time, to pull over into the hard shoulder there.

Nervously, each and every member of An Garda Síochána moved over to the side of the road, wondering just how much trouble they were in. Was it the penalty points thing? Was it about

the way whistle-blowers' lives are destroyed after they voiced concerns about corruption?

'Oh fuck,' said one guard in the back seat. 'Is it the way we've been just entering whatever figure we felt like into the breathalyser statistics?'

'Or is it how we sorta magically appear in force anytime a government interest is being protested against, while simultaneously being "short of numbers" when it comes to tackling

TRENDING This disgusting piece of shit can't remember where he was when 9/11 happened

9/11 was very bad. On that everyone can agree. But we never thought we'd hear ourselves saying there was something worse than westerners losing their lives until we heard about this horrible excuse of a human being who doesn't even remember where he was or what he was doing when it happened. The prick.

We here at *WWN Politics* pride ourselves on never, ever taking a stand on an issue, be it trivial or serious, until such a time as we can see that enough people online are thinking a certain way about things and it's safe to cash in without damaging our

brand. At that point, we write up a quick article that says something like 'a lot of people are starting to feel this way' or 'we don't agree with X celebrity here'.

This strategy means we don't take the risk of having a genuine opinion that might adversely affect our ad revenue. Content is king of course, by which we mean we'll do anything for money and don't actually care about content at all. Plus, the three of us on the writing staff don't want to make life hard for the 179 sales people we employ here at *WWN Politics* – we're not monsters.

Anyway, we've reached the point with this 9/11 story now because loads of people have been giving out about this guy, this piece of shit, Andrew Stanning. Judging by his face he looks like a normal guy, but that was until we found out that this shitebag can't remember where he was when terrorists flew into the Twin Towers. No, seriously, we're not making it up. It's almost like he wants the terrorists to win.

'Ah yeah, dunno where I was actually, long time ago when you think about it, which is mad,' explained the obviously pro-ISIS Dubliner in a private Facebook Messenger conversation with the drugs and crime ravaging towns and cities?' suggested another.

The guards watched as the nation of Ireland walked methodically around them saying nothing but taking notes in a small black jotter.

'Is it that we're pricks?' asked one garda sergeant, head in hands. 'We're pricks and bullies and self-serving arrogant bastards. I'm telling you, we were grand all the way up the road until we just got too fucking smart, that's when they pulled us over. Nóirín, what'll we do? Ah Jesus, Nóirín, they're at the window, what are you going to tell them?'

Sitting in the driver seat, the beleaguered commissioner snapped at her passengers, 'Would youse shut up for a minute? I'm trying to think.'

The public rapped on the driver's window with one knuckle and made a wind-down motion.

'Ah, how're ye, Irish public?' asked O'Sullivan, winding down the window and trying to decide what the fuck she was going to say next.

'Listen, is it about the scandals? Yeah, look, I know they're piling up at the minute, but I swear I'm going to get them sorted at the weekend. If you want, I can get them done straight away. I've just been up against it lately, sure you know yourself, ha ha ha ha.'

Not buying it for a second, the public repeated itself again, slowly, 'Get. Out. Of. The vehicle.'

Calmly and without hesitation, O'Sullivan floored the boot and tore away from the hard shoulder

with the entire garda force in the back seat screaming at her, 'What the fuck are you at Nóirín?'

'They're after us now! We could have talked our way out of it, like we always do! What have you done?' asked one experienced garda.

'Shut up, shut up, shut up,' said O'Sullivan, glancing periodically in the rear-view mirror as the public closed in on her and her organisation. 'Shut up, shut up, shut up, shut up, shut up, shut up, shut up, shut up, shut up, shut up.'

TOP 5
Politicians in Ireland 2017

As has been the case since we started compiling lists in 1931, this list remains blank due to a lack of suitable candidates.

a friend, which was shared with us after it was screengrabbed. We reproduce it here without his permission because the world deserves to know what a piece of shit he is. We're still working on finding out where he works so we can pressure his employer into firing him.

Stanning (20) probably thinks it's gas craic altogether that Ground Zero is a thing. It speaks to what a piece of shit the young man is, that he is unable to reach back and perfectly recall an event that happened when he was three years of age.

While we don't condone shaming people on the Internet, unless our marketing people say it would be good for business, *WWN Politics* thinks it wouldn't be a bad

thing if someone flew a plane into his face. See how much he likes it.

EDITOR'S NOTE: Check back later when our exclusive 'People need to stop giving Andrew a hard time, this is everything that is wrong with the Internet' goes online.

Wonderful World of Science

Groundbreaking research suggests white people can also be terrorists.

How Ireland would look under Shania law

REGARDLESS of our stance on immigration, refugees and a multicultural society ... the vast majority of people in Ireland are on the same page when it comes to Shania law: we are not in favour of it.

Considered a barbaric, outdated system of social order, Shania law has been banned in most western countries, and with good cause. Here are some of the terrifying, unthinkable things that could become a reality in Ireland should Shania law be implemented.

Gender confusion

We're living in an unprecedented age for non-cis people, with gender divides finally being addressed in a bid to bring happiness to all. Shania law would place all this is in jeopardy. Men who feel like women will start to feel like men, and women who feel like women might feel like men. Where does the madness end?

Lack of enthusiasm

Activities and emotions that would have brought you joy before will be removed under Shania law, replaced by a general sense of meh. You could watch someone ramp their car over 13 burning buses and land perfectly on the other side, and it still wouldn't impress you much.

No divorce

When you get married under Shania law, you get married for life. It doesn't matter if you and your partner get sick of each other after 10 years, they're still the one. You want a divorce? Not under Shania law. There are no concessions to any non-religious doctrine. There's Shania law, and secular law, and never the twain shall meet.

12 MONTHS A GUARD *Month 1*

Well, I'm finally here! It's where I've always wanted to be since I was just a little boy: training to be a guard. I made sure to work very hard in the last few weeks so that I am in peak physical condition; gotta make sure that I pass those fitness tests! Although, to be honest, some of the other folk in my class don't seem to have, eh, put in quite as much work as I have. Still, my 500 fellow recruits are all delighted to be here! That 500 number was one that was read out by the senior guard who welcomed us, but by my count, there's like 60 of us or so. I think they have to say 500 new guards for PR reasons. We all got our uniforms earlier today. Well, when I say we all did, due to cutbacks we actually have to share one uniform between every three recruits. Plus we don't get a Copper's gold card each, which is a shame. Ah well! Off to my first class, 'How to walk'. Can't wait!

Heron problem in Dublin needs to be addressed now, says government

THE government is to assemble a task force aimed at dealing with the ever-increasing heron problem across Ireland, particularly in inner-city areas.

In Dublin in particular, the slim, long-beaked birds have become ever-present along canals and even on the city's streets, with many of them getting in the way of people who want to inject themselves with class-A drugs.

The new section of An Garda Síochána will be tasked with tackling both herons and the source of herons, with many calling for the problem to be addressed at the root rather than targeting it on a bird-by-bird basis.

'You've got herons coming into the country, with nobody even trying to stop them,' said one anti-heron campaigner *WWN* spoke with.

'Our main fear is that the cops are just going to move herons from one area to the next, without solving anything. Sure, move the herons away from Portobello, move them on to the Royal Canal, move them on to Talbot Street. Get them away from so-called decent areas, that's all that counts. Don't do anything that might actually make a difference. This has been going on for years, sticking a band-aid on a broken beak.'

Meanwhile the HSE has admitted that large numbers of people attending A&E have heron-related illnesses and injuries, adding that 'neither the money nor the political will' exists to do anything to change this.

TRANSPORT NEWS

Government tells culchies to move to Dublin if they want decent public transport

THE government has recommended moving to Dublin for any culchie with an interest in public transport and getting from A to B, amid fears Bus Éireann could become insolvent.

'Regardless of whether or not Bus Éireann folds, if you want to get somewhere on public transport, living in Dublin is a sure-fire way to do so,' Minister for Transport Shane Ross explained to the country's culchie population. The minister then repeated his words a second time, only much more slowly, in order to ensure that everyone understood.

Public transport, usually associated with providing the public with a variety of options and ways to get to certain locations without putting profit at the forefront of its concerns, differs in Ireland to other nations in that successive governments have pledged to make all services 'a pain in the bollocks'.

'If you want timely and affordable transport, or even a bus that passes through the town three or four times a year, you should move to Dublin, lads,' added the minister, regaling reporters with the tale of the time he used a bus once.

Incurring losses of €8 million in 2016 due to increased competition on busier routes, Bus Éireann confirmed it was contemplating switching to 'Dublin only services'.

'Given the choice, who'd want to live outside Dublin, in fairness?' said a spokesperson for Bus Éireann Dublin Only. The government confirmed that any culchies complaining only have themselves to blame for living outside Dublin.

Hooded Fianna Fáil members meet to discuss best time to seize power again

BENEATH the foundations of a building in an undisclosed location in Dublin's city centre, members of Fianna Fáil gathered together in robes to determine the perfect time to retake power in Ireland, *WWN* has learned.

'The children's hospital budget looks to be spiralling out of control, maybe we could piggyback on that and pretend we care,' one figure whose face was obscured by a hood offered, causing faint murmurs of discussion to ripple through the room.

'Yes, I agree, and we can pretend Dear Leader didn't set up the HSE, and that he now has all the answers. We just need the souls of five or six more independent TDs and power will be ours,' another figure added, bellowing from a dark corner before cackling with unconfined delight.

A number of members of Ireland's largest opposition party then stepped forward, brandishing knives. Raising their right hands in unison, they used the knives to cut into their flesh, allowing their blood to leak into a chalice.

Turning to face a large portrait of a brown envelope, the cloaked figures began chanting, 'We give you this offering so that you may return, we give you this offering so that we can earn.'

'Eh, well, would there, eh, em, be room for eh, another return of eh, someone, eh, else?' another figure, caged up in the corner asked the chanting masses, but received no reply.

The room returned to silence when a man entered carrying a lengthy scroll.

'Fuck sake, lads, not even 30% in the latest poll, we'll have to wait a while yet,' the man shared to groans of disappointment.

EXCLUSIVE REPORT

Gerry Adams smuggles Armagh across the border while no one's looking

AS Ireland, Northern Ireland and Britain continue to be distracted by Brexit and negotiations to form a new Stormont Assembly, it is believed that Sinn Féin leader Gerry Adams has smuggled the county of Armagh south of the border under the cover of darkness.

Placing the 1,326 km² county under a loose-fitting jumper and taking the back roads, it is alleged Adams drove south to his County Louth home, making use of Ireland and Northern Ireland's soft border while it is still in place.

'We can confirm that the alarm was raised by a member of the public after they spotted Slieve Gullion poking out of a car driven by a bearded man in his 60s at approximately 3 a.m. this morning,' the PSNI and An Garda Síochána said in a rare joint statement.

'Brexit, the negotiations, International Women's Day, the run up to Paddy's Day, Tuam, that Barcelona match, we all got a little distracted ... really, we should have seen this situation coming,' the police forces added.

Serious questions will be asked of forces monitoring the border as they failed to spot the roughly 175,000 population of Armagh in transit under Adams's jumper, believed to be XXXXL in size. While it is not yet clear if Adams plans on smuggling more counties south in the future, Unionists have attached large bike locks to Fermanagh, Down, Antrim, Tyrone and Derry just to be safe. Searches for Armagh in a number of abandoned industrial estates south of the border have failed to result in any leads.

Elsewhere, British Prime Minister Theresa May has not ruled out placing Northern Ireland on eBay in search of the best possible price in the event of a stalemate in the Assembly negotiations.

Inquiries into gardaí now outnumber actual guards

WITH the launch of yet another investigation, inquiry, commission of investigation, investigative commission of inquiry or the investigative commission into various actions of members of An Garda Síochána, *WWN* can confirm that inquiries into the gardaí now dwarf the number of guards on the streets.

The inquiry has been instigated by Minister Frances Fitzgerald and will seek to ascertain whether or not garda whistle-blowers were subjected to unfair punishment and intimidation. It brings the number of external investigations into the gardaí to over 13,000, eclipsing the number of current gardaí, which stands at 12,850.

'The cost isn't important here, what is important is ensuring whistle-blowers are heard and the intimidation of them ceases,' a solicitor with responsibility for dragging out the length of the inquiry for as long as possible confirmed to *WWN*.

Commending herself for her decision, Minister Fitzgerald said, 'This government is committed to reacting to things after the horse has bolted, paying through the nose for it and ultimately learning nothing, as is a government's duty.'

While many have welcomed the inquiry as it represents a very public backing of current and future whistle-blowers in the force, others have praised it for its ability to earn them money.

'I'm charging by the hour here, this is going to be great. If we fuck it up and have to have an inquiry into the inquiry even better, but let's not get ahead of ourselves,' suggested one retired judge who is hoping to get the nod to head up the inquiry.

The government denied it had any more money for new gardaí, new training, new equipment or the reopening of garda stations, but admitted that an unlimited cap on the cost of inquiries into why it had no money allotted to these things was in place.

> **Did you know?**
> 100% of politicians have evolved to the point of requiring no back bone. Fascinating.

EXCLUSIVE REPORT

Calls for Taoiseach to 'take out Trump' on St Patrick's Day visit

RENEWED calls have been made for Taoiseach Enda Kenny to 'take out Donald Trump' while presenting the American president with a bowl of shamrock on St Patrick's Day 2017 at the White House, *WWN* can confirm.

Kenny is facing increasing pressure to assassinate Trump by any means necessary on 17 March. He has been told that, in taking such an action, he would become an international hero and the soundest Taoiseach that ever lived.

'The Secret Service wouldn't think of searching him and he could easily strap on one of those suicide vests handy enough,' one supporter of the assassination plot suggested. 'Or pack in some Semtex underneath the shamrock and Bob's your uncle. It's the least he could do. Now that he's stepping down as Taoiseach, he may as well go out with a bang.'

Republican pyrotechnic experts confirmed that as much as four pounds of C-4 explosives could be hidden in the shamrock bowl, enough to take out Kenny and Vice-President Pence as well and perhaps several other members of Trump's administration, if detonated at the right time.

'Kenny's martyrdom would go down in history as one of the bravest decisions any politician ever made,' another man told *WWN*. 'Sure what age is he now, mid-sixties? What has he to look forward to being an ex-Taoiseach? Join a few boards as a money-grabbing director, give an auld talk for silly money here and there? That's all okay but this plan would make him a global hero and he should definitely consider it.'

In response to the radical requests, Kenny confirmed that he will take out Trump: 'Of course I'll take him out, it's important for Irish businesses and the economy to wine, dine and lick the president's arse, which I hear he's into, by the way.'

Irish property prices set to increase by 30% by end of this headline

THE latest news emanating from the Irish property market suggests that due to a shortage of available houses, prices will have been driven up by as much as 30% in the time it took you to read this article's headline.

The government, prospective home owners and homeless charities all expressed their concern but declined to comment on the record for fear that any lengthening of this article could see further price increases.

'I mean, depending on how long I ramble on about current market factors and confidence in the market, or some shite like that, prices could be rising another 50 to 60%, and I could probably rip you off a bit more,'

explained local estate agent John Healy.

With increased demand for housing increasing and the lack of supply in the country by no means lacking, supply and demand may still be mentioned at least every three seconds by vested interest groups involved in the property sector, Healy suggested.

'Look, I just figured the longer this article goes on, the greater chance I have of buying

a 172-reg Audi A5,' Healy added, while simultaneously telling a local Waterford couple that they should think about offering €30,000 over the asking price, just to show they are serious about a property with a specific and clearly stated price.

Breaking the government's silence on the latest price increases, the Minister for Housing pleaded with members of the public to resist reading the above headline.

Worrying number of child refugees growing up to be adult refugees

A new report has found that a worrying number of refugees under the age of 12 are continuing to grow, with a large majority of them reaching adulthood in only a matter of years.

A staggering 99.9% of refugee children who have been processed in European countries are currently ageing at an alarming rate, raising fears as to who or what they may turn out to be when they reach 18.

In one instance in the UK, an 11-year-old Syrian orphan managed to reach puberty after being granted asylum only two years ago, despite gaining entry as an innocent child with little or no concept of religious fundamentalism, yet.

'What if these children start forming their own opinions or belief systems?' one concerned Roscommon man told *WWN*, following news that 80 such refugees are to be homed in the area. 'Yes, we were told that half of

these poor souls are children, but no one ever said anything about them growing up into adults – it's false advertising and a lot of people in Ireland now feel cheated.'

Ireland has already agreed to take in 200 additional unaccompanied children from the now disbanded refugee camp at Calais, with the majority of them expected to mature in as little as 10 years.

Minister for Justice Frances Fitzgerald was not available to comment on the matter.

Nation suspends use of 'proud to be Irish' phrase after remains found at Tuam

A long-standing turn of phrase expressing pride in the achievements of the country of Ireland and its people has been suspended indefinitely, pending a review, after the discovery of the remains of infant children in a septic tank.

The move will see people refrain from using the phrase 'proud to be Irish' to express pride following various sporting events or triumphs in the arts or business worlds.

'Yep, at the moment I don't feel like it means all that much really, does it? Might just hold off using it until the country earns the phrase,' the Irish public explained, still trying and failing to comprehend the circumstances that led to the deaths and burials of newborn babies and toddlers in a septic tank.

The Commission of Investigation into Mother and Baby Homes has confirmed that the remains of children, ranging in age from approximately 35 foetal weeks to 2–3 years old, have been found on the site of a former mother and baby home in Tuam, prompting an outpouring of grief, shame and anger, as well as significant pause for thought.

'I think it's best we park the "proud to be Irish" phrase for the foreseeable future. It doesn't really carry any weight anymore; I'm not sure it ever did now I think about it,' added the Irish public, barely able to speak, such were the horrors it was again confronted with.

It is unclear when the phrase will be reintroduced into circulation, if ever.

Elsewhere, a local church apologist confirmed he will be waiting for the full facts of the Tuam investigation before blaming the Catholic Church, while also pointing out, 'Now is not the time for point-scoring against a religious organisation that has shown itself in Ireland, time and time again, to be violent, misogynistic and sociopathic in its words and actions.'

Government agree to cull Kerry by giving them the drink-driving laws they want

IN the largest project of its kind ever undertaken by an Irish government, the cabinet has formally agreed to alter the drink-driving laws for Kerry in an effort to cull the county's population.

Unlike previous attempts to carry out similar culling projects in County Cork, the people of Kerry are 100% behind the efforts to permit them to drink as many pints as they want before driving on rural Kerry roads and onwards to certain death.

'Three pints minimum before being allowed to drive at all seems the least the government up in their big Dublin offices with their big Dublin heads could do,' Danny Healy-Rae of the Sure I Drink-Drive All The Time And I've Killed Nobody (SIDDATTAIKN) lobby group shared with *WWN*.

By allowing the people of Kerry to make up their own laws for driving home from the pub, the government hopes to reduce the population in Kerry to zero over time, thus freeing up some of the money that is normally reserved for appeasing rural TDs.

'We tried ignoring Leitrim for six or seven years, but this is the first time a controversial government policy like this has been embraced by the people it's designed to wipe out,' explained one cabinet member.

While full details of the cull have yet to be decided upon, it is thought it may involve leaving Kerry to it.

Pro-Life group not all that interested in children once they're born

A pro-life group speaking at a meeting of the Citizen's Assembly this weekend admitted to giving 'much less of a shit' about foetuses once they are born.

Citing their relative disinterest in the affairs of children who are either orphaned, in the foster care system, subjected to abuse or live in poverty once they are born, the Respectful Alliance Against Genocidal Women Who Can't Be Trusted (RAAGWWCBT) explained that when it comes to children their focus is very much on the unborn iteration.

'We have an unending capacity for compassion towards children when they are in the womb of women we frankly can't trust, but look once they're born, that's someone else's problem,' explained a RAAGWWCBT spokesperson in a calm and measured voice while holding up a sign written in her own blood which spelled out the word 'murderers'.

'I know, it's quite surprising, but honestly, I'm really not all that fussed as long as children are born; that's the important part. If they go on to suffer, that sounds like something those do gooders at Amnesty would look after,' she added.

The neglect of children in Ireland is well documented, with more and more examples of the suffering many have endured coming to light each and every day, so it is believed organisations like RAAGWWCBT will have to state their complete indifference to such things on a more regular basis.

'Ireland's adoption system, poverty, violence, deaths once out of the womb, all that stuff is just a million miles away from the issue we're most passionate about, which is other people's wombs,' added the spokesperson for RAAGWWCBT, who went on to explain that when asked about such issues in the future they would just smile their odd blank smiles until people felt uncomfortable enough to walk away.

Gerry Adams diagnosed with selective Alzheimer's

EXPERTS in neuroscience have diagnosed Sinn Féin leader Gerry Adams with a new form of Alzheimer's disease that causes the victim to lose huge chunks of memory relating to the same subject.

Although Alzheimer's patients normally experience a gradual loss of memory from across their whole life, the newly named 'Adams disease' causes the sufferer to have zero recollection about one particular topic, no matter how much experience they had with it over the years.

While Adams has endured years of being accused of hiding the truth about his involvement in the armed Republican movement, the whereabouts of 'the Disappeared' and dozens of murders committed in the name of 'a free Ireland', this new information has led many to call for Adams to be left alone due to his illness.

'The man is ill, would youse quit badgering him about the 'Ra,' said Dr Harold Jennings, who pioneered the research into the diagnosis of Adams disease.

'For years he says that he doesn't remember things like that, and for years people have called him a liar ... but this new research shows that he truly doesn't remember anything about paramilitary activity, blacked-out vans, deaths, things like that. You can ask him all you want, but it's just not in that head of his. It's pointless, like thinking a lad in a wheelchair will climb a ladder if you ask him enough times.'

Adams himself has come out and denied having Adams disease, which Dr Jennings describes as being 'classic Adams disease behaviour'.

Wonderful World of Science
There is no conclusive reason why people continue to agree to drink rounds of shots while on nights out.

Roscommon told to think of brown tap water as 'craft water'

AS 'boil water' notices remain part of everyday life for residents across a number of locations in Ireland, a number of leading figures doing nothing to solve the problem have suggested people in Roscommon just think of it as 'craft water'.

'It's probably got that strong taste too, maybe not hops, perhaps an earthy flavour? You can show off to other counties like all those craft beer pricks do,' explained a spokesperson from Irish Water, who had previously confirmed some 456 times that the problem would be solved imminently.

'You bring that into a pub now, and you can charge Dublin prices, €6, €7 and sure nobody will bat an eyelid cause ya said it was craft,' added the spokesperson trying to make the best of a bad situation.

The Environmental Protection Agency has confirmed the need to approve the water supply in a number of locations as part of its Remedial Action List; however, Irish Water have insisted residents could simply adopt a 'glass half full of browny-looking shit water' outlook.

'We're trying to fix all the problems, but for the time being, think how fancy you'll feel talking about all the different flavours and "accents" the craft water has. And the water even has some of the same side effects of the worst craft beer: diarrhoea,' the spokesperson concluded.

TRENDING Waterford woman tweeting non-stop about Trump has no interest in Irish politics

A ferociously passionate Tramore woman has continued her constant stream of tweeting about Donald Trump without letting her complete disinterest in Irish politics deter or hinder her in any way.

Retweeting any tweet that confirms her own thoughts on the inept leader, Alannah Mahon remains highly critical of people who refuse to wake up to the fact that the 21st century is now at a terrifying crossroads thanks to the precarious position of American politics.

Consuming endless articles on American politics, Mahon has yet to turn her insatiable desire to read about a world left on the brink by the divisive billionaire and professional sexist into ample fuel with which to engage with Irish politics.

'It's sickening what this means for the poor; women especially,' a despondent Mahon said of a recent Trump policy, unaware that the political landscape of Ireland is also worthy of intense scrutiny and examination.

'The only winners here are big businesses, but that's US politics in 2017 for you,' added Mahon, fully realising the gravity of a climate and culture that sees politicians allowed to operate without any opposition or resistance.

'Apathy is the root cause of all of this, and we're all paying for it,' continued Mahon in a reply to the same person she always has these conversations with on Twitter.

'Totally agree with you; so, so depressingly true,' responded Alan Corless, who just like Mahon can never recall the name of his local TD.

HEALTH NEWS

Maternity hospital to respect rights of married mothers, confirms spokesnun

THE Sisters of Charity have confirmed that the new €300 million national maternity hospital will always respect the rights of the mother and the baby, as long as the mother is married, a spokesnun told *WWN* today.

Sister Gertrude Dingleberry, a member of one of 18 religious orders that were included in the €1.5 billion redress scheme with the state in 2002 for child abuse, said the new maternity hospital would not generate any revenue for the Sisters of Charity, and also advised the nation not to worry about them taking sole ownership of the hospital, a decision made by the Department of Health.

'We won't receive one red cent from this takeover, so please don't even think of asking for the rest of that €3 million compensation we owe the victims of child abuse in our industrial schools,' Sr Dingleberry said, while blessing hospital blueprints with some holy water. 'We'll get it right this time. God was on holidays during those dark days of abuse, but he's back now to guide us through the running of this new maternity hospital.'

The congregation, which owns the country's largest public and private hospital on St Vincent's campus, said it will 'reach out to all creeds and backgrounds' and promised to 'give a good service to women who are married'.

'As long as they treat God right, we'll treat them right,' Sr Dingleberry added as she showed this reporter a section at the back of the hospital for unmarried mothers. 'And we'll even deliver the babies of those who got pregnant out of wedlock in this specially designed wing of the new hospital, which will have its own self-catering and laundering facilities.'

Asked what the large area beside the proposed wing called 'Pit' was for, she declined to answer and abruptly ended the interview.

An online petition against the ownership has so far received more than 76,000 signatures.

NAMA inquiry to be finished before next property crash, promises government

THE government has given a firm commitment that any potential inquiry into the sale of NAMA's Project Eagle property portfolio will need to be concluded before the next catastrophic property crash, *WWN* has learned.

Speaking exclusively to Ireland's leading news publication, a Fine Gael insider sought to reassure the voting public by stressing that this latest inquiry will be different from other recent disappointing inquiries.

'We've got to learn from the past, and any independent inquiry should be held to a higher standard than others in recent memory, which is why we're pushing to have the inquiry wrap up just before the next property crash,' the insider confirmed.

Learning from the mistakes of the last government as well as those of the previous Fianna Fáil-led governments, the NAMA inquiry has been allowed the option to report five years later than planned, to run well over budget and to make use of some leeway regarding how soft and inconsequential its final summation can be.

'Of course, first we've got to make the terms of the inquiry and its remit very vague and ambiguous – this will take at least six months, then after that there will be a period in which we might have to rush through emergency legislation so that the inquiry can actually start. The pressure will be on at this point as, obviously totally unrelated, the property market will be lurching to yet another combustible crescendo,' the Fine Gael source added, only this time sounding almost human-like in his delivery.

While experts have yet to agree when the next property crash will take place, news that any possible NAMA inquiry will be wrapped up before then has been greeted warmly.

WWN REVIEWS:

The New IRA

WWN reviews the latest release from genre-defying, Queen-denouncing purveyors of RepubliPop The New IRA.

Despite activity on their old fan message boards proving less frequent than sexual congress between a couple in their 90s, The New IRA have insisted on touring around the country trying to rouse interest.

And yet with these gigs poorly received and sparsely attended, The New IRA are still concentrating on their dwindling careers, which carries all the hallmarks of a group completely out of ideas.

There's no beating around the Republican bush, The New IRA are a pale imitation of a cover version of a bad song and their latest release is only marginally less offensive than U2's last album.

In truth, it is hard to assess their new oeuvre with enthusiasm, knowing some of the key minds behind their seminal works are no longer part of the group. Sure, their work carries with it some of the same exposure and column inches, but you get the feeling their work evokes a time and genre that has long since lost any semblance of credibility.

Many die-hard fans admit to the fact they simply don't view The New IRA as the band of upstarts they were once so fond of in the 60s and 70s.

One long-time fan remarked recently, 'They had some bright ideas back in the day, but this latest stuff is like Oasis and their album *Be Here Now* ... the New IRA are definitely in their drug phase, their fuel-laundering phase. I've certainly lost interest.'

A tired cliché which offers nothing new despite the name.

Zero stars.

We schedule patient appointments three hours early for the fucking craic, admits hospital

HOSPITALS up and down the country have finally admitted to scheduling appointments for patients way earlier than needed, just for 'shits and giggles'.

Many patients attending hospital for scans, check-ups or outpatient procedures are told to be there at 8 a.m. and subsequently left to sit in the waiting room for hours on end while doctors and nurses try to stifle their giggles as they walk past.

The curious practice, which heaps hours of unnecessary suffering and misery onto already vulnerable people, is said to help hospital staff 'chillax' during the day, and keep their minds off the pressures of their stressful jobs.

'Look, see that lady out there in the waiting room? Her appointment was for nine this morning, it's gone past lunchtime now,' giggled one hospital manager, speaking exclusively to *WWN*.

'Oh, we could have given her an appointment for 3 p.m., instead of having her sit out there for six hours, but where's the fun in that? I'm working an 18-hour day here, gimme something to laugh about.

'And yeah, sometimes patients get wise to this and don't turn up at the time on their appointment card ... we just cancel those straight away. "Sorry love, your card says 8 a.m., it's 10 a.m. and you've missed your slot" ... even if there was no chance they were getting seen for another four hours. You'd want to see the looks on their faces!'

Pope to visit zero mass grave sites during visit

A preliminary itinerary for the 2018 papal visit by Pope Francis has outlined several high-profile meetings at government buildings, churches and of course the Phoenix Park site visited by Pope John Paul II in 1979, as well as absolutely no visits to the former sites of Magdalene laundries or mother and baby homes around the country.

Pope Francis made the announcement of his visit earlier this week, prompting fleeting thoughts in the minds of those affected by the Catholic Church's views on 'fallen women' over the last hundred years that they might be getting some sort of apology from the pontiff at a special ceremony or something.

However Franko's 'bucket list of places to visit in Paddyland' features zero mention of visiting people whose lives were torn apart by paedophile priests or the subsequent Vatican-endorsed cover-up, or indeed of the mass-grave site of over 800 babies at a mother and baby home in Tuam, County Galway.

'We're aiming to keep this trip light,' said one Vatican official, browsing TripAdvisor. 'Wave at friendly crowds, bless a baby or two ... just the JP visit all over again, except this time we kinda have to deal with all the shit that has come to light over the last 30 years.'

It has also been confirmed that Pope Francis will be following the tradition of posing for a picture of him sipping a pint of Guinness, while officials at the Irish Tourist Board come in their trousers.

This staunch pro-life supporter got the babysitter pregnant, what happened next will amaze you

WE love astounding and heart-warming stories here at *WWN*. If our mind isn't blown at least eight times a day, it's a tragedy. So you can imagine how thankful we are to have stumbled upon this story of a babysitter becoming pregnant after sleeping with a devoutly religious father of four.

Dáithí McDrone, with an address near his local church in Waterford, is an avowed pro-life supporter who firmly believes abortion, under all circumstances, to be murder.

However, after learning the 17-year-old babysitter to his four daughters is now pregnant following a recent lift home administered by McDrone himself, the religious man has become an expert in flights leaving for the UK first thing tomorrow morning.

'I knew Ryanair prided themselves on good value, but Jesus, did you see the price of flights to Manchester or London, at such short notice? A life saver,' the married man shared with *WWN*.

'Now I know London has some great tourist attractions, but I hear Manchester is good value for money and Ciara will like it I'm sure, a 17-year-old in a big city,' added the irregular church attender and selective commandment follower, hoping we didn't know he really wasn't talking about tourism.

McDrone was keen to add that his trip to Manchester with Ciara is purely coincidental and that nobody should read into it all, as he's booked separate seats on the plane.

'Manchester, they have that shopping centre, don't they? Well, of course they do, that's why I'm going there in the first place, yeah, the big shopping centre thing and the football team, they have one of them. But, no, actually it's a conference, that's right, I've to suddenly go to Manchester on short notice with the babysitter in floods of tears because of a work conference,' McDrone concluded.

Consider all at *WWN* amazed. Great story from Dáithí.

'I'm the only one creating jobs around here,' local drug dealer slams government

WATERFORD drug dealer Richie 'The Grater' Harrington has today slammed the Irish government for ignoring the young people in his council estate, stating that he has been the only one creating jobs in the area over the past 10 years.

Mr Harrington, who has been wholesaling illegal drugs since 2006, currently has 34 foot soldiers under him, with 'runners' ranging from eight-year-old trainees up to mature dealers in their late 40s.

'Business is booming and I'm actually expanding out to the estate next to us ... once I sort out a couple of fellas,' the 34-year-

old entrepreneur explained. 'It's great to be able to keep so many young people employed, but the turnover is high with lads getting murdered, beaten and imprisoned, so I'm constantly on the lookout for new skin.'

The Grater, whose signature punishment is grating those in debt to him with a cheese grater, credits the Irish government for his success. He claims that he wouldn't have a multimillion-euro tax-free business if it wasn't for the state's neglect of rural Irish towns like Waterford and neighbouring Clonmel.

'I can't imagine what it would be like if there was enough gardaí to handle our crew,' he continued. 'Or indeed, if there were decent paying jobs that actually offered people more than the social welfare or, better yet, an education system developed to combat some of the poverty found in council-estate Ireland.'

'Man, give me 10 minutes in the Dáil and I'd have this place in tip-top shape,' he concluded, before blowing a snot to the ground and walking off.

MOTORING NEWS

17% of Irish motorists not driving it on ta fuck

THE Road Safety Authority has confirmed today that as many as 17% of drivers on Irish roads are not driving it on ta fuck, claiming that their lack of speed actually causes accidents as opposed to preventing them.

An analysis of forensic collision investigations conducted by the RSA shows that slow drivers account for twice as many accidents in Ireland than previously thought. The report urges such drivers to keep in line with the speed limits.

'If you're one of those motorists who goes 30 kilometres per hour under the speed limit, then you could be endangering the lives of the impatient drivers behind you,' said an RSA spokesperson. 'Either drive it on ta fuck or pull in out of the way until you grow a pair. It's people like you who infuriate other drivers, forcing them to take their lives into their hands by overtaking on our already treacherous roads.'

The study shows that rural Ireland had the largest proportion of accidents caused by 'some cunt who won't drive her on ta fuck', with the majority of their vehicles being tractors, Nissan Micras, Ford Kas or just two pricks on bicycles who won't move into single file because it's in the stupid law somewhere.

'You know what, fuck these guys,' added the RSA spokesperson, 'shunt them off the road if you have to.'

Waterford motorist tests positive for joint he smoked in Transition Year

A 36-year-old Waterford man has been charged with driving under the influence of drugs after being stopped at a checkpoint by gardaí on the Old Tramore Road this morning.

Conor Casey, a full-time delivery driver, could be facing a ban from driving, despite the fact that he smoked the substance in 1996 down the back lane during a Transition Year lunch break.

'I knew I should have never bowed down to peer pressure like that,' Casey later told *WWN* after being released from garda custody, now also facing redundancy from his driving job. 'It's my own fault and I should have known better than to be driving with cannabis in my bloodstream. I haven't been stoned in 21 years, but the law is the law, and it's nobody's fault but mine.'

The stoner has become the first motorist in the country to be caught under the new drug-testing regime for drivers, which tests for serious drugs like cocaine, opiates and cannabis for some reason under a new law launched today by the gardaí and the Road Safety Authority.

'The new test has already stopped one maniac from killing dozens of people this morning,' Minister for Transport Shane Ross was all too eager to point out. 'We expect to catch many more dope drivers over the coming months, and save millions of lives across the country in the process.'

'Cannabis is the most common drug detected on Irish roads, and obviously that's a bad thing, because driving on cannabis is bad, because we said so, without doing any research into its effects on human drivers. Sure, you may not be stoned at the time of driving, but that's not our fault if you smoked it in the past.'

It is unclear yet whether stimulants like caffeine, codeine, tobacco, cough syrups or various types of solvents, including glues and aerosols, will be also tested under the new law, and if indeed gardaí are capable of counting the correct number of tests without inflating them, but one thing is for certain: those who are caught could face disqualification from driving for a minimum of four years.

Meanwhile, the RSA has reported a 67% drop in Ireland's traffic since the new law was introduced this morning.

'Novelist' told to order a coffee or get the fuck out

'HEY, Hunter S. Thompson … you've been nursing that empty cup for over two hours now and we're about to hit the lunch rush, so you either order something or get the hell out of here!'

WWN is on location at one of the city's busiest coffee shops, Coffee Bean an Tí, where the problem of 'writers' clogging up the limited seating space while they soak up the free WiFi and browse YouTube has hit an all-time high.

Coffee Bean an Tí owner Cam Wilson told us how he has to shoo at least 30 of what he refers to as 'woolly-hat-wearing cunts' out of the shop each day. If he doesn't do this, customers who would actually spend money in his coffee shop don't come in because it appears 'too crowded' from the street.

Wilson spoke angrily about how 90% of the laptop brigade do nothing throughout the day except update their social media bios in a bid to find the best way to refer to themselves as 'writers'.

'If you can afford an iPad, then you can afford a fucking latte,' said Wilson, who's just had it with this shit.

'Quit sitting there pretending you're working on your first novel when in actual fact you're only here because it's warm and there's free WiFi. I'm trying to run a business here. Go be fucking useless elsewhere.'

Wilson then kindly allowed *WWN* to write this article in the cafe, as long as we ordered at least one €7 sandwich and a €4 bun.

Armed TV licence enforcers to be deployed nationwide

A crack team of specially trained TV licence inspectors is to be deployed in a bid to recoup the €40 million in unpaid fees every year, Communications Minister Denis Naughten has confirmed.

'TV licence enforcers' are to be recruited and trained alongside the Garda Emergency Response Unit. They will be equipped with military-grade automatic weapons and body armour to help them in their mission to clamp down on non-payers.

'The weapons are only a precautionary measure that will aid enforcers to reclaim the fee from licence dodgers,' said Minister Naughten. 'If television

owners refuse to cough up, then they can expect to be roughed up a bit and verbally warned. If they continue to refuse, our specially trained team is authorised to administer a good old-fashioned kneecapping, but hopefully it won't ever come to that.'

It is understood the TV licence enforcers will also be able to search a home for TVs without a court order, and any device with an Internet connection will warrant the €160 fee, even if the user doesn't watch any of the national TV stations.

Once formally approved by the government, the Department of Communications will be able to

use a public tender to hire the new TV licence enforcers.

'Anyone with a background in paramilitary activity should apply, as they have to be handy with the butt of a gun,' Minister Naughten added, hinting at hiring some of the country's 5,000 unemployed IRA members. 'Our plan is to hit the elderly first, you know, to break the lads in, and then we'll work our way through the low earners, basically anyone who depends on the welfare system.'

With a budget of €200 million for hiring, training and arming the enforcers, even the government's most vocal critics will fail to see a flaw in their plan to recoup the €40 million in unpaid licence fees.

'Even if it's just the *Late Late Show* on a Friday night, you're gonna get capped,' the Minister warned.

'But where are you really from?' black woman with Irish accent asked

A Waterford-based black woman with a thick Irish accent, usually referred to as an 'Irish person', has once again been asked politely by one of the country's citizens 'But where are you really from?' *WWN* can confirm.

The question was posed by a well-meaning middle-aged man called Sean Carty. It occurred at a bus stop and marked the 46th time Ardmore local Cora Adeola has been accosted by a well-meaning member of the public so far in 2017.

'No, I know, but I mean where are *you*, ya know, from, like,' Carty ventured once again upon being told by Adeola that she is from Waterford.

Carty was prepared to launch into a fresh set of questions before Adeola cut their conversation short and produced a sheet of paper with a set of prepared questions and answers.

'It skips past the usual "Now is it your mam or dad that's the, you know, foreign one?", so it's just much easier this way,' Adeola shared with *WWN* when this reporter also crossed the street to ask her where she was really from.

Language skills are another point of interest among well-meaning members of the general public. A common question is 'When did you learn English?' and Adeola often encounters confusion when she speaks as Gaeilge, 'You speak Irish, that's mental stuff' being a typical response.

'I understand the curiosity, but it would be nice if they started off with a normal hello and didn't just want to figure out why the fuck I'm here,' Adeola confirmed, before refusing to answer this reporter's follow-up question about when exactly she lost her original accent.

TECHNOLOGY

Dyson hand dryers recalled after sucking the life out of 23 people

DYSON has recalled the entire supply of its signature Airblade dryers after the total number of fatalities as a result of using the machines reached a staggering 23 this week.

The Airblades became the market leader in post-piss hand-washing and drying technology after Dyson's patented technology created a dryer that was more energy-efficient than its competitors and dried hands in less than 10 seconds.

Unheated air travelling at 400 mph helped make the airblade the hand-dryer of choice across the world after its UK launch in 2006 and its US launch in 2007. However, the very thing that made it a success is now killing innocent hand-drying individuals everywhere.

'The air circulation system is highly effective but there is a sweet spot within the Airblade that causes the user to be sucked in by the 400 mph air, and essentially the air is moving so fast in a suction vacuum that the life is literally sucked out of the person using the dryer,' John Hingley, Chief Safety Officer for Dyson, shared with *WWN*.

CCTV footage, too graphic to show our readers, is circulating online of Surrey pensioner Alvin Criggdon in the toilet of his local cinema. Sadly, Criggdon became the latest victim of the rogue Airblades when he walked passed the dryer.

'Mr Criggdon was actually happy to stroll out of the toilet without washing his hands, the vileness of which we can talk about on another occasion, but he walked by the Dyson and it automatically switched on, sucking him into its path and that was it – the life was sucked right out of him,' Hingley admitted.

Criggdon's deoxygenated corpse was found by cinema cleaners and has become the final nail in the Airblade's coffin, as over one million units have been recalled today.

TRENDING RTÉ
Player down as more than seven people log on at the same time

IRELAND'S national television broadcaster RTÉ has apologised to online users after its player was down for more than three hours last night.

IT staff at the station worked round the clock in a bid to pinpoint the cause of the intermittent service. In a statement published moments ago, they explained: 'After some general diagnostic checks we have found that last night's issue was down to seven people streaming on the player at the same time. Obviously the sheer amount of people online congested our servers and that is why users experienced lagging. Thankfully it is very rare for more than three people to log on to the player at any one time, so we don't expect this problem to happen again anytime soon.'

The RTÉ Player, which was built in 1978 by Aonghus McAnally's cousin John, hosts some of the station's top-tier programmes for Internet users to watch. However, the dated interface has come under fire over the years, with calls from licence fee payers to bring it into the 21st century.

'It's like something some lad in his first year in software development in college would make last minute for an assignment,' one viewer told *WWN*. 'And who the fuck wants to watch three minutes of adverts on the Internet? If I see an advert on a viral video for five seconds I'm outta there, yet these fools think I'm gonna stay watching three minutes of ads for some shite.'

RTÉ has apologised for last night's outage and confirmed it is looking into upping the number of people able to watch the player at one time to ten by the year 2025.

Cocktail sausages at half ten voted 'best thing about weddings'

THE distribution of miniature sausages during the nightly intermission of a wedding reception has been voted the best part of the entire matrimony process in a recent survey conducted among four drunk lads at an afters in Waterford.

The quartet of men, who had been drinking since the early afternoon at the wedding of a lad they knew from school to some girl from Kilkenny, or possibly Kildare, declared the 'plate of budleys' to have been the highlight of the day, and the perfect snack to refuel them for another hour or two of 'bucklepping about the place'.

Indeed the platter of cocktail sausages, valued at around 79 cent, was deemed to have been even better than the €49-a-head five-course meal they had eaten earlier in the day, and the four men made short work of polishing them off.

'Jaysus, them cocktail sausages were lovely hi,' declared Declan Hanlon, spokesperson for the group.

'Best bit of the whole day. You have your drink, a bit of jiving, and then just at the right time, when you're saying to yourself I'd go for a feed right now, out they come with the sossies. Great timing, great sausages, best part of the day altogether.'

Having finished the plate that landed at their table, the four men then headed to the bar again, helping themselves to any leftovers they encountered on the way.

BREAKING NEWS

GARDAÍ in Dublin are today celebrating a small but significant milestone in battling the ongoing Kinahan/Hutch feud after they arrested the character who appears to be the Kinahans' most significant figure in Ireland, Mr Silly.

The Mister Man, who is believed to be in his late 60s, was arrested at his home in the city after an early morning raid by the Emergency Response Unit in conjunction with detectives investigating the cartel's main henchmen.

'We believe Mr Silly may have been running firearms and money for the Kinahans since the late 90s, and he is understood to be a violent and very dangerous criminal, with ties to a number of murders in the city, including the shooting of Mr Rat last week,' a Garda source told *WWN*.

Bloodbath fears as gardaí arrest notorious Kinahan henchman, Mr Silly

Gardaí found over €40,000 in cash at Mr Silly's home, with laminated books containing the names, addresses and even hand-drawn, coloured depictions of 49 Mister Men associates. His wife, Little Miss Social Welfare, was also arrested, but she was later released without charge after being questioned at Store Street Garda Station.

'The information in these books describes a highly sophisticated gang of criminals, and this find could fuel a further bloodbath,' warned one detective.

Mr Silly will be held for questioning for 72 hours. Gardaí are expected to charge him over a botched assassination attempt in the city, where Mr Silly dropped his driving licence at the scene after his gun failed to fire due to his forgetting to load it with bullets.

'He's not the sharpest tool in the box,' pointed out one garda.

Meanwhile, tabloids have asked An Garda Síochána to refrain from further arrests until such a time as journalists can give all criminals nicknames that dehumanise the violence innocent people are exposed to by the gangs.

Co-worker knows a quicker way you could drive home

DESPITE nobody ever asking for better travel directions, one worker at a prominent Dublin accountancy firm has taken it upon himself to suggest alternative time-saving routes to his co-workers at all times.

With nothing much to talk about due to a lack of personality, Olliver Gahan finds himself asking his co-workers questions such as 'D'you have far to come in the mornings?' and 'D'you drive or take the bus?' during petrifying 30-second silences in the canteen of Lehanne and Hamble, located in Ballsbridge.

Upon learning the current path that his disinterested co-worker takes, Gahan then launches into a Garmin-worthy list of routes that 'are much quicker', going into incredible detail as to which roundabout to turn at and how to know when 'you've gone too far'.

'I'm actually grand with the way I come to work at the minute,' said fellow accountant Lisa Denehy, speaking exclusively to *WWN*. 'But that didn't stop Olliver from telling me a way that would save me 10, maybe 15 minutes that involved a series of one-way and residential streets, and a few turns that 'are grand if the guards aren't out'. I stopped listening halfway through if I'm honest, but he seemed happy to bang on.'

Gahan has stated he will continue to dole out this free advice, despite everyone in the office wishing on a daily basis that he would find a path to a new job elsewhere.

Varadkar's triathlon marred by presence of homeless people in Phoenix Park

IT should have been a routine photo opportunity for the Taoiseach to showcase just how 'cool', 'ace', 'class' and 'down with the young 'uns' he is, but things took an unsavoury turn for Leo Varadkar as he had the misfortune of cycling past a number of homeless people while completing the cycling portion of the Dublin City Triathlon over the weekend.

Sources close to the Fine Gael leader described him as 'shook' but admitted a collective sense of relief as media photographers refrained from taking photos that could be spun to highlight the disparity in fortunes between the 'haves' and 'have nots' that make up Ireland's citizenry, instead preferring to take 4,000 photos of Varadkar in various states of exercise.

'Could you imagine the damaging context that would provide? Leo on a bike and a homeless lad being all homeless and that. The headlines could have read "get on your bike Leo, time to help ALL of society" but thank Christ everyone just sort of thought better of it since we're still revelling in everyone around the world thinking we're sound for having a young leader who ticks a few nice boxes,' the source confirmed to *WWN*.

Authorities assured *WWN* that a number of homeless people, who were residing in Phoenix Park at the time of the triathalon, were given a stern talking-to by the Taoiseach's handlers and agreed to refrain in future from stumbling into the background of a good photo opportunity for the Dublin TD and former Minister for Health.

'It's a massive park for God's sake, and if they're looking for shelter there's a good few trees that are out of the way of people who get up early in the morning to work. They should know better,' the source added.

Taoiseach Varadkar completed the triathlon in a time of 1 hour, 39 minutes and 36 seconds and marks the first time he has completed anything of note while serving in public office.

DRUG NEWS

Gardaí seize enough cannabis to supply Galway city for 10 whole hours

GARDAÍ and Revenue officers seized a massive 1,873 kg haul of lethal cannabis resin at Dublin Port over the weekend, enough to supply Galway city for 10 whole hours.

The seizure, with a street value of €37.5 million, comes as part of ongoing joint investigations targeting organised crime in Ireland, with this latest bust expected to cripple Dublin-based gangs.

'There's no coming back from this,' a source close to the Kinahan cartel explained. 'The boss man probably bought the hashish for €300 a kilo in Morocco, which would have cost him over half a million euro, wholesale. I wouldn't be surprised if Christy Kinahan just handed himself in after this find. He must be devastated.'

The seizure is expected to leave tens of thousands of hash addicts strung out for hours.

'This amount of soap bar would keep Galway's druggies smoking for up to 10 hours,' Assistant Garda Commissioner John O'Driscoll claimed. 'This blow to Ireland's billion-euro drugs trade couldn't have happened without the hard work the gardaí and Revenue staff have put into this operation ... and, of course, the vulnerable informant we've risked the life of, who will probably be gunned down in a hail of bullets in the next week or two. But yeah, we did great. I'm fucking stoked, if I'm honest.'

Since its introduction to Ireland in the mid-20th century, cannabis has killed a staggering 75 million people in the Republic, and is responsible for almost every violent crime recorded on the island, including the Troubles in Northern Ireland and the violent England v. Ireland football clash in Lansdowne Road in 1995. Cannabis has also been called the 'gateway drug to alcohol'.

Culchie wakes up from coma speaking fluent Dublin

DOCTORS at University Hospital Limerick have said they cannot explain why a County Tipperary patient has suddenly woken up speaking Dublin, after spending three months in a coma following a severe car crash.

Peadar Walsh, a 24-year-old culchie from Rosegreen in Tipperary, was put under an induced coma in July when his brain began swelling after he hit his head during the car accident.

'Peadar began to wake up slowly last Friday, which was great news for the family at the time,' Dr Rashid Mohammed explained. 'However, things took a turn for the worse after he began stringing sentences together in what we can only describe as Dublin talk.'

First to realise the brain injury was the student's mother, Joan, who said that she got an awful fright when he greeted her yesterday morning.

'He said something like "Wasta bleedin' story, ma?",' Mrs Walsh recalled, visibly shaken from the incident. 'Then he started asking if 'the Dubs' won the All Ireland. He has his poor father's heart broken with this carry on.'

Speaking to this *WWN* reporter earlier, the son of two seemed to be fully coherent and claimed to have no knowledge of his previous life as a culchie. He said he couldn't wait to get back to the 'big smoke' (i.e. Dublin), despite only visiting the city once before for a school tour in 2005.

'De nurses in heor are bleedin' rapid!' Peadar said, giving a cheeky-chappy wink to a Filipino nurse. 'I'll tell yis one thing for naughtin': if I don't dip me wick soon me balls will turn blue, wha'? Are you another culchie? 'Tis like the bleedin' 1960s down here, an' all.'

Following our brief interview, family members and doctors agreed to re-induce Mr Walsh into a coma for another few months in a bid to give his brain some time to heal properly.

'Hopefully he'll be back to himself soon; otherwise we'll have to leave him asleep,' his mother insisted. 'I'll be fucked if I'm listening to that crap for the rest of my life.'

Wonderful World of Science

Despite €3 billion in research, we're still no closer to keeping both sides of the pillow cold.

Did you know?

98% of local racists can't be racist because they 'know a black lad'.

Ireland's secret shame: we meet the kids forced to pick stones for weeks

IN yet another example of a shameful and long-forgotten way Ireland treated its young people and children over the years, a damning new documentary is about to lift the lid on the hundreds of thousands of kids in rural Ireland who were forced to spend days, sometimes weeks, picking stones out of the ground in fields across the country.

The backbreaking, seemingly pointless exercise was mainly carried out by culchie kids who were forced by their fathers and uncles to do it ahead of ploughing or sowing seeds. On occasion, visiting cousins from towns were also coerced into helping them.

These kids were often paid nothing for their labour, and were instead assured that it was great to be out on a good day picking stones and throwing them into a transport box at the back of a tractor to be dumped further up the field.

'We did our best, but they would always yell at us for missing even the smallest of rocks,' said Cian Drury, one of the kids interviewed for the upcoming exposé *Stone Mad*.

'We didn't know why we had to pick stones. It just seemed so useless. I had a friend who picked strawberries all summer and made enough money to buy himself a BMX. I had to spend my summer picking up fucking aggregate and got nothing except a slug of flat TK orange out of a jumbo bottle.'

If you have been a victim of stone-picking, please contact your local authorities.

BREAKING NEWS

Hunt is on to find €2 scratch card winner

THE hunt is on this evening for Ireland's latest winner after a mystery player matched €2 on a scratch card, which was found on a footpath on O'Connell Street in Dublin city centre.

Punters crashed the National Lottery's website trying to check for updates to see if the winner's identity had been discovered.

The winning scratch card was sold in a local Tesco Express store in the city, where manager Jeremy Aherne reduced all the shop item prices by 50% in celebration.

'So far I've lost the business twelve grand since opening today,' Aherne said, popping open a bottle of champagne like he had won the €2 himself. 'There's a lot of speculation, with customers coming in to ask if the winner has come forward, but even if I knew I wouldn't tell them; that's up to the winner themselves to decide.'

The shop is already being dubbed the luckiest in Ireland after selling a *Winning Streak* ticket containing three stars to a regular customer last month.

'He wasn't picked from the drum to go on *Winning Streak*, but he was damn close I'd say,' Aherne added.

The lucky scratch card player will have 90 days to claim the €2, before the winnings vanish back into the National Lottery vaults, along with the winner's hopes and dreams.

Horror as man comfy on sofa realises phone is on mantelpiece

THERE was heartbreak and dismay for one Waterford man last night when, right at the moment he achieved peak comfort on the sofa, he realised that he had left his phone on the mantelpiece.

Declan Brennan (33) thought he had it all: a can of beer within reach, his favourite show streaming on the telly and the perfect arrangement of couch and cushions underneath him, ready to keep him in bliss for the next hour

or at least until he needed a slash.

Tragedy struck the Waterford native mere seconds into his cosiness, as it dawned on him that his phone wasn't within reach and in fact the iPhone 4 was all the way across the room, requiring him to get up and get it or face an hour of telly watching without the facility to

piss around on Facebook during the breaks.

Solemnly accepting that he would never fully realise the exact level of comfort he had fought so hard to achieve, Brennan got up to get his phone, tears in his eyes.

'You never get that level of ooooh yeah again,' said Brennan, fidgeting around while trying to get back into the position he was in just seconds ago.

'This is like lying in a fucking hedge right now. Why, why didn't I remember to take my phone from the mantelpiece before I settled down? If ever there was an argument for living with someone, this is it.'

EMPLOYMENT

GOOD news on the jobs front this morning as local county councils are to roll out dozens of hole-staring positions to suitable applicants across the country, with as many as 250 jobs set to come on stream by 2019.

Although once a valid and lucrative career path, the role of 'man staring into hole' has diminished in recent years as during the economic downturn local authorities were forced to curtail the amount of money they were spending on people gazing into an opening in the ground.

With money starting to flow into local projects again, county council officials have been quick to advertise new hole-gawking vacancies, with the first of the posts expected to be filled as early as this summer.

Jobs boost as council to hire 250 new hole-staring experts

'Yep, we're getting 10 new hole-staring experts in July,' said Seamus Dargan, Head of Planning for Waterford County Council.

'With the extra manpower, we should be able to spend our entire budget this year. That was

a problem we had last year; we didn't use up our allotted cash and so, of course, we had it cut back this year. They won't give it to you if you don't spend it! So we'll have our 10 new staff go and spend a few hours every day looking into a hole; some are qualified to just lean on a shovel, but some can also shake their heads and drink tea.'

Although the positions for hole-looking staff are expected to be snapped up quickly, the council has no plans to employ more people in the 'filling up holes and leaving the road as good as new' department.

NATIONWIDE ALERT

Robin enters Waterford home, killing three

GARDAÍ in Waterford have issued a nationwide alert this afternoon following an incident where a small bird casually entered a family home in the east of the city and later killed three of its occupants.

A robin redbreast was later identified by eyewitnesses, with one neighbour stating that the bird flew into the house after several previous failed attempts.

'We believe the robin tried to gain access through the sitting room window first, and kept hitting off of it, trying to break in,' detective Tadgh Browne told *WWN*. 'It then got in through a back door, sending the elderly residents into a terrible frenzy.'

It is understood the occupants were highly superstitious and panicked when the bird entered the house, leaving 67-year-old Theresa O'Brien, her husband John (71) and neighbour Kevin Tobin to fend against the creature for themselves.

'All three victims appeared to have suffered from exhaustion while trying to get rid of the bird and succumbed to dehydration and eventual death,' added the detective. 'They were heard shouting at each other to "get it out of here before someone dies" for several hours.'

'This isn't the first time a robin has been connected to a number of deaths in the area, and we would advise people to keep their doors and windows closed for the time being, while we continue our investigations.'

The bird is believed to have a 20 cm wingspan, weighs 16–22 g, with a brown and grey plumage and a distinctive red breast.

Since 2010, over 3,350 deaths have been linked to robins breaking and entering into Irish homes.

Taoiseach Enda Kenny was not available for comment on the phenomenon.

Smug prick passes driving test on first go

THERE were bitter scenes this morning at a Waterford office after one man arrived to work with the news that he had passed his driving test that morning on his very first go, much to the annoyance of those who had to take their test multiple times before eventually passing it.

Declan O'Malley (27) was delighted with himself to have passed his test following months of practice, lessons and being a good driver at all times. O'Malley had studied the rules of the road until he knew them off by heart and is in general a safe and competent driver, attributes that helped him secure a full driver's licence after his first attempt.

This did not sit well with many of his co-workers who failed their tests multiple times, for reasons

such as 'the tester was a bollox', 'it's all just a money racket' and 'they needed to fail someone to keep their quotas up'.

'Look at him there, Mr "I'm such a safe driver",' said Mark Hanlon, who is sitting his test again next week for the fifth time.

'What, just because he's so safe on the road and knows how to keep himself and other motorists safe? He was just probably in the right place in the queue. If he'd gotten a different tester, they would have failed him. That's how it works; they failed me four times, and not just because I kept mounting kerbs and turning without indicating, it's because the tester was hungover or something like that'.

O'Malley now intends to continue a lifetime of safe motoring, despite his co-workers' assurances that he can 'drive however the fuck he likes' now that he's got a full licence.

TRENDING Country calls for separation of Church and bouncy castle rental businesses

'THERE comes a time to say enough is enough,' said Kathleen McMarron, speaking at a rally of concerned parents looking to bring about the end of the Catholic Church's ties to the world of large-scale inflatable children's entertainment.

'How much longer are we going to allow these two entities to remain entwined, one feeding off the other? If we stand together as one and say "no more", it can happen tonight!'

McMarron, herself a mother of three, was lashing out at the common practice of hiring a bouncy castle or other such inflatable to celebrate First Communions and Confirmations, a routine that rakes in millions of euro each year for both the Church and the castle hirers.

'With kids showing a lack of interest in religion until they see that they get a party with a bouncy castle, it only made sense for the Church to cosy up to Mick's Bouncy Fun or whatever crowd were hiring them out,' said McMarron, amid jeers from some priests and lads with generators in the crowd.

'It's all one and the same now. The kids don't give tuppence for the Body of Christ, they just want to invite their pals over to have a go on a big slide. It suits everyone: the Church, the bouncy lads, the kids – everyone except the parents who have to pay for it all. It'll be tough explaining to my kids why they're not getting a party when their pals up the road are, but I believe that this unholy union must come to a stop!'

Her sentiments were echoed across the country, where bouncy castles were burned in protest, resulting in hundreds being hospitalised after breathing in huge amounts of melted tarpaulin.

12 MONTHS A GUARD *Month 2*

Everything is going great here at garda school! We got our stab-proof vests, so that'll be a great help when someone tries to stab us directly in the torso. Arms, legs, neck, face … criminals rarely aim for those places. But as the top guards say, only dead guards make the headlines. As long as we're not killed, they don't mind us getting stuck with a syringe or two. Also today, we got firearms and weapons training. A senior member of the force came in and talked us through pistols, shotguns, semi-automatic rifles, Uzis, machetes, samurai swords, and all of the other different weapons that the criminals of Ireland use on a daily basis. Then we got handed sticks. I was a bit concerned that we would be expected to tackle vicious drug gangs with nothing more than a baton, but then we were given an intensive course in shouting, so we're more than ready for 'em now!

Kid on bottom half of double-buggy wondering why he deserves this shit

WHILE his sister lounges in the open air, mere inches above his face, one Waterford toddler is wondering why he had to be the one confined to the hell that is the bottom tier of his parents' new double-buggy.

Liam Kelly (3) has to make do with the lower deck of the over-under child carrier that his mam is currently pushing around Waterford city centre, while his eight-month-old sister, Hannah, gets to stretch out in comfort above him.

With nothing to look at except the black fabric of the seat above him, Liam is searching his soul to find a reason as to why his sister got the good seat while he is forced to put up with this bottom-half bullshit.

'I feel like I'm a friggin' Chilean miner down here,' says Liam, who can't even move his hands at the minute. 'When I saw them coming with this buggy at first, I thought, oh, that's nice, it's got a lot of room at the bottom for groceries and what have you. I didn't think I'd be the one who got slid into it every time we leave the house. What the hell did I ever do to deserve this crap?'

Hannah Kelly is unavailable for comment due to her being unable to speak just yet.

Leinster to be renamed Dublin

STARTING in 2018, the province of Leinster is to undergo a complete rebranding, and is expected to be known simply as 'Dublin' from 2019 onwards.

The decision to rename one-quarter of the country as Dublin comes following a new report that states almost half of the country's economic growth is emanating from Dublin, with the surrounding counties becoming little more than satellite towns to the capital itself.

With the 'Dublin city region' now sprawling from Gorey to Dundalk, officials see no reason to retain the illusion that Leinster is a province made up of separate counties, and have pulled the trigger on a scheme that will see new postcodes implemented by this time next year, followed by changes to road signage and sports teams.

'So, for example, Drogheda will now become Dublin 137,' said a spokesperson for the project. 'Dublin will win the Leinster championship every year, except it'll be called the Dublin championship and they'll win by default because there are no other counties. Estate agents will be able to stop saying that houses in Navan are "in driving distance to Dublin" because they'll actually be in Dublin. Taking your child to a hospital in Dublin won't seem so bad because, even though you're in Carlow, technically you'll be starting and ending the journey in Dublin.'

'And, of course, house prices will soar across the region once they get Dublin in the address line. It's great news for everyone in Leinster! Maybe not for the rest of the country, but let's face it, those lads were always going to be ignored no matter what.'

Nobody wants to hear about your 'meal prepping', gym pricks told

THE nation's enthusiastic gym goers who feel the need to post pictures online of a week's worth of meals have been told to save themselves the time and effort as nobody cares, *WWN* can exclusively reveal.

Meal prepping, the technique by which gym pricks find yet another way to inform people that they will go or have been to the gym, has grown in popularity in recent months as avid narcissists realised the general public have cottoned on to how attention-seeking traditional gym selfies can be.

'No matter how I dressed my gym selfie up, be it with a "it's been a long journey", "feel so much happier" or "positivity is the key", people have copped on to the fact I just want to be showered in a masturbatory downpour of likes,' explained Waterford man Gavin Hassion.

'So I had to get clever. How can I get likes which praise me for exercising? By posting pictures of food for lazy fat arses to drool over, of course,' revealed Hassion.

Despite the best efforts of gym pricks to entice the wider public into sharing, commenting and liking these 'meal prep' photos, the lazy portion of the nation has resolved to tell meal preppers to 'fuck off with that shite' as a picture of 12 chicken breasts and 40 hard boiled eggs is the last thing they want to see.

'Oh you've made seven days' worth of increasingly unappetising-looking food, yeah, fuck off pal, you're making me feel ill,' explained Tramore couch squatter Andy Deeley.

'Come back when you're serious about this. You'll have all my praise and attention when it's a takeaway version, Chinese, Thai, chipper, pizza,' concluded Deeley.

Local straight man thinks every gay man fancies him

A local heterosexual has convinced himself that the majority of gay men, if not all of them, are magnetically drawn to him and his masculine aura.

Drowning in his own self-congratulatory praise for being so frank about gay men, and not even making a big deal about it, Dublin-based Waterford man Paul Kane (28) spoke about his predicament to *WWN*.

'I wish I could explain it. Gay men like Derek in accounts and

the lad working in H&M are all gagging to ride me, but obviously I'd be doing the riding if there was any riding to be done ... I mean c'mon, look at me.

'There's twinks and bears or something like them yokes that the gay lads love, but I think they're mad for me cause I'm not that. I'm just raw straight sexiness,' said the local man who almost had sex last year with a woman.

'I pass by the lad working at the Inglot makeup counter on my lunch break, just you know, to brighten up his day, bless him,' added Kane, unaware of how full of himself he sounded.

'Some lads who aren't as comfortable with their sexuality and masculinity would be totally not okay with the attention I get, but I just take it as a compliment. But I'd fear being swamped in the George, you know yourself, they'd tear me limb from limb, I'm gay crack,' Kane concluded.

Kane failed to provide any concrete evidence to back up his claims of being desired by gay men, but it is believed such proclamations stem from one party in 2007 when a presumably gay man passed comment on Kane's jacket, calling it 'really nice'.

Local youth pleads with younger brother to stop hitting himself

'WHY? Why are you doing this to yourself' cries 12-year-old Michael Guinan, desperately trying to prevent his eight-year-old brother Liam from repeatedly smacking himself in the face.

'Stop, please stop hitting yourself ... stop hitting yourself!' he continued.

The situation in the Guinan household is not an isolated one. Across the country, dozens of younger brothers have taken to self-harm, with only their older siblings attempting to stop them.

In the Guinan family's Dungarvan home, older brother Michael admits he has to stop his little brother from self-harming at least once a day, maybe more if there's nothing on telly and it's a really boring day.

Michael tells *WWN* that he does his best to help his brother by grabbing his hand and pleading with him to stop, but sometimes Liam will just keep punching away at himself until their mam shows up.

'I just want him to stop hitting himself,' says Michael, described locally as a pup. 'Sometimes he even does it with both hands, slapping himself on the cheeks while crying and moaning. No matter how much I tell him to stop, he just keeps at it until he starts crying for mam to come in, like a big baby.'

The elder Guinan brother also confides that sometimes Liam will hit himself twice for flinching.

MEDICAL NEWS

Man in critical condition after pulling the stomach off himself

A County Waterford man remains in a critical but stable condition this afternoon after pulling the stomach off himself at his home.

Emergency services were called to the scene at approximately 3:45 p.m. after a neighbour reported 'loud moans' emanating from the man's home.

'I also heard several different women screaming in the apartment at the same time,' longtime neighbour Theresa Dunne recalls, 'but the ambulance lads later said there was only one person in the house, Mr Clark, and that I may have been hearing his computer as it was on when they went in.'

Dermot Clark (45) was later rushed to University Hospital Waterford where doctors carried out an emergency procedure to reattach his stomach to its original location below the rib cage.

It is believed Mr Clark pulled the stomach off himself while 'exercising', with doctors treating the condition as a 'rare case'.

'For one to pull the stomach off themselves in such a way is utterly bizarre,' Dr Rashid Petal explains. 'I have no idea what exercise he has been doing, but there is a lot of bruising and tenderness around the groin area, and his underpants were soiled in a milky white secretion – which I have sent off for analysis.'

Since records began, there have only been 12 instances in Ireland where someone pulled the stomachs off themselves. Interestingly, all 12 cases were male.

MOTORING

New drink-driving laws to affect people who can drink loads of pints and still be grand

NEW legislation currently being proposed by Minister for Transport Shane Ross will see a serious clampdown on all people who drive after drinking, even those who insist that 'they're grand and are only going up the road a little bit'.

During a speech at a meeting of the Oireachtas Transport Committee, Ross stated that the current numbers of people who persist in drink-driving is 'unacceptable', and that new laws would mean that people would be classed as 'over the limit' after less than one pint.

If implemented, this could have serious repercussions for people who are 'grand to drive after a few pints' and have never hit anyone while driving, not just lightweights and careless people.

The new laws will grant no concessions for people who 'just don't want to walk back for the car in the morning', nor will they give leniency for drink-drivers who didn't even go to a nightclub that night.

'I think it's a disgrace, to be honest,' said one local man who normally has three, maybe six pints before heading home when the roads are quiet.

'It's one thing to clamp down on people who drink-drive and cause accidents, but it shouldn't affect those of us who have done this sort of thing for years and never hit anyone. Guards should be instructed to accept that if the driver says he's grand to drive, then he's grand to drive, just wave him along.'

The new legislation has also been dismissed by some geniuses for being 'a cynical ploy to let guards fine more people', as opposed to something that will help save lives on Irish roads.

Miracle teenager survives on his own for almost six hours with no WiFi

IN what has been hailed as 'a miracle', one Waterford teenager has reportedly survived in his home with no connection to the Internet for almost six whole hours.

Answering to the name 'David Gowan', the 16-year-old was found in a distressed state yesterday evening, walking through a Dungarvan neighbourhood holding his Samsung Galaxy above his head looking for a signal and muttering incoherently.

The emergency services were notified and David was brought to a nearby Starbucks and hooked up to their WiFi immediately. It remains unclear as to how the teen was left without Internet for such a long period of time, and a search has begun to find David's

parents, with fears that they may have other kids without even a single bar of coverage.

'David survived without access to any social media or video sharing sites for the better part of an afternoon,' said an amazed member of Waterford's child protection services.

'No GIFs, no memes, no porn. It's incredible to see him in such good condition, considering what he went through. There's grown adults who can't go without

Internet for that long, let alone teenagers. God love him like, he didn't even see the new *Star Wars* trailer yet.'

David was not available for interview, with rumours circulating that the poor youngster had lost the ability to speak in anything other than normal English, having not used emojis for so long.

Did you know?

100% of barbers admit to giving all men 'short back and sides' regardless of what they request.

Driver on M1 in thrilling 'race to Dundalk' with total stranger in other lane

THE driver of a 2012 blue Skoda Octavia travelling from Swords to Dundalk may not be aware of it, but he's currently involved in a neck-and-neck race up the Pale with Adam Jennings, who he nonchalantly cut off while merging onto the motorway.

Jennings (33) has made it his morning's work to 'beat that bastard in the Skoda' up the road, and has stayed on the tail of his nemesis while they both travel at speeds of up to 130 kilometres per hour along one of Ireland's busiest roads.

Motorway racing, where a driver will choose a totally oblivious fellow motorist to 'race' over an unspecified distance for no good reason whatsoever, has always been a popular sport among those road-users with little or no time to concentrate on driving carefully.

However, this morning's race has been classed as 'one for the ages', with Jennings '09 Toyota Corolla occasionally overtaking his Skoda-driving foe, only to lose ground while stuck behind a slow-moving lorry, before sinking the boot again to make up lost ground.

'If I get out of the toll plaza quicker than he does, victory is in sight,' said Jennings, focusing more on the race than on his three small children in the back seat.

'This is Schumacher–Hill. It's Prost–Mansell. Two drivers. One road. One goal – get to the slip-road for Dundalk south before the other. Let's GO!'

UPDATE: Although Jennings is claiming victory, judges ruled the race a 'no-contest' after the Skoda peeled off for Collon. Jennings continued the rest of the journey without a rival, before racing a Ford Transit from Ardee to the Dundalk Applegreen for the hell of it.

Rollie smoker treats himself to pack of real fags

'IT'S like a little present to myself,' said Waterford man Kenneth Muldoon, unwrapping a pack of Marlboro cigarettes like a child on Christmas morning.

Muldoon (23) is a regular smoker but is limited to smoking hand-rolled cigarettes due to also being too broke to afford 'real fags' most of the time.

Resorting to 'making do' with rollies that look like the inside of a bookie's pen, Muldoon splashes out on proper cigarettes every four weeks or so, whenever he has a spare tenner in his pocket or if he just feels that his lungs are due 'a treat'.

'Rollies are alright, but it's like putting together a Kinder Surprise toy every time you want a smoke,' explains Muldoon.

'And they're a nightmare when you've a few pints on board, trying to put together a cigarette like Lego with a filter stuck in the corner of your mouth while you get bumped by people from all sides. So it's nice to just open a pack and boom, there's a smoke waiting for you. Open it again, there's another! And another and another! It's just the most magical experience in the world.'

Muldoon also states that real cigarettes seem healthier, and are basically good for you if you smoke enough of them.

Couple posting pictures of their 'little outdoor adventures' told to fuck off

A local Waterford couple, who seem to spend their weekends engaged in 'little adventures' if the photos they post on social media are anything to go by, have been politely told by everyone they know to fuck off.

Peter and Sarah Sealing's latest exploit was marked with an album uploaded to Facebook entitled 'another little outdoor adventure', drawing more frustration from friends, family and co-workers who have become tired of being reminded that they did absolutely nothing with their weekend by comparison.

The photos mark the 37th album the Sealings have shared on social media this year, each one chronicling a different outdoor adventure in which they have taken part.

'We can't be any clearer when we say fuck off, fuck right off with your walks and your hikes and your hillside coffee shops,' one comment below the photos read, which at the time of this article's publication had received a modest 4,000 likes.

Speculation has been rife among the couple's Facebook friends as to the motivation behind the photos. The general conclusion drawn is that both Peter and Sarah are full of themselves and want everyone to be impressed by a stroll along a beach or up a mountain.

'Sorry if how proactive we are rubs people up the wrong way, but we just love, love, love, being out and about, we couldn't imagine spending the week on the couch, ya know,' Sarah explained.

Sarah also pointed out a little-known fact that an outdoor activity technically might as well have not happened at all if evidence of it, in the form of 600 pictures, isn't uploaded to Facebook and Instagram shortly afterwards.

Far from being deterred by being told to fuck right off by everyone they know, Peter and Sarah are expected to upload pictures from a 95k 'fun run' they are taking part in this weekend.

Wonderful World of Science

A study published in *The Lancet* predicts that 2189 will be the year when Irish people stop freaking out when referred to as British.

Did you know?

RTÉ cancelled the highly popular *Bosco* show when its star was found to be trafficking Eastern European prostitutes into Ireland.

Dublin drugs crime criminal gang plot murder daylight horror criminal attempt

DUBLIN, our capital city, is besieged yet again by murdering drugs criminals in yet another death plot plan carried out by masked gunmen in broad daylight.

Shot dead! The victims were known to gardaí for their links to drug-related shootings and gang-related violence and mob-style executions and fire-based arson and penis-based rapes.

As children played in a schoolyard mere miles away, feared criminals, in retaliation for attacks from other feared criminals, struck fear into the hearts of the fearful in the cool air of a February morning, while wearing masks and brandishing an arsenal of shotguns, pistols, uzis, machetes, drugs, pitbull dogs, AK-47 assault rifles, and fistfuls of dirty drug money.

'Murder. Murder killing drug scum plots, linked to known criminals,' said one tabloid journalist, reaching into a glass bowl filled with gang-related phrases in a bid to produce an attention-grabbing headline for tomorrow's paper.

'Blood crazy killing drugs epidemic capital city. Thugs shotguns drugs, gardaí powerless, streets equal warzones, links to crime syndicates. Costa del Scum! Spain! Dublin, murder! Aghhhh!'

This journalist then went back to work compiling a 24-page pullout for this weekend's edition, which will consist of the same four words over and over again.

Yes, Dublin is once again in the vice-like grip of drugs gangs launching murderous plots to assassinate known drug lords with links to crime families, with the gardaí powerless to stop the carnage leaking out onto the streets in broad daylight.

Local woman who never wins anything would love to win Facebook competition

A Waterford mother of three has issued a heartbreaking missive on her Facebook page to accompany the sharing of a competition for cobblelock paving by a local company. In it she stresses how she would love to win the €1,000 worth of paving slabs as she 'never wins anything'.

Janet Kirkham (36) took part in the 'like and share to enter' competition posted on Facebook by 'Hannigan and Sons – Asphalt, Patio and Paving Specialists' in which one winner will have their driveway revamped with new paving in a colour of their choice.

The competition was the sixth that Mrs Kirkham entered that day, each with a note added about how much she would love to win the weekend away/gas boiler service/€80 hair voucher/DVD/ miscellaneous prizes.

In all instances, no competition had asked more of entrants other than to like their page and share the post, but that didn't stop Dungarvan native Kirkham from adding a little plea with each shared post, with her desire to win paving bricks proving to be particularly heartbreaking.

'xXx would love to win dis, never win anything,' wrote Kirkham while sharing. 'Kids love playn football in driveway, would be great if had better surface so lots of love for this prize, can move d car out of way LOL LOL share this page would love to win!!!!'

As the draw nears, the entire nation holds its breath.

BREAKING NEWS

Parent posts inspiring statement their toddler clearly never fucking said

TODAY in an incident many experts are consigning to the 'shit that never happened' category of the Internet, a Waterford toddler gave a powerful speech about the state of the world, which was then transcribed by her mother onto social media despite the fact nobody buys for a second that the kid said anything of the sort.

'I asked little Tanya what she thought of all the wars and poverty in the world, and here's what she had to say,' wrote Jane Kelliher on her Facebook page this morning, lying through her virtual teeth.

'She's only two and a half, isn't it amazing how much we can all learn from children? #lovemybaby, #soyoungsowise.'

The statement was followed by a lengthy and grammatically perfect musing that the 34-year-old mother clearly wrote herself about how the world could be so much more if its people would just put down their weapons and come together to help end poverty and hunger once and for all, combined with a picture of little Tanya wearing a pair of *Frozen* pajamas while eating a Babybel with the red cover still on it.

So far the post has failed to go viral worldwide, prompting the Dungarvan native to make a second attempt at claiming her daughter is a philosopher some time next week with a post about how the toddler came up with the perfect solution to climate change by planting more flowers.

Rural drug dealer thinks he's Tony fucking Montana or something

A County Tipperary man thinks he's Tony fucking Montana or something after selling a bar of weed in four weeks, sources close to the man revealed today.

Aidan Lyons (19) who got the nine ounces of contraband 'on tic', reportedly told everyone how much of a big player he is now, claiming he may soon be 'known to gardaí' if he's lucky.

'If I keep this up I might make the *Sunday World* and even get a proper nickname like *The Beast*,' Lyons told *WWN*, in a townie accent he picked up since starting to deal last month. 'I'm after banging out nearly two ounces a week in three-gram bags. At this rate,

I'll be driving a 5 series in no time,' adding, 'the world is mine.'

However, friends have since pointed out that Lyons has retrieved very little money from his sales, as he gave half of it away on the book to people he doesn't really know or trust.

'Poor auld Aido has lost the run of himself,' friend Patrick Greene explains. 'Everyone suddenly became his friend when he got the bar of weed. Now they're not even answering their phones when he's ringing, which could be dangerous for him as he owes the real dealer two grand.'

Lyons, who sold 10 panadols for €300 to a lad in school once, claims he will get the money back 'no matter what', by using intimidation tactics he learned on the mean streets of Kilusty, the tiny village he grew up in.

'Yeah, there's a few lads not answering their phones, so I've threatened them with knocking on their parents' door if they don't text back,' the absolute hard man concluded.

UPDATE: Aidan has since broken two of his legs after 'falling down the stairs', and now has an irrational fear of being outside.

Did you know?
67% of good-for-nothing losers lack self-confidence, research shows.

THE Insurance Squad raided a brokerage and seized insurance premiums with an estimated street value of €5 million.

Car insurance has become one of the most detested criminal elements in the country, with even hardened drug crime lords looking down on insurance companies as nothing more than detestable vultures.

Operating as a criminal cartel, insurance companies have long bled the country dry by making their customer base dependent on their products before jacking up the price of premiums year after year.

With the government either powerless to stop this crime wave or just happy to ignore it, insurance companies have been left unchecked until earlier this

Car insurance with street value of €5 million seized in dawn raid

week when the decision was made to step in and 'kick some ass', resulting in the daring dawn raid this morning.

'We kicked in the doors of a local brokerage and dragged the CEO out in his boxers,' said a spokesperson close to the taskforce.

'Inside, we found dozens of premiums that would have cost millions if they had hit the street. Look at this: we've got one for a 36-year-old man who drives

10,000 km a year, one for a 19-year-old girl on a provisional licence, another for a 56-year-old woman with no previous claims or convictions … these are the kinds of premiums that would have had devastating effects on the pockets of ordinary citizens, so we're glad to have them off the streets.'

Fears are now growing over retaliatory attacks from the insurance gangs, with sneaky terms and conditions or excess hikes expected in the coming months.

HOUSING NEWS

Dublin landlords now looking for 35 years' rent upfront

THERE have been renewed calls to Housing Minister Eoghan Murphy today for more rent protection after it was revealed that some Dublin City landlords were requesting up to 35 years' rent upfront from potential tenants as a deposit.

In the latest revelation, some tenants have had to pay hundreds of thousands of euro to landlords in a bid to secure

rental accommodation, with one Dublin family even offering up their first-born child as insurance.

'It's an awful amount of money to pay upfront, but what other choice do we have?' asked renter Damien Woods, who handed over a €757,000 deposit for a one-bedroom apartment in the city centre on a 12-month contract. 'I'm pretty sure I'll get

it all back when I move out next year, but it's really unfair on those people who don't have the money to rent and need to work in the city.'

Meanwhile, several Irish banks have denied they are facilitating unscrupulous landlords by offering 'deposit mortgages' to customers at a 45 per cent interest rate, claiming instead to be helping people acquire the rental accommodation of their dreams.

'There's not enough houses being built, so how else do you expect us to make back the money we owe the country?' asked an AIB spokesman. 'We're even offering mortgages on treehouses now. Have you seen our television advert? Yeah, that's about how desperate it is right now. So stop worrying your little heads about it and just trust us property people to do our thing.'

Rural newborn twins already feuding over who gets family farm

A six-day-old pair of identical twins in Leitrim have become the youngest siblings in the history of Ireland to feud over who gets 'the lower field', *WWN* can exclusively confirm.

Born just last week, Ian and James Mulderne have refused to speak to each other for four of the six days they've been on this earth, amid a bitter dispute over who will inherit the seven-acre piece of land that their parents own just outside Mohill, County Leitrim.

Although feuds between siblings over property and real estate are an inevitable and inescapable part of Irish life, the Mulderne boys have broken the record for youngest warring members of the same family by a good eight years, beating the previous record set by an eight-year old Carlow girl and her 10-year old brother over who gets the family house when mammy and daddy pass away.

Speaking to *WWN*, Jeanette Mulderne spoke of her hopes that her sons would put their differences aside and reunite.

'They overheard me talking to my husband Paul, about how Ian was a better sleeper than James,' said Jeannette, in tears.

'That must have made James think that Ian was going to be getting the lower field, leaving James with just the two acres at the top of the hill with no road frontage on it. Since then, we've had to take them everywhere separately ... I don't know how we're going to get through the christening.'

BREAKING: Although there doesn't seem to be any resolution to the rift between the brothers, they have agreed to at least 'be civil' to one another.

TRENDING Parents arrested after kids found spoiled rotten

A south Dublin couple have been released from Dún Laoghaire Garda Station this afternoon after being charged with child neglect.

Sarah and Declan Ronan from Vicar Road were stopped and arrested by gardaí while exiting their luxury home shortly before eight this morning. The arrests followed numerous complaints from family members about the way they treat their two young kids.

'We received an official complaint from the children's grandmother and aunt that they have been spoiled rotten over a period of up to eight years,' investigating Garda Martin Bridges confirmed. 'Upon further investigation this morning, and acting on a warrant, we intercepted the couple transporting the children to school in a 171-D Range Rover Sport, despite the school being only a two-minute walk away.'

Gardaí then issued the warrant and carried out a search of the family's stately home. 'On further examination we found dozens of expensive items littered around both children's bedrooms, including two 55-inch smart TVs, 14 top-of-the-range games consoles, thousands of euro worth of designer clothes and a huge collection of expensive toys,' he added.

Gardaí contacted Child Protection Services who took the two children, aged seven and eight, into care, where they will get the attention they deserve.

'This is probably the worst case of spoiled children we've ever seen,' said one care worker. 'The poor things didn't even know how to open a car door by themselves. When we offered them tea, they insisted on chai or Earl Grey, the poor pets. They don't even wipe their own arses.'

Mr and Mrs Ronan were charged with child neglect and spoiling their kids rotten and were released on bail pending a court appearance next month.

In Ireland, spoiling your children rotten comes with a mandatory five-to-ten-year sentence.

Shit about to go down on dancefloor as wedding guest takes off tie

REVELLERS on the dancefloor of a Waterford wedding were on high alert at the weekend, after one guest loosened his tie just enough to let everyone know that 'oh yeah, this shit just got real'.

Tramore native Sean O'Massey had maintained his decorum throughout the wedding ceremony of his friend Pat Shefflin to Jane Farrell, and also kept a lid on himself throughout the meal and the speeches.

With his top button still done up and his tie still impeccably tied, O'Massey was among the 100 guests who clapped and welcomed the newlyweds onto the floor for their first dance as a married couple at approximately 8:45 GMT, after which the 35-year-old was seen to untie his top button and loosen his tie by 40 mm or so, signifying to the congregation that they need to 'stand the fuck back, this is happening'.

'A day of drinking kicked in all at once when that tie got loosened,' said one onlooker.

'It was like the tie was holding all the drink in Sean's head, then when he untightened it, the alcohol just surged through his system. It was an instant transformation, from mild-mannered wedding guest happily enjoying a beautiful day, to someone who could dance to any song for any length of time, rhythm be damned'.

The situation escalated later in the night when 'Walk of Life' came on, at which point O'Massey's tie went from around his neck to around his forehead in less than a second.

12 MONTHS A GUARD *Month 3*

We had a special guest lecturer today: a guard who had served on the force back before the advent of camera phones and social media. He brought us through his rose-tinted memories of a time when guards weren't constantly monitored by the public, or brought up on a social media trial by a bunch of crybabies and 'leftie sadsacks who can't take a truncheon to the shin without writing an essay about it'. We were warned that these days the conduct of gardaí is being held up to closer scrutiny than ever before, so if we are going to lay into someone, we've to have a good look round first to make sure there's nobody live-streaming it. 'The only live-streaming back in the day was coming from a broken nose,' our lecturer mused, wistfully. Meanwhile, I've taken on extra tasks due to being the only recruit who has a car. Driving fellow recruits to and from their digs, flying down to the bookies to put on bets for the senior guards, taking uniforms home to my mam to have them cleaned ... I'm keeping my petrol receipts to claim it all back, but nobody seems to know who I submit them to and my superior just laughed when I asked him.

Waterford man awarded €179k after receiving bad pint from city night club

A Waterford man who was served a 'bad pint' in a local city bar has today been awarded €179,000 damages by the High Court, *WWN* can reveal.

Mr Justice Anthony Barr made the award to Brian Phelan (47) against Egan's Nightclub over a questionable pint of Budweiser that was poured by barman James Macky on 17 March last year, forcing the construction worker to miss the following day's work.

Phelan, a grandson of four, told the court that he felt 'poisoned' by the bad pint, the effects of which were delayed until the following morning at 6 a.m., as he was waking up to go to work on a building site the following Friday, leaving him no other option but to phone in sick and forfeit a day's wage.

'I was out all day drinking with friends and I was in great form until I hit Egan's Nightclub,' the victim told the court, now caressing his pot belly which was protruding from under his untucked Ben Sherman shirt. 'I remember ordering a round of jägerbombs with the round of beers, because it was Paddy's Day like, and the barman handed me the pint.

'Now, as drunk as I was at the time, I could see the pint looked a bit off, flat or something, so I asked the young fella to put a head on it. Anyway, I took back the thing, thinking it was grand, and the next thing I knew I was absolutely fucking dying in the bed with the alarm going off, Judge. The whole fucking day after I was literally pissing from me arse,' he calmly demonstrated before the court, with a bucket and a squeezy bottle full of yellow liquid.

Barrister acting for the nightclub, Derek Saint John, admitted his client's liability after taking into account Mr Phelan's 40 long years' experience as a drinker, opposed to the barman's four years in the job, stating the claim of negligence was advanced, leaving the judge's task to only assess damages.

'This seems to be a clear-cut case of being served a bad pint,' pointed out Mr Justice Anthony Barr, with every member of the courtroom nodding in agreement, including the publican himself, 'and a bad pint is a bad pint; it's a crime and you will be rewarded a significant compensation for your trauma.'

In a landmark decision for the nation's drinkers, and on the basis of guidelines on damages set down by the Court of Appeal, Mr Justice Anthony Barr awarded €170,000 to the now delighted Phelan, who was making pint gestures to a rowdy swarm of 'lads' at the back of the court.

The judge also agreed special damages of €9,000 for 'just being a pure fucking legend of a man for bringing it to court', ending proceedings with the question 'scoops?' to the courtroom.

⭐ TOP 5
Responses to chuggers on the street 2017

5 'La la la la, can't hear you.'

4 'Fuck off following me.'

3 'Sorry, I've no notes or small change on me and I don't own a debit or credit card or a chequebook.'

2 'Stop it. I don't want to hear about how little kids just need €2 a month to live, I'm late for pints with the lads'

1 'Where did you get that photo of me? God, what do you want??? Okay, okay, €10 a month, will that keep you off my back? And you'll destroy the photo once I sign up, yeah?'

Man had no idea co-worker was a Protestant

A Waterford office worker has expressed surprise and shock after discovering the man sitting opposite him in work for the past two years is a Protestant, *WWN* can reveal.

'I just hadn't a clue, it's mad,' office worker Cormac Nellin shared with *WWN*, still wrestling with the revelation.

Nellin made the discovery earlier this morning when discussing with Aaron Kilbride the impending baptism of his youngest child. Kilbride, not previously known for willfully hiding any deep and dark secrets, was forced to disclose to Nellin that none of his own children were baptised as he was an atheist with his own parents being of the Protestant faith.

'You wouldn't think it to look at him would you?' Nellin said of Kilbride while spreading the news around every one of his co-workers, who were not sure what the big deal was. 'A Protestant like. Wasn't sure we had any in Waterford.'

'Ah, you can see it now though, when you properly look at him,' Nellin said, visually comparing Kilbride's pale skin, glasses, short hair, beard and shirt with another co-worker Derek Devlin's shirt, beard, short hair, glasses and pale skin.

'Chalk and cheese,' Nellin said, laughing to himself, noting how foolish he was for not seeing the startlingly obvious before.

It is believed Nellin will spend the rest of the working day periodically staring at Kilbride in wonderment and slight suspicion.

Women's GAA teams getting 14% less ham sandwiches and Club Orange than men

ALTHOUGH great leaps have been made in the past year to promote women's GAA as equally exciting as its male counterpart, new statistics have shown that ladies playing football or camogie receive 14.4% fewer sambos after each match.

Under the standard GAA pay structure, male participants in games such as hurling, football and handball receive up to four ham sandwiches, a swig out of a two-litre bottle of Club Orange, and a good hard slap on the back after each match.

This can be increased to a carvery dinner and a big feed of drink after significant matches, such as selling out Croke Park at €60 a ticket.

However, women receive just 86% of this total amount, as evidenced by yesterday's All-Ireland Ladies GAA final where the victorious Cork senior team didn't even get a full sliced-pan's worth of sandwiches after defeating Dublin by one point.

'Women are underpaid in almost every profession in Ireland, and now we're getting done when it comes to refreshments as well,' said Maureen Hanillan, spokesperson for the GAA Gender Gap Awareness Association (GAAGGAA).

'Our women train as hard as the men, play as hard as the men and are as committed as the men, and they don't even get crisps? It's time for equality. Christ knows it's not like we're asking for actual money, we know it's the GAA we're dealing with, but if the men are getting cheese on their sandwiches, we want cheese on our sandwiches.'

Dozens of women hospitalised by local fanny magnet

THERE were grisly scenes in Waterford city centre this afternoon, after dozens of women suffered severe pubic injuries when a local fanny magnet walked into town.

Sean Coughlin (34) attracted vaginas to himself with such force that, in some extreme instances, women reported that their genitals had been ripped away from their bodies. Reports have confirmed that Coughlin was wearing his best Ben Sherman shirt at the time, as well as lashings of Lynx Africa, amplifying his fanny magnet abilities. Women of all ages were left rolling on the floor, clutching their groins in agony, as

a specialist garda team bundled Coughlin into the back of a van and whisked him out of town to limit the damage to the nether regions of the rest of Waterford's female population.

'You can't be a pure fanny magnet and just wander around town,' yelled one doctor over the screams in the A&E of Waterford Hospital.

'I've got 30 women in here, all with their fannies torn right

off. One woman needed 150 stitches to re-attach her vagina, and she was one of the lucky ones. There's 10 women out there whose fannies flew into the River Suir as the cops drove your man away.'

Appeals for fanny magnet regulations have flooded social media following the incident, with campaigners pleading with confirmed fanny magnets to stay out of populated areas.

Police ordered to round up and shoot anyone referring to themselves as 'digital influencers'

A worldwide order issued by a record number of nations will see everyone referring to themselves as a 'digital influencer' shot on sight, *WWN* has learned.

At the behest of the public, governments have instructed their police forces to deal swiftly and fatally with individuals whose heads are 'stuck so far up their arses they think a picture of themselves accompanied by a complimentary phrase about a brand will suddenly drive up the company's sales of items, services or products.'

'Some lad on Instagram was giving it the "I'm a digital influencer" like he has the same influence on empty-headed fools as Kim Kardashian does or something. He's a trainee fucking hairdresser showing off

his Nike Air Jordans his mam bought him, for Christ's sake,' shared irate member of the public Ciaran Littleton, who is believed to be in favour of the shooting order.

While there are no official numbers, experts estimate that there are as many as '23,000 fucking eejits who consider themselves to be digital influencers' in Ireland currently. Those suffering from these vivid delusions of grandeur have been instructed to cop on to themselves but many fail to listen.

'I threw up a picture of my new iPhone on Snapchat and Instagram and then I find out Apple have sold one billion iPhones, those events are not a coincidence. People take my advice on products,' explained

one insufferable digital influencer, Dublin man Eoin Healy.

Gardaí in Ireland have already begun to enforce the new crackdown on so-called digital influencers.

'You can influence me hoop, you narcissistic spanners,' head of the Digital Influencer Termination Unit, Garda Vincent Lonergan, shared with *WWN*.

'We don't take shooting anyone lightly, but this'll be great craic altogether,' Garda Lonergan explained as his unit broke down the door of a 26-year-old woman, who despite only having a following of 789 people on Instagram and still living in her parents' house, thinks any recommendation she gives a dress on ASOS will result in it being sold out within seconds.

Did you know?

In Dublin, you are never more than 3.5 metres away from someone who refers to themselves as a 'social media influencer'.

Waterford armed forces bombard Kilkenny rebels in battle for Ferrybank

WATERFORD armed forces have today bombarded rebel strongholds in the north of the city this morning in their latest bid to reclaim the disputed Ferrybank region from the grasp of Kilkenny fundamentalists.

Airstrikes pounded key locations on the hill, forcing the rebels to retreat into civilian areas, with some reports on the ground stating that they are using Waterford children and GAA players as human shields.

So far 367 casualties have been reported in the region, many of those innocent civilians who had no opinion either way in the ongoing dispute.

'We just want to live in peace here without all this fighting,' said eight-year-old Amir Hassan, who moved to Ferrybank from Iraq in 2011 with his family. 'Who cares about county borders here? We're living on a tiny island here. How is this ridiculousness even possible?'

The Blue and White Helmets, known locally as the Waterford Civil Defence, have stated that as many as 58 civilians have been killed in this morning's airstrikes on Ferrybank, with more expected over the coming weeks.

'This is our land because we live here and support the Kilkenny hurling team,' said John Paul Phelan, leader of the Kilkenny Indigenous Society In Slieverue (KISIS). 'We will stop at nothing to defend what is rightfully ours. God is great!'

The 5,827 acre area, which generates an annual revenue of €110 million in agriculture and thoroughbred hurlers for the Kilkenny regime, has long been disputed by both sides. Sources on the ground believe hurlers are the real goal here, with Kilkenny producing 1,200 barrels of hurlers a day.

Record number of Kevins being referred to as 'Kev'

THE latest figures released from the Institute For Recording Nickname Usage (IFRNU) suggest that a growing number of Kevins are insisting people call them 'Kev', leading to a record number of Kevs.

'Just call me Kev,' confirmed 79% of Kevins surveyed by the IFRNU, in the largest study of its kind ever conducted in Ireland.

'While "Kevin" communicates a formality normally associated with any and all first names, Kevins eschew such conventions preferring to appear relaxed and chilled out about formal name calling. Nearly four in every five Kevins now identify as a Kev, it's really fascinating stuff,' explained lead researcher Dr Kev Fagan.

However, the IFRNU research is not good news for every Kev in the country, as some of the study makes for uncomfortable reading.

'A lot of Kevs turn violent if you persist with calling them Kevin despite their laid-back insistence that Kev will do fine actually,' added Dr Fagan.

The study suggests that Kevs have such a nonchalant and easy-going nature that when people call them by the more formal 'Kevin' they immediately turn to violence to correct any name-calling that suggests they are anything but relaxed people.

'There's a complex series of psychological phenomena at play as well, which begs further studying, but some Seans, Eamons and Nialls have taken to changing their names to Kev as well, keen to feel that warm and jovial response all Kevs feel when introducing themselves as "Kev" to the general public.'

Royal family relocating to Ireland because of Brexit

THE Brexit exodus has officially begun with news coming in that the British Royal Family are now planning to move to Ireland in the hopes of securing a better and more stable future for the monarchy.

In a statement issued today by Buckingham Palace, the Queen and her husband, Prince Phillip, are expected to move to the Emerald Isle in January 2019, just three months before Brexit is officially executed. They are looking to build a 700,000-square-metre palace, which will eventually house the entire royal family, on the Hill of Tara in County Meath.

'As a result of the financial uncertainty brought about by the UK leaving the European Union, Her Majesty Queen Elizabeth II has decided to relocate to Ireland for the foreseeable future,' read the statement. The Royal Family's spokesperson insisted that the move will not get in the way of the Queen's duties, 'All speeches, including the Queen's Christmas message, will be streamed live from her new home, but will come with a few minor changes.'

Due to 'fair balance' in Irish broadcasting laws, the format of the Queen's addresses will have to alter slightly to include Irish rebel songs in the background.

The songs include 'A Nation Once Again', 'Come Out You Black and Tans', 'Rifles of the IRA' and the classic 'Give Ireland Back to the Irish'.

Planning permission for the Queen's new home has already been submitted, but is also subject to several conditions laid out by Irish law.

'Unfortunately, the Queen will not be able to fly the Union Jack over the property, as that has been illegal in Ireland since the establishment of the state in 1921,' explained Meath County Councillor Gerard Holden. 'It's probably for their own good, as a lot of people around here are not that happy about them building on such a historic location. In fact, they really couldn't have picked a worse place, being the Royal Family.' Holden concluded, 'But I'm sure people will warm to them ... eventually.'

IRISH Water has announced that they will tackle the massive water leak crippling supply to Drogheda with as much pace and enthusiasm as Irish people tackled paying their water bills, *WWN* can reveal.

Thousands of people in the Meath/Louth area are now entering their fourth day without water, after a burst main at a key water treatment plant in Meath caused shortages to approximately 70,000 homes.

In an official statement on the matter, Irish Water has pledged to sort out the problem later this week, or maybe next month, or after they go on holidays, or whenever they fucking feel like it, frankly.

'Yeah, nobody was calling us when we were looking for payment but all of a sudden there's a burst pipe and you come crying to us. "Oh, come fix

'We're in as much of a rush to fix leak as you were to pay the bill' – Irish water

our water for free. We never gave you any money, but now there's no water in my tap and I need you to fix it." Yeah, we'll be right there, pal. It's our top fucking priority,' said a spokesperson for Irish Water.

'Yeah, free water falls from the sky and goes directly into your taps without any pipework or infrastructure or maintenance. Why would you bother paying

for that? And look what's falling from the sky now, free workmen with free materials to fix the leaks in the free water system. We'll have you fixed up in no time, promise!'

As the situation unfolds, the government has pledged to 'not touch this one with a bargepole' and urged citizens to accept that 'they're on their fucking own'.

WWN WORLD NEWS

Apple stuns world by unveiling some sort of phone-type device

IN a move that stunned the globe and sent share prices skyrocketing, tech giants Apple took a quantum leap ahead in technology and unveiled their latest device: a phone.

Dubbed the iPhone 7, the gadget is said to be groundbreaking in every way, from its ability to take pictures to its ability to usually take calls as long as you're standing at a certain angle to the horizon at the time.

The new device, unveiled by Apple CEO Tim Cook during a glitzy 40-day conference, sent shockwaves round the world as country after country woke up to the news that Apple had finally said, 'Fuck computers, we're gonna make a goddamn phone.'

'I can't believe it can play games and only costs about the same as my first car,' said one man, who up until now has communicated with his friends and family using a series of drumbeats on the hollowed-out carcass of a dead cow.

'Truly, this is an incredible time to be alive. A phone, with a touchscreen and a camera … what will they think of next?' said one impressed woman, shaking her head in wonder.

Adding to the general amazement at the announcement, Apple revealed that the new device would not be compatible with the standard headphone jack that has been around for the past 40 years. Just because.

BRITISH NEWS

'Just try to fucking leave, I dare you,' Prince George tells Scotland

ADORABLE king-in-waiting Prince George has informed Scotland to 'just try to fucking leave, I dare you' after news emerged that the Scottish National Party is looking into the possibility of staging a second Scottish independence referendum.

Taking a break out from reading *The Art of War* by Sun Tzu at playschool, the delightful toddler made a slitting-throat gesture while looking menacingly in the direction of Scotland.

'If you fuckers leave, where am I going to dump all those dead bodies?' queried the young royal, whose trademark outfits resemble those of a demon child from the 1940s. 'Glasgow is

supposed to be the place where I send my most hated enemies.'

Citing economic uncertainty and the fact that over 60% of Scotland voted to remain in the EU, SNP leader Nicola Sturgeon confirmed a second referendum would have to be considered.

'You know I could just turn a Trident missile on all you Irn-Bru-swilling, heroin-loving ginger pricks at any moment, so don't even think about staging

another vote,' the cute prince warned, while producing what looked like the scalps of several red-headed Scots who had previously 'tried to defy him'.

Prince George then wondered out loud if it was possible to deep-fry a human being.

Palace insiders praised the prince's remarks, stating, 'He's really coming on with his speech, so many words. You can't shut him up these days.'

MIDDLE EAST NEWS

America generously donates $38 billion to impoverished and war-torn Israel

IN a kind-hearted and generous gesture to one of the world's most impoverished and war-torn countries, the United States of America has offered to donate a whopping $38 billion to the desperate people of Israel over the next 10 years, *WWN* learned today.

The donation, which represents the largest pledge the US has made to any country, will enshrine funding for Israel's reconstruction programme and expansion across the West Bank. It will help get the fragile nation 'back on its feet' after years of oppression from Iran and terrorist groups like Hamas, who razed Israel to the ground over the past decade.

'I was debating with myself for ages what to spend this extra money we found in our never-ending banking reserves on. Regenerating impoverished cities? Ending the escalation in racism? Gun control? Drug addiction? Water pollution? And then I remembered poor old Israel!' outgoing President of the United States Barack Obama explained.

'There is no other nation in the world I can think of that truly deserves this ludicrous sum of money,' Obama stated. 'No doubt Mr Netanyahu will spend it wisely, for the greater good of mankind.'

The donation, known as a Memorandum of Don't Tell Everyone our Dirty Secrets (MODTEODS), will see $3.8 billion a year in aid delivered to the cash-strapped state.

Following news of the donation, Prime Minister Benjamin Netanyahu requested another $10 billion 'if America could spare it', but later settled on the agreed $38 billion and a few stray airstrikes on Israel's enemies.

'$22,000 per Palestinian ought to do it ... cheers!' the Israeli PM said, thanking America.

OUTGOING American President Barack Obama has ordered one last drone strike this evening in an emotional goodbye to his eight years in office.

Visiting the White House situation room for what is expected to be his last time, the teary-eyed 55-year-old gazed at the freshly printed mission sheet, pausing for a moment before greenlighting its proposed strike on an al-Qaeda stronghold in Yemen. He then wiped a single tear from his cheek.

'I'm really going to miss this old place,' he told his military personnel, who began relaying the strike order over the phone to a 24-year-old drone operator in Texas. 'Bin Laden, Gaddafi, so many great memories we've had here, guys. Some sick-ass shit, some stuff I'll take with me to the grave. Delicate stuff. Stuff I hope my successor has the balls

Emotional Obama greenlights one last drone strike 'for old times' sake'

to carry out when the time arises – at least with Hillary, you'd know that crazy bitch would just blitz anything, no questions asked.'

Watching the situation room's high-resolution screen, Obama hummed the national anthem eerily in the background to the black and white images streaming from the multimillion-dollar unmanned aircraft as it flew to its target in Sana'a, West Yemen.

'Is that a school?' he asked, before then correcting himself. 'Ah, a mosque! I nearly shat myself there. It would be a bad week to kill kids; so close to Christmas and that.'

Timing his instruction 'Engage target' to the peak of his 'The Star-Spangled Banner' rendition, 'O'er the land of the free ... ', the next former president of the United States of America climaxed the song as two AGM-114 Hellfire II air-to-ground missiles simultaneously pummelled the ground below.

' ... and the home of the brave!' he finished, before bowing to his applauding peers.

'America needs to leave the US,' Farage tells Trump rally

OUTGOING UKIP leader Nigel Farage urged Republicans at a Donald Trump rally in Jackson, Mississippi last night to leave the United States if they want to make America great again.

Appearing before 15,000 activists, Farage was flanked by the presidential candidate as he delivered his speech comparing the union of states to the European Union and advocating that America should 'Amexit' immediately.

'Why should you bow down to the United States?' Farage asked the detached crowd, who had no idea what he was on about but applauded like seals regardless. 'America is better off without the US, just like Britain is better off without the EU. Do as I say and everything will be alright.'

Trump, who is trailing his Democratic rival, Hillary Clinton, in the opinion polls, has backed the UK's planned exit from the EU.

'This man obviously knows what he's talking about, m'kay?' the US business tycoon told the rally. 'We need to stop the immigrants from coming in. We need to take America back for the rich native white people who originally owned it. My granddaddy did not come all the way from Germany to have America taken from him. We need to make this country great again, like in World War II when we blew up the Japs and ended the war.'

To end the rally, Trump and Farage were handed a semi-automatic pistol each and they fired several rounds in the air in celebration of their new alliance.

America tries to ignore pale horse that just appeared beside Trump

'STAY on Trump, stay on Trump,' barked the director in the TV control room, trying his best to maintain a sense of calm order following the sudden appearance of a ghostly pale horse onstage with the newly sworn-in President of the United States in Washington DC.

'Camera 2, stay on Trump. Cameras 3 and 4, wide crowd shots only, okay? Keep an eye on the horse, and keep him out of shot.'

A hush fell across the assembled crowd at the inauguration ceremony when the animal appeared to the left of Donald Trump just as he was sworn into office as the 45th president of the United States. It was cloaked in mist and curling its lips back to reveal some very sharp un-horselike fangs.

The arrival of the horse, whose mane on close inspection seems to be made up of the shrieking, miniaturised souls of the trapped dead, was accompanied by what many described as a 'terrifying peal of thunder', or perhaps the bellowing roar of some dreadful horn or similar wind instrument, blown with gusto by some unseen heralder of doom.

Despite the clear ramifications of the appearance of such a beast, Americans are currently doing their best to assure each other that everything is fine, and that sometimes pale horses just show up and it doesn't really mean anything about Trump, America, the world, or indeed the end of days.

'The pale horse? Yeah, that's probably ... that's probably just a stray horse that wandered onto the stage,' said one inauguration attendee from under his sweat-soaked 'Make America Great Again' cap.

'It's nothing to worry about. It's certainly not a harbinger of anything. It's just a horse showing up, saying hello in its own horsey way. Now, let's just all go home and hug our loved ones, everything is going to be just super,' added another Trump supporter.

UPDATE: A skull-faced rider has now appeared on the back of the pale horse, but onlookers continue to assure each other that it is 'just part of the show'.

'We've only €8 billion in the bank' – Vatican defends not paying abuse compensation

ACCORDING to the man responsible for the Holy See's finances, Cardinal George Pell, the Vatican is unable to pay the remaining balance of €568 million under the redress scheme set up to help survivors of clerical sexual abuse, as it has only €8 billion in the bank.

'What do you expect Irish orders to do, pay the amount they are legally obliged to instead of just dodging it and leaving the taxpayer with the bill?' asked the cardinal, who admitted in 2014 to finding hundreds of millions of euro just 'tucked away' in the accounts of various Holy See departments. 'To do so would require an awful lot of effort on our part. Besides, most of the victims have been paid ... just not by us, and isn't that all that matters?'

The Vatican's latest comments come after a report by the Comptroller and Auditor General, published by the Department of Education, which found that the Catholic religious congregations who ran residential institutions where children were abused have paid just 13% of the compensation they owe, despite revenues exceeding €300 million year-on-year.

'If we're being honest, this isn't a Catholic Church problem, it's an Irish problem,' explained Pell, who is himself embroiled in the unfolding Australian Catholic Church child abuse scandal.

'Plus, our finances are very complicated,' Pell explained, perhaps referring to the Vatican Bank's questionable past when they were caught money laundering for the Mafia and former Nazis. 'We have our fingers in a lot of pies, managing €5.9 billion of assets on behalf of 17,400 customers, and we have gold reserves worth over $20 million with the US Federal Reserve, so it's not as easy as signing a cheque. But we do have a few spare Michelangelo paintings if they want to go splitsies?'

The Vatican City has a rich economy relative to its size: it has a population of only 800 people and its nominal GDP per capita is $365,796 – making it the richest state on the planet by this measure.

'Any chance of that trillion dollars you owe us?' Chinese president asks Trump

CHINESE President Xi Jinping has reportedly asked American President Donald Trump if the US has the $1.051 trillion it owes the People's Republic of China. It's the second time he's had to ask since meeting Trump last week and his officials stress that 'he hates asking', but China has a few bills of its own.

Speaking over the phone yesterday amid tensions off the North Korean peninsula, Xi explained that he could really do with 'that few quid'. China owes $4.3 trillion in national debt. As a transcript of the conversation shows, the Chinese premier pointed out the pressures of keeping a nation of 1.3 billion people alive.

Xi: 'Our GDP per capita is the 91st-lowest in the world, below Bosnia and Herzegovina, so you can imagine the crap I'm getting back home, Don. We also have 1,548,498 prison inmates to feed, so shit keeps piling up. I hate asking for that few quid, but you know yourself.'

Trump: 'Tell me about it, we have 2,193,798 prisoners to feed, with only a quarter of the population you guys have, so things are tight here too. Did you ever try just killing them?'

Xi: 'Yeah, officially we get rid of 3,000 a year, but unofficially ... '

Trump: 'I get ya, I get ya. I like your style, Jinping ... can I call you Jinping? You're a great guy. I love those mobile execution vans you little guys have got. Very inventive. I tell you what, I'll ask my money guys to get onto your money guys to see what we can do about that debt.'

Xi: 'Don, that would be great. We've a mountain of unopened bills here, so it would be much appreciated.'

Trump: 'Who the hell do we owe this money to anyway? Everyone is always on about this debt, and I never know, ha ha.'

Xi: 'Ha ha, me too. No idea, but the envelopes look very official and scary.'

Trump: 'Okay, we'll get the ball rolling ... Oh yeah, I nearly forgot, we'll probably make a move on North Korea pretty soon, so if you guys could back off a little?'

Xi: 'Sure thing, but we'll need to flex our muscles a bit and make it look like we're opposed to the whole thing.'

Trump: 'Deal! God, I love this job.'

Xi: 'Me too. Golf this weekend?'

Trump: 'Now you're talking like a president!'

CALL ENDS

Backpacker returns from 12-month trip with wisdom, knowledge and a penis like a sock full of old strawberries

LOCAL man Ciaran Farrell has returned from a year-long backpacking trip around Southeast Asia with a newfound awareness of his place in the world, a deep respect for the cultures and customs of others, and a penis that looks like it could honestly fall off at any moment.

Farrell, who headed off on a nine-country trek just after completing his college degree, spoke to friends about how amazing it was to fully immerse himself in the ways of the indigenous populations of each region he visited. He spoke about how his mind was opened to the new tastes, sounds and sensations that he encountered along the way, and how his dalliances with a never-ending stream of sex workers has left him with so much venereal disease that every trip to the bathroom 'feels like I'm pissing fingernails'.

With a glowing tan that makes him look far healthier than he currently is, Farrell met some of his old friends for his first pint soon after arriving home to Tramore, and regaled them of tales of his experiences, his new outlook on life and the fact that his penis now resembles a bin bag in a butcher's shop.

'I walked along a beach in Thailand just as the sun was rising in the morning ... I was the only person for miles and the serenity is something I will never forget,' said Farrell, scratching at the tip of his cock through his jeans.

'Just the night before I had sat on the sands with a group of musicians, poets and writers from all over the world. It's that kind of experience that has really changed me as a human being, I just ... I just learned so much. It was a true awakening. Then I had a five-way with three girls and a ladyboy for less than the price of a taco chips over here. I felt that for the next month, let me tell you.'

Although his friends were horrified to learn about the state of Farrell's penis, they are most concerned about the fact that he owns a necklace made out of seashells.

Dozens shot in America, probably

IT'S more than likely that reports will come in later today that dozens of people have been shot in America after a shooter goes on a rampage in a school, or possibly an office.

Statistically speaking, America has a mass shooting every few days, so it's pretty fair to say that there's more than likely one going on either now or as this article goes to the presses.

The victims will probably be mostly innocent bystanders, and the overall death toll will include the shooter, who more often than not ends each rampage with a self-inflicted gunshot wound to the head or head area.

'Our thoughts and prayers are with the victims of this occurring or soon-to-occur incident,' say the majority of US political figures in pre-written statements that they keep in their desks ready to have the blanks filled in at a moment's notice.

'The people of [insert place] are a resilient and strong community, and we know that the actions that took place on [insert date] may shake them to their core, but they will endure, and so will these United States. God bless us all, now, or soon.'

As and when the race of the shooter is revealed, *WWN* will confirm whether this latest incident was the work of a troubled loner, or a cowardly act of terrorism.

TRENDING Government to keep changing Health Minister so no one fully gets the blame

THE government has vowed to continue changing the person in charge of the Department of Health in a bid to distance party members from fully getting the blame.

Outgoing Taoiseach Enda Kenny confirmed that swapping different ministers every so often had greatly benefitted the government, and advised the incoming Fine Gael party leader to follow suit.

'It just works, you know?' Kenny addressed his party peers in a closed meeting this afternoon. 'If things get too hot under the collar, just pass the buck onto whomever it is you want to see fail, because believe me, it's a fucking shit show in health and they are doomed to fail.'

'Also make sure the Health Minister is someone young, so the voters can't get too mad at them,' he added. 'God loves a trier, and so do our naive electorate.'

Kenny went on to suggest that a two-year period for a sitting Health Minister is enough for any politician to bear, pointing out the amateurism of the previous Fianna Fáil government who kept the same person in the position for four to five years.

'The idiots had Mary Harney there for more than six years,' he laughed. 'And where's she now? Anything above two years is just professional suicide. Imagine having the same person working on something that length of time – they might actually get somewhere with it.'

Kenny finished by pointing at Simon Harris, the current Health Minister, and shouting, 'One more year, young man, hang in there!'

Eric Trump defects to North Korea

THE highest-ranking US defector in years has said that the days of the country's leadership are 'numbered' and that its attempts to control outside information are not working due to facts being freely available online.

'I am sure that more defections of my colleagues will take place, since America is already on a slippery slope,' said Eric Trump, defector and son of President Donald Trump, during a news conference in Pyongyang, the capital of North Korea. 'The traditional structures of the American system are crumbling; so I know more will follow me.'

Paraded in front of a bank of photographers and an adoring crowd, Eric bravely told the story of his daring escape from the clutches of the authoritarian regime in America. Still visibly carrying the psychological scars from his ordeal, his denunciation of the Trump-Tower-based regime was littered with apprehension.

'He demands 100% loyalty; you will not be hired to any public position unless he knows he can control you. It was a case of fleeing now, or staying around long enough to be the next person on his list,' Eric explained. 'He wanted me to sign a contract agreeing to donate my first-born's hair to his wig.'

North Korean officials deny that the younger Trump's defection was secured with the promise of pioneering gum reduction surgery.

'We have not sweetened a deal of any sort, Eric Trump has fled a tyrannical regime and is welcome to enjoy the many freedoms our citizens enjoy here,' a spokesperson said.

'Can all the migrants from the countries we invaded go away now please'

BRITISH Prime Minister Theresa May has politely asked all the foreign migrants currently living in the United Kingdom to kindly 'pick up their shit and leave' at their earliest convenience.

In what has been hailed as her toughest address yet, the Conservative Party leader listed out a torrent of Eurail and airport departure timetables in a bid to help those who 'may not have left yet'.

'There are a couple of planes headed to India at six o'clock,' she pointed out, sifting through pages of printed-out timetables. 'The Eurotunnel would probably be your best bet though as it's cheaper. Plus, you'll be on mainland Europe within the hour and can easily just grab another train to wherever the hell it is you're going. Please leave the keys of your homes under the doormat or wheelie bin, where I'm sure we'll find them.'

This latest request comes just days after Mrs May proposed that UK companies compile a name-and-shame list of all their foreign employees, in the hope that it will force them into hiring only British passport holders in future.

Closing her speech, the 60-year-old turned to the country's six million Irish workers, confirming that they, too, will have to look elsewhere for work, despite having similar skin tone and hair colour to their British neighbours.

'And that goes for you Paddies too,' she barked, holding a crossed-out Graham Norton postcard in her hand. 'We don't even rule parts of Ireland anymore and ye're still coming over here pestering people for jobs with your God awful slang and ridiculous accents. I hear Syria will be dishing out construction jobs soon, once the Americans and Russians are finished demolishing it. We'll give ye a good reference.'

With that, May raised the podium microphone over her head, stared at the bemused crowd and then dropped it, before walking off the stage to Dr Dre's 1992 gangsta rap song 'Nuthin' But a "G" Thang'.

God dies after battle with short illness

THE Vatican has today confirmed the untimely death of God the almighty and creator of the universe after losing a 'brave battle with a short illness' at his heavenly home.

Pope Francis led tributes this morning from St Peter's, sending his condolences to God's only remaining relative, Jesus, who has been sitting at the right hand of the Lord for the past 2,000 years.

'His untimely death will no doubt touch billions of people across the world,' an emotional Pope Francis told followers. 'The Catholic Church passes on its condolences to his only son, and to all his staff, the Angels Gabriel, Michael, Peter and all the saints, and to you, our brothers and sisters.'

Details surrounding God's illness are still vague, but sources believe God was coming to the end of his life for the past 500 years and has been 'training' his son into the family business.

'Jesus will now sit on his father's throne and take the wheel, so to speak,' a Vatican insider explained. 'This death was inevitable as God was reaching the ripe old age of four billion years old, which is absolutely incredible when you think about it.'

'It's a sad day for everyone here. This year has really been the worst.'

Jesus is expected to take some time off before transitioning into the almighty father role as Master of the Universe in February 2017.

R.I.P.

'I'll kick the face off of any cunt who challenges our charitable status' – Buckfast monk

CAMPAIGNERS calling for Buckfast Tonic Wine to lose its charitable status over links to violence have been warned by monks not to even think about it, stating they will 'kick the face off any cunt' who challenges it.

Speaking from his quarters in Buckfast Abbey, Devon, Brother Decco Ward told *WWN* that he was sick to death of the stigma attached to the popular alcoholic drink, pointing out that his order is not responsible for people's behaviour when drunk.

'What the fuck are we supposed to do, follow every ned, chav and scumbag round while they skull it back?' he said, while drinking a can of the fortified wine, which is laced with caffeine. 'Yeah, we've made €10.3 million in a year, and yeah, we didn't pay tax on it because we're a religious order, but you don't see anyone complaining about the revenue that bottles of water from Lourdes make every year, do you? Those Holy-Mary-loving fuckers in France are minted.'

The National Secular Society, which works to challenge religious privilege, has claimed that Buckfast Tonic Wine is a scourge on society and called it an 'abuse of the charitable system'.

'Buckfast is a tonic wine and it is not meant to be drunk for the craic,' Brother Ward added, standing up in a stagger and throwing a combination of mock punches through the air. 'But if those motherfuckers at the National Secular Society want their go, I'll fucking give it to them.'

Encouraged by Police Scotland, the Scottish Labour Party previously tried to ban the wine, but backed down when three million angry protesters took to Glasgow's streets and caused £23 billion in damage.

Mexico agrees to build wall following large influx of American refugees

MEXICAN President Enrique Peña Nieto has confirmed today that a proposed plan to build a wall along the border with the United States will now go ahead. The plan is a bid to stem the flow of 'American refugees' currently attempting to migrate from the Trump-led nation.

Peña Nieto, who previously dismissed Donald Trump's proposal to build a 35 to 40 foot concrete wall at the cost of $8 billion to the Mexican taxpayer, made the dramatic U-turn yesterday afternoon, following reports of a large-scale immigration of people wishing to leave the 'land of the free'.

Over 500,000 people are already queueing at various border controls along the current Mexican–US border, forcing the Mexican president to temporarily restrict access to non-Mexicans wishing to escape Trump's America.

'We've been queuing here since Friday,' one father of four told *WWN*. 'We've been made stay in a refugee camp along with other Americans. All I want to do is find a better quality of life for my family. Now we're stuck here in limbo.'

Peña Nieto said he will continue the ban on all immigrants until the wall is built, and urged Americans not to waste their time attempting to cross the border without the appropriate documentation.

'Our borders are currently overwhelmed with overweight men, women and children from the United States of America,' he said. 'We now have no other choice but to close our border posts and build this wall to help secure our country.'

Emergency pop-up McDonald's restaurants have been erected along the border to help feed the starving American refugees.

Separately, the Mexican navy has reported saving several hundred people from drowning after they tried to cross to Mexico on makeshift rafts. In a harrowing incident, one desperate family attempted to make the crossing on board their 400-pound father, who later had to be sunk after emergency rescue crews failed in their attempts to hoist him to the helicopter.

'Go find your own shite.' Fed-up St Anthony steps down

THE Vatican has confirmed its first-ever saint excommunication since its establishment, following an outburst from the now former saint of lost things, Anthony.

Born Fernando Martins de Bulhões, also known as Anthony of Lisbon and of Padua, took to the heavens on Monday to lambast those 'idiots' who continue to pray to him for help in finding missing items, many of which, he says, are insignificant and a total waste of his saintly time.

'We regret to inform our followers that St Anthony of Padua has been excommunicated after an outburst on Monday evening,' a Vatican spokesperson confirmed.

It is understood the saint began ignoring prayers over three months ago, leaving many Catholic worshippers in limbo when trying to find their missing objects.

'It used to be important things like locating lost souls or people who had gone missing,' Anthony stated, 'but now it's all "find my iPhone" this, "where's my car keys" that. You people are absolute time-wasters and you can all go find your own shite from now on as I have had enough of your ungrateful bullshit. Not once have I received a thank-you prayer in my 900 years working for this piece-of-shit religion. So I'm out.'

The Vatican was unable to comment on whether a replacement saint of lost things will be hired but did confirm that there is now a 12-week backlog in prayers as a result of Anthony's excommunication.

The Vatican also blamed the former saint for failing to find millions of euro intended for a redress scheme set up to help survivors of clerical sex abuse in Ireland, stating that 87% of the money still owed to victims is currently lost somewhere in the Vatican Bank.

'I lost because hackers showed America what a complete fucking lunatic I am'

IN what is being hailed as Hillary Clinton's most honest interview to date, *WWN* visits the former secretary of state's home in Chappaqua, New York.

Greeted at the front gates by her husband, former US President Bill Clinton, this reporter was immediately patted down by him personally and told to leave my car outside the property.

'Don't worry, pal, you won't get a ticket here,' Bill said, winking, before pressing his brittle index finger against his right nostril and hocking out mucus onto the ground.

As we walked up to the converted farmhouse, Bill pointed to a barn to the side. 'I wrote my book in there,' he advised, as if giving an important history lesson.

'And that's not all I get up to in there, if ya know what I mean,' he quipped, gyrating his pelvis in and out and mimicking a sex noise.

Bill led me to the house but stopped at the entrance. 'This is as far as I'm allowed to go,' he said, with a deep sadness in his eyes.

With that, he skipped off towards the barn while I rang the doorbell.

An African-American butler by the name of Hos answered and led me into a large living area, where a rather frail Hillary Clinton beckoned me in.

'C'mon now, don't be shy,' she said, coaxing me over with her wide, pale-blue eyes. 'I hope you didn't let that Bill into the house.'

'No,' I replied.

'Good! I don't have the energy to be chasing him out again but some of the staff here are female, and we also have pets in heat, so you know yourself.'

Before I could take out my pen and notepad, the 69-year-old stopped me in my tracks, stating that the interview will be short and sweet as she just wants to 'get a few things off her chest'.

'I lost the election because hackers showed everyone what a complete lunatic I am,' she blurted out, grimacing with the pain of truth. 'They got me real good … there, I've said it!'

Startled by her honesty, I asked her if she really believed the Russians helped Donald Trump to win the election.

'It doesn't matter who hacked our e-mails. The horrendous content contained in them is still the same. I'm actually a horrible person who instigated several civil wars around the world. I'm also responsible for the loss of countless innocent lives during my time as secretary of state. We tried to blame the Russians for my losing, but the real truth is I lost because I'm a terrible human being, okay?'

'So what about this anti-fake news concept you've been lobbying?' I asked.

'Fake news, ha ha, yeah, that was Bill's idea. We were desperate and a bit sore after losing, so we started blaming everyone but ourselves. Like, all the news you get these days is questionable. It's all bullshit, even the presidency is a load of bollocks. To think any elected president in the White House has any control over corporate America is just delusional. Bill's presidency taught us that very quickly. So we just wanted to make more money for our foundation and ourselves, is all.'

With that, Hillary stood up abruptly and ushered me to the front door, where a dead bird lay on the doormat.

'Oh, Bill, God loves a trier!' she exclaimed, kicking the carcass away.

'Look, you must go now and tell the world what I just said to you. Tell them from now on I'm only going to tell the truth. We have a presidential race to run in three years. Time is of the essence.'

Leaving the Clinton residence, I could not help but wonder if I was just another pawn in a Clinton game. Was she playing me?

I hesitated to write this article, but I've taken a journalistic oath to report what I see and hear, so there it is, laid bare before your very eyes.

Wonderful World of Science

How do you sleep at night? No, seriously, you've done such awful, terrible things.

First corpse removed from White House in rolled-up carpet

WHO had 21 days? Sources monitoring the White House announced that the body of a currently unknown person was removed from the premises last night rolled up in a carpet with only the feet sticking out, before being loaded into the back of a black SUV and vanished into the Virginia countryside by the Secret Service.

In news that some people described as 'inevitable', the suspicious activity basically confirms that at some stage between yesterday morning and yesterday afternoon, someone entered the White House as a living, breathing person and left in a less alive, more dead manner.

With only the feet of the deceased visible, sources have estimated that the dead person is almost certainly a woman, due to the presence of high heels and stockings.

Reports that a strong smell of urine was detected from the rug have yet to be confirmed, but experts are confident that the liquid seen leaking from the material 'certainly wasn't Pepsi'.

'If I was a guessing man, then what we have right here is some sort of piss-related sex game gone terribly wrong,' said one man who watched the entire sordid affair unfold as he walked his dog.

'Young lady, White House, Trump, piss everywhere, it gets a bit out of hand, Secret Service step in to clear up the mess – rug, van, drive, dig, bury, back to the White House in just over an hour. They won't be happy with that time, but I'd imagine they'll have plenty of opportunities to improve on it over the next four years.'

Although the White House has yet to comment on the matter, witnesses confirmed that a new rug was delivered to the Oval Office earlier today.

Irish people in Australia somehow not getting killed by spiders every two days

AMAZING new statistics have shown that a remarkably small percentage of the approximately 70,000 Irish people currently living in Australia have run afoul of the many different species of poisonous antipodean creatures that are available to kill them.

Australia, located almost as far away from Ireland as you can go without coming back the other way, is currently home to the world's most poisonous snake, the world's most poisonous spider, the world's deadliest shark and that lad you used to know at school who held an electric fence for an hour on a dare.

As such, it was once feared that the vast majority of the Irish population migrating to Oz in search of work following the economic crash in 2008 would all be dead within a week. Their 'ah look, I'm sure he's harmless' mentality when encountering the region's huge range of deadly beasties was expected to be their downfall.

However, *WWN* can report that the number of actual cases of Irish lads getting drunk and putting funnel-web spiders into each other's beds 'for the laugh' remains remarkably low.

'It's amazing the restraint that people are showing when it comes to throwing box jellyfish at each other on the beach,' said one spokesperson for the Irish embassy in Canberra. 'Some people are coming from a background where the most dangerous creature they've ever encountered is a badger, to a land that has dozens of ways to kill you just while you're walking around. Their lack of preparation for these dangers, coupled with the fact that Irish people generally have that "ah sure I'll be grand" was a worry to us. So yeah, we're pleasantly surprised with the figures.'

Bowl of shamrock wilts and dies moments after touching Trump's hands

THE traditional meeting between the Irish Taoiseach and US President, which takes place in and around St Patrick's Day each year, took a worrying turn this morning, *WWN* can exclusively reveal.

Taoiseach Enda Kenny has spent the week in the US banging the drum for Irish businesses and for the undocumented Irish in the US and defending the EU. The day before St Patrick's Day, however, has long been considered to be the most important day of this trip as it is the day he met newly inaugurated US President Donald Trump. Handing over the traditional bowl of shamrock, a symbolic gift that speaks to the strong and prosperous relationship between the two countries, Kenny was horrified to witness the shamrocks immediately wilt and die as soon as the bowl made contact with Trump's small hands.

'No, everything is fine, this isn't a bad sign or a harbinger of doom. Ireland still loves you, Donald. Say and do what you want, it doesn't matter to us, we'll still lick arse with the best of them,' a panicked Kenny shared with Trump as the media's cameras flashed intensely.

'D'ya remember when I said you were racist? That was gas.

But, Jesus, if you don't remember then I never said it, okay?' Kenny added, sweating profusely.

While no experts have yet come forward to explain why shamrock would suddenly wilt once placed into someone's hands, members of the public have been invited to draw their own conclusions.

'No, here look, we've another bowl. Oh God, oh God, oh God,' the Taoiseach added, while handing over a fresh bowl of shamrock to Trump that also immediately wilted and died.

Trump then delivered some empty remarks that were void of any trace of genuine human sentiment and which focused on how great the Irish people are and how beautiful their country is.

A spokesperson denied making sure they got the smallest bowl possible for the shamrock in an effort to make Trump feel like he has giant hands.

AMERICAN NEWS

Mike Pence praised for swallowing own vomit when shaking hands with gay couple

GOOD news stories about the Trump administration are at a premium these days; however, even the enemy of the American people 'the media' will be quick to heap further praise on Vice-President Mike Pence following a kind gesture befitting the most noble of statesmen.

Shortly after speaking at CPAC to an audience of American conservatives, Pence was introduced to a stream of members of the public in the crowd and happily shook their hands and stifled any urge to vomit when he learned that two of them were in fact homosexuals.

'This is the kind of unifying leadership we need. VP Pence could have vomited directly onto those hell-bound heathens, but he didn't for the sake of uniting the country, which was a magnanimous decision,' shared one CPAC attendee. 'This is what real leadership looks like.'

Pence, who could be seen using a tissue to dampen the edges of his mouth where a small droplet of vomit had escaped, held a stern smile and politely stared into the distance beyond the two men as they shared their concerns about the Trump administration.

'The media are going to make a big deal about this, but he used bleach to wash his hands *after* the homosexuals left the room. And he's been called the most awful things, it beggars belief,' explained another CPAC attendee.

The office of the vice-president denied separate claims made by some CPAC attendees that he was the lesser of two evils when compared to Donald Trump.

TRENDING

Unemployed supporter finally starting to think Trump might be full of shit

THE slow-dawning realisation that perhaps US President Donald Trump may not be keeping some of his election promises, and has no intention of ever doing so, has led one of his loyal supporters to suspect the 71-year-old might be completely full of shit.

When asked what gave it away, 49-year-old Kentucky native Gabriel Jones was reluctant to definitively label Trump as someone who goes back on his word or fails to deliver on his promises, but he was open to the possibility of no longer taking everything he says at face value.

'Well, I was delighted he was putting America first, ya know, and "greating-it" again. I couldn't wait for the mine to reopen in my town so I'd get that job back, with free healthcare, a large pension, the works,' explained the doe-eyed and reasonable father of two.

Jones confirmed he would never apologise for voting for Trump as his vote was 'a vote for my family, their chance at not just surviving but prospering'. However, the sneaking suspicion that the ignorant billionaire, who has thus far presided over the most chaotic and dysfunctional presidency in living memory, was full of shit persisted.

'I have to question his actions as president. I mean, I still see Muslims on the TV in America and he hasn't imprisoned Hillary Clinton. Women still seem confident enough to answer back to me and that black family across the street hasn't been evicted or arrested or shot by the police yet,' observed the still perfectly reasonable Jones.

Jones also lamented Trump's failure to pay for dry-cleaning his favourite hooded white sheet.

12 MONTHS A GUARD *Month 4*

Today's module was all about keeping our streets safe and clean by moving on any and all homeless people we see while out on the beat. This works hand in hand with what we learned last month about not getting filmed by the public because they tend to get very vocal when they see four of us clearing a homeless lad in a sleeping bag from the doorway of Brown Thomas while up the road there's a gang of lads shooting each other in the face. Clearing homeless people seems easy enough, and it gives me a chance to work on my garda-talk, such as 'move out of the way there', 'I'm going to have to find you in breach of the peace' and (has to be said quietly, this one) 'get the fuck up you dirty hoor or I'll break every fucking finger you have'. I have to admit, I felt bad the first time I pepper-sprayed a homeless old woman, but after a while you get used to it when everyone else is doing it and the senior guards seem perfectly fine about it.

Margaret Thatcher's erection breaks through coffin at news of snap election

REPORTS from several British news outlets have confirmed that the coffin of former British Prime Minister Margaret Thatcher is in serious need of repair after the corpse occupying the plot became aroused when learning of plans by the Conservative Party to further consolidate its power in an effort to impose its policies on the public.

'The whole thing will need replacing, it's been shattered by the force of a blunt instrument right in the middle of the coffin,' explained a groundskeeper at the cemetery where the former Conservative leader is buried.

It is believed that current Prime Minister, Theresa May, instructed an aide to attend Thatcher's graveside in order to relay the good news that May herself had masterminded a snap election, which could ultimately see the dismantling of the NHS and a clear mandate for the Tories to continue cutting essential public services while loosening regulations on corporations.

'Oh, she would have bloody loved that,' confirmed one long-time Thatcher supporter, who beamed at the news of her potent erection.

'It's just a shame she won't be here to see the police beat the living shit out of anyone who protests whatever punishment the Conservatives have in mind for the poor once the election is over,' added the supporter, who praised May's decision to pretend the election is all about providing her party with a clear mandate for Brexit negotiations.

'We're already saving £300 million when we leave the EU, imagine what we'd save if we didn't spend any money on the NHS at all,' concluded the supporter.

Cemetery workers have expressed concerns for their own safety were the Conservatives to attempt to reintroduce the Poll Tax or abolish the Human Rights Act, stating, 'Thatcher's erection upon hearing that sort of news would be hard to contain and the damage to nearby graves would be truly irreversible.'

Stormont talks begin as Arlene Foster finishes every sentence with 'Fenian bastards'

AS the results of Northern Ireland's Assembly elections see Sinn Féin and other Nationalist parties close the gap on Unionist parties to just one seat, the hard task of reaching a compromise in order to achieve stable governance in the North begins.

WWN has learned that these negotiations are already underway as DUP leader Arlene Foster, who faces calls from within her own party to step aside, has offered a conciliatory olive branch to Sinn Féin by ending each and every one of her sentences with the phrase 'Fenian bastards'.

'There is a real chance of a new era of non-sectarian politics, which is very much based on the pressing issues in Northern Ireland, chief among them the economy,' explained political negotiation expert Martin Arnold.

'I think the fact that Arlene is ending her sentences with "Fenian bastards", rather than starting a sentence with that phrase, is a really solid sign of progress,' added the expert.

Sinn Féin, a party led by Gerry Adams, has been asked to enter any negotiations without a 'big shit-eating grin' following an election that saw a higher turnout and vote capture for Nationalist parties than in the previous elections 10 months ago.

'Sinn Féin is committed to practical solutions for all the people of Northern Ireland, and we hope to reach an agreement with the DUP,' a tired Adams explained, having spent the weekend without any sleep, seemingly too excited by the thoughts of a United Ireland.

Trump: Latest drone strike on Syrian school 'better than Obama's'

PASSIONATELY defending his record on killing innocent civilians with drone strikes against the record of his predecessor, Barack Obama, US President Donald Trump has claimed that a drone strike that killed at least 30 innocent people in a Syrian school has surpassed any innocent loss of life under the Obama regime.

'My drone strike was the best, believe me,' Trump defended his action, batting away statements from journalists who seemed to suggest that Obama had the superior civilian death toll having carried out 20,000 drone strikes over eight years.

This latest statement could possibly be yet another example of a lie shared by the current US President.

'No, mine is the best, believe me. Killing innocent people in a school, it's the best – everyone is saying it,' Trump added, clearly incensed that there were people attempting to give Obama credit, even suggesting that Obama's strike on a hospital in Afghanistan was the best erroneous drone strike ever carried out by a self-proclaimed leader of the free world.

The president went on to deny that his much vaunted plan to defeat ISIS was nearly identical to that of the previous administration – both involving targeted and precision mistakes that lead to the loss of innocent life, followed by no accountability.

'Wrong,' countered Trump, shutting down one journalist. 'We're going to mess up drone strikes on such a level, it'll make your head spin. I'll get two Nobel Peace Prizes, believe me.'

Responders to the scene of the drone strike said the difference between the two methods was 'unclear to them'.

Elsewhere, there were further problems for President Trump as he threatened to set the KGB on members of the Republican Party who don't vote for his replacement healthcare plan for Obamacare.

Planet now 47% Facebook data centres

A recent survey of the planet's surface performed by NASA has found that almost half of the Earth is now entirely covered by some 23,000,000 Facebook data centres, raising fears it may be totally consumed by 2070 if legislation is not introduced to curb the phenomenon.

The survey found that a total of 92,543,000 km² of the planet's landmass is currently taken up by the storage facilities, which houses the information of almost two billion users.

'If Facebook continues to grow like it has been over the last decade, they could run out of room and may have to start seeking alternative planets or moons to house their servers on,' lead researcher of the survey Dr Ren Schneider points out.

Last year, Facebook bought over 22 countries, including Ireland, to help expand its global operations and provide quicker and faster loading times for its users' hilarious videos and status updates.

'Is the development of modern technology slowly killing the planet? Yes. Is it worth it for faster loading times and auto-loading videos? Definitely!' defended a Facebook spokesman earlier. 'Your information is very important to us, from the instant message spat with your wife in 2009, to that dick pic you sent her sister in 2012. It's important we build massive warehouses to store and process all this valuable information for people in the future to laugh at.'

He added, 'Man, can you even fathom the amount of money your great-great-grandchildren will pay for your vintage messages? And the absolute gas they will have scrolling through your late-night drunken rants on news publication pages? It's a fucking goldmine.'

NASA admits it has known about alien life for years, just forgot to mention it

'SORRY. We just kinda assumed everyone knew about it,' NASA spokeswoman Trish Chamberson told a packed press conference at their headquarters in Washington DC today, after it was revealed the space agency has known for years about alien life, but just forgot to mention it.

'There are so many films, documentaries and TV programmes on aliens that we thought everyone was aware of them by now,' Ms Chamberson explained to the shocked crowd of reporters. 'Greys have been visiting our planet for thousands of years. Who do you think built the ancient pyramids and all the other megastructures across the world? C'mon guys, it's quite obvious.'

During the two-hour briefing, NASA scientists confirmed previously speculated information about UFOs and alien technology, confirming that four separate races of aliens are in regular contact with NASA, and have actually asked the agency to say hello to everyone on the planet for them.

'We do apologise for this mix up, the whole thing just slipped our mind,' another scientist explained. 'We were so busy back-engineering their technology, we simply forgot all about it. They even have a base on the far side of the moon, and are currently mining several planets in our solar system for minerals. They've only started on Jupiter recently, hence the new rings around it. It's all good though, they're a nice enough bunch. They don't talk much but are always complaining about our nuclear weapons, claiming they affect parallel universes every time they're triggered.'

The disclosure comes after 70 years of countless sightings and abductions, raising questions as to why it is they are here.

'The aliens are actually harmless and only interested in the planet's natural resources,' the briefing concluded, 'which shouldn't cause us any problems whatsoever.'

North Korea continues missile assault on sea

THE Korean Central News Agency has issued a statement in which it has praised the country's military for a decisive strike on the body of water between itself and Japan, claiming to have knocked out several key shoals of fish as well as creating 'an enormous splash worthy of a king'.

Dubbed 'Operation Hit The Water', North Korea launched two ballistic missiles yesterday, with a 50% success rate. One missile exploded on launch, with sources close to the North Korean military expressing that this was 'exactly what we wanted it to do'.

With North Korea now launching one successful missile strike against the Sea of Japan every 19 months or so, many believe it is only a matter of years before the country are ready to take aim at something that isn't a huge, empty space.

'Our Glorious Leader has struck a hammer blow against our enemy, water,' beamed the newsreader for the CNA.

'Kim Jong-un has once again shown that he is the man to protect us from waves, fish, plankton and kelp. Our missiles hit the 977,980 km² area target, exactly as we planned. Nothing can stop North Korea. We can hit any sea we want, as long as it is directly adjacent to our border and the wind is in our favour.'

The celebrations continue as the one boat owned by the North Korean navy travels to the impact site to retrieve the missile for use later in the year.

State of 'I'm going to do whatever the fuck I want' declared in Turkey by Erdogan

AS a crackdown on civil liberties in Turkey continues, President Recep Tayyip Erdogan has declared a state of 'I'm going to do whatever the fuck I want'.

Similar in many aspects to a state of emergency, the state of 'I'm going to do whatever the fuck I want' will see the office of the president, a largely ceremonial post, take on an even more politicised and undemocratic approach to restricting basic freedoms of non-AKP party members and supporters.

'I treat Turkey like my own private game of *Sims*,' Erdogan, a noted goat fucker, explained on Turkish state television. 'I do what I want, maybe I build a wall around a *Sims* character, blocking them in and forcing them to urinate themselves. These are just the things I like to do to enhance the security of the Turkish people. Or maybe I play *Call of Duty* and round up everyone and execute them, who knows.'

Erdogan announced that the state of 'I'm going to do whatever the fuck I want' will last for a total of three months before being extended again and again for an indefinite period of time.

Small print in the 'I'm going to do whatever the fuck I want' measures also allow Erdogan to continue to move Turkey further away from being a secular state.

'Democracy must be maintained,' Erdogan confirmed as he wrote up a list of newspapers, journalists, teachers, hairdressers and vegetables he didn't like.

'Brussel sprouts were part of the plot against me,' he went on to confirm.

There is expected to be little meaningful opposition from international leaders as a stable Turkey remains the only thing keeping myriad Middle Eastern problems and conflicts from spilling over into far more important places such as Europe and beyond.

Melania Trump blinks the word 'help' in Morse code

EXPERTS in Morse code are claiming that America's First Lady, Melania Trump, blinked the letters 'H.E.L.P.' during her first official appearance at the White House on Wednesday to welcome Israeli Prime Minister Benjamin Netanyahu and his wife, Sara.

Standing outside the South Portico of the White House with her husband, President Donald Trump, the 46-year-old wore a tailored white skirt suit while waiting for their guests to arrive. She then turned to the cameras and desperately gave them a series of long and short blinks, which was later translated as a common SOS, or help signal.

'This isn't the first time Melania Trump has secretly sent Morse code with her eyes,' one decryption expert told *WWN*, in Morse code. 'While she was dancing with the president during the inauguration, she blinked the words "Jesus fucking Christ, what have I gotten myself into" while calmly waltzing with her husband.'

Following the signal for help, Melania went on to greet her guests with a kiss. The group exchanged pleasantries while posing for some photos before Melania began a new series of blinks, which were subsequently translated to mean 'these two men are lunatics and need to be stopped'.

'It's quite clear Melania is trying to reach out to the American public and warn them about something big, or that she may even be in danger herself, perhaps held against her will,' the expert added.

Mrs Trump, who can communicate in five different languages as well as Morse code, has apparently spent the past month in her apartment in Trump Tower, with friends suggesting she is 'miserable' in her new role and just dying to get a good night out with the girls.

'This will be different from Iraq, Vietnam, Gulf War, Afghanistan and Libya,' America confirms

THE nation of America confirmed that any further military action in Syria will result in a better outcome than in any of the previous 4,556 military interventions carried out by the western country over the previous 50 years.

While it is still unclear if the Trump administration will add to the recent missile strikes against the Assad regime, America has confirmed that no matter what, they have learned from previous mistakes and that it will be completely different this time.

'We'll only fly a "Mission Accomplished" banner on an aircraft carrier when we're totally certain we've nuked Assad in the face,' confirmed a smattering of the 320 million people who make up America.

Some critics have been quick to point out that those in leadership positions in America might not be best placed to plan, carry out and oversee a regime change in a divided country.

'America!' America responded, dispelling any doubts that could be had about a poorly thought-out plan of military action in a nation located in the Middle East.

'Oohrah,' screamed the section of Americans who have never actually served in the Marines or any section of the armed forces.

Further assuaging fears earlier today, President Trump confirmed he had never eaten in the Al Nusra chain of Indian restaurants when asked for his thoughts on the terror group Al Nusra.

On the potential for the creation of power vacuum in Syria, Trump was clear on his vision for the war-torn country.

'There won't be a power vacuum, I won't allow it. We'll only use American-made hoovers, the best,' Trump explained.

Terror engulfs America as Kim Jong Un threatens to cut healthcare for 22 million US citizens

THE tyrannical leader's threat could cause the deaths of millions if he carries out his planned attack on the US healthcare system.

Both Republicans and Democrats in America have been locked in emergency meetings since late last night after receiving a threat from despot and North Korean leader Kim Jong Un.

While news of yet another missile test led to the issuing of robust language by the US government, which warned of consequences if missile tests continued, the White House has officially declared a state of emergency across the nation after Jong Un threatened to rescind medical coverage for 22 million Americans, many of whom have pre-existing conditions.

'This barbarity is something only a Republican should be able to carry out. Kim Jong Un is threatening our very beliefs as Americans and we must stop him,' confirmed House Speaker Paul Ryan earlier this morning.

The news that North Korea is seeking ways to dismantle the US healthcare system in a bid to cause endless suffering has left millions of US citizens in a state of abject panic and terror.

'President Trump is in the middle of making America great again, and now this bozo Kim is trying to destroy our country. We won't stand for it,' one Florida native told *WWN* from his nuclear bunker. 'I've never heard of such evil in my life.'

'When someone makes a threat like this, threatens the American people on a scale we've never seen before, we must respond and respond bigly,' President Trump shared with media in Poland, where he is meeting with world leaders.

In a bid to protect the healthcare of Americans, President Trump has instructed the army to stand guard outside hospitals throughout the country, acting against his own advice and the advice of the Republican Party.

Toddler banging on pots and pans appointed as new White House Communications Director

'HEY! Look at me. I making music,' exclaimed newly appointed White House Communications Director, four-year-old Tabatha Charles, as she banged on several pots and pans with a pair of drumsticks in her first press conference this morning in Washington DC.

The toddler, daughter of billionaire property developer and Trump's friend Jonathan Charles, was carefully placed in front of a packed press room at the White House, where she proceeded to bang strategically placed red pots in a very loud and amusing fashion, much to the admiration of the press.

'Oh my God, she's so adorable,' one CNN journalist commented, ignoring several important questions on his notepad relating to the investigation into Donald Trump Junior's ties with Russia. 'I'd say she could bang those drums all day.'

Following 40 minutes of laughs and giggles from amused journalists, Tabatha Charles continued to fend off concerns from some of the more sombre journalists in the room about the situation in North Korea, stating that she was tired, wanted her mammy and had a 'poopy in her diaper'.

'I really hope she lasts longer than her predecessor,' voiced *Fox News* journalist Todd Richardson, referring to the firing of Anthony Scaramucci after holding the post for less than 10 days. He continued, 'She's a breath of fresh air and actually a lot more informative than Scaramucci or Bannon,' adding in awe, 'Oh. My. God. She has brilliant rhythm for a child.'

Following 20 minutes of selfies with the new Communications Director, the congregating press waved Ms Charles 'day-day' as her mother took to the stage to carry her home.

'This fat shaming of Kim Jong-un has to STOP'

In the latest entry of our WWN *Voices series, we give a platform to those we really shouldn't. This week sees Gráinne Halligan Nelligan, a person and* Guardian *reader, criticise those poking fun at Kim Jong-un's very public struggle with his weight.*

PEOPLE are quick to rush to ridicule in this day and age, and no one is exempt from online scorn, not even tyrannical dictators. Case in point, Kim Jong-un, who would be judged on his merits as a dictator were it not for the fact that in recent years it appears he has gained a little weight.

This simply isn't fair. Kim should have the opportunity to have his deplorable human rights record challenged, but instead any discussion about him devolves into speculation on his weight.

Some people will observe that he is currently eating as much as 70% of his impoverished nation's food supply. However, instead of judgement, we should seek to understand how Kim has come to resemble the Marshmallow Man from *Ghostbusters*.

Mocking the man and not trying to see past his tyrannical reign for what it is, a cry for help, really puts the blame at our feet. We need to acknowledge that it is not his fault that he is addicted to cheese. This is a guy who lost his father just a few years ago and we shouldn't forget that.

'There's more chins than in a Korean phonebook' – not only is discourse like this unhelpful, it is entirely inaccurate and racially insensitive. 'Chin' is not a common Korean name, nor is 'Phat'.

So, anonymous online 'hate brigade', if you're going to brutalise a despot with your horrific words of hate, try to stick to the factually accurate ones.

I don't know Kim personally, but like many dictators in the public eye, he is probably under immense pressure to conform to society's expectations of him.

It would be foolish to think that we haven't forced dictators to idealise the slim figure of Hitler, or the stocky muscular frame of Stalin. This needs to stop. It is not Kim's fault he can't seem to grow facial hair.

Until such a time that we can accept dictators for who they are, regardless of their body type, there is little hope that we will ever come to truly know them.

Kim, if you're reading this, I hope you accept my apology on behalf of everyone.

MIDDLE EAST NEWS

Touching moment police present tear gas to Native Americans for Thanksgiving

NORTH Dakota policemen have been praised for offering Native American Indians several hundred litres of tear gas in an emotional ceremony at Standing Rock this afternoon.

Keeping with the American celebration of the blessings of the harvest, police officers lined up in a show of solidarity with their Sioux brothers and offered up the lachrymatory agent to their welcoming faces, keeping with an age-old tradition spanning back centuries.

'Obviously everyone here is very emotional right now,' police officer Todd Chamberson explains. 'The natives here at the reservation are openly weeping at our kind-hearted gesture. I just wish the rest of the world could get on like we do and live in harmony with one another'.

Standing Rock reservation resident Abedabun Yazzie was so overwhelmed with the touching gift, he was stuck for words.

'Oh my fucking eyes! Help me, help me, I can't see. It's burning me. My eyes, I can't see,' he thanked, before accepting more tear gas. 'Argh, my skin feels like it's on fire. Why are you doing this to us? Leave our land alone. My fucking eyes.'

Celebrations at the ancient Indian site are expected to last right on into the New Year, with even more policemen and women expected to arrive with more gifts throughout the Christmas period.

'It's great to see everyone so involved,' added Officer Chamberson. 'Only problem we have now is that the local people are now pretending to be Indians too. I just hope we have enough tear gas to go round.'

Trump confirms Muslims must wear crescent moon with star armbands

EVERY Muslim in America from 17 February will be expected to wear an armband with a crescent moon with a star on it as part of a new law to be passed by American President Donald Trump, *WWN* can reveal.

Over 3.3 million Muslims living in the United States will first have to be registered under the new law, with failure to do so resulting in a mandatory six-month prison sentence.

'This is just a precautionary measure to ensure the safety of our country,' a spokesman for the Trump administration explained the move. 'We have already built several detention centres across the country to help deal with any objection from the Islamic community that could arise,' adding, 'hopefully it won't come to that.'

The new armbands, which are to be manufactured in the US and not China, are to be distributed across America from next week at a cost of $49.99 to each wearer, with discounts of up to $10 for those who can prove that they're the good Muslims, and not the bad ones.

'If there are any objections, we will simply seize the property and assets of those Muslims who clearly have no desire to put America first. Their property will then be given to responsible citizens who are ready to help America's cause,' the spokeperson added.

The move comes just days after President Donald Trump issued a ban on all Muslims entering America from Muslim majority countries he doesn't like the sound of, or has no financial dealings with, raising racial fears and forcing hundreds of thousands of people to protest the ban around the world.

The move has been widely welcomed by many Americans who voted for Trump.

'It's only an armband, no big deal. The only Muslims objecting to wearing them obviously have something to hide, there's no other reason you'd kick up a fuss about it,' shared one American we spoke to.

TRENDING
Bomb community devastated after losing mother

THE global bomb community is said today to be in mourning following the passing of the mother of all bombs (MOAB) after it was dropped on a cave and tunnel complex used by Islamic State fighters in eastern Afghanistan.

Missiles, grenades, IEDs and many more explosive devices joined together in solidarity for a minute's silence this afternoon, marking the GBU-43/B Massive Ordnance Air Blast.

'She will be sorely missed,' one warhead at a nuclear missile base in New Mexico told *WWN*. 'There's an eeriness in the air here and I think I can speak for every other warhead here when I say there won't be another bomb like her. She was the best mother a bomb could have.'

Most of what is publicly known about the GBU-43 is that she weighed a massive 21,600 pounds and created a mushroom cloud that could be seen 20 miles away from the blast.

'Her weight killed her in the end,' one sibling explained, while pointing at North Korea. 'I suppose the only consolation here is that she died doing what she loved: maiming and ripping people and terrain to smithereens.'

The mother of all bombs, who leaves behind millions of children worldwide, was first created in 2002 ahead of the US-led invasion of Iraq, which went on to result in the loss of half a million lives during the Iraq War. However, it wasn't until yesterday afternoon that she could add to that figure.

R.I.P.

Updated Nativity set to feature Palestinian kid taking rifle butt to face

UPDATES have been made to the classic cast of the Christmas Nativity in a bid to make it more relevant to the Holy Land™ today, with the addition of new characters such as an IDF soldier dragging a Palestinian teenager around the back of the crib and smashing his face with the butt of his rifle.

Manufacturers have made the changes after it became apparent that a tranquil scene of a family snuggled safely in a Jerusalem dwelling with a roof just 'wasn't realistic', even in the context of a woman made pregnant by a ghost giving birth to the son of the creator of the universe.

New additions to the diorama include the aforementioned terrorist/Palestinian child being 'interrogated' by the Israeli army, a queue of Palestinian civilians being herded out of their homes before the bulldozers get sent in and, on more expensive sets, a Palestinian hospital being hit by heavy artillery fire.

'The donkey and the three wise men, they're all still there, even though you'd struggle to find those things in Israel right now,' said Karl Lungrof, one of the designers of the new-look Nativity.

'And the rest is just there to show that the Holy Land you read about in the Bible isn't some mythical Middle Earth kind of place; it's real, and it's still there, and it's still a place where a family have to flee in terror due to the threat of death by a tyrannical regime. Oh, and I forgot to show you this ...'

Lungrof paused to find and flick a switch on the back of the crib.

'It lights up! Pretty sweet, yeah?'

Is a war really a war if it isn't trending online?

IS the immeasurable suffering experienced by innocent civilians in a war-torn region happening at all if it is failing to trend online? It is a question that has plagued philosophers and meme-generating websites for centuries.

'If a refugee from Eritrea, a country I imagine you know very little about, could maybe dress up as a Pokémon in a blue and gold dress while carrying a gorilla on his shoulders, there's every chance that when he's murdered he could trend on Twitter for several hours. That's the sort of thinking-outside-the-box we need, but sadly, people ignore our advice,' Alyssa Morton, Head of GIF Procurement at BuzzFeed, told *WWN*.

Can conflict, complete with bombs and bullets piercing flesh, making orphans of children, widows of women and widowers of men be considered to be happening if the opposing sides have yet to be boiled down into a fun list complete with GIFs of cats, Kanye West and children falling off trampolines?

'The simple answer is no,' lecturer in philosophy at Harvard University Timothy Schlubmann explained to *WWN*. 'Conflicts in Yemen, Darfur, Eritrea, Ukraine and elsewhere can't really claim to be wars until they launch a ridiculously good-looking corpse meme.'

At this point our minds began to wander and we took to our phones to look at the latest *Hey Arthur* meme doing the rounds. However, frustratingly, the lecturer continued to speak.

'Existence is conditional, conditional to being of consequence, of ascertaining tangible meaning, and to being shared in dialogues. This is where Sudan fails and cat GIFs succeed. I'm not condoning the cat-GIFtification of the conflict in Yemen, but if you want to exist at all and be acknowledged ya gotta up your meme game,' Schlubmann cautioned.

Questions still remain on what war-ravaged areas can learn from World War II and Vietnam, among other wars, which managed to gain the public's attention without ever trending online.

'Lists are hilarious, memes are hilarious and civilians taking cover from renewed air assaults need to be aware of this when creating content on Snapchat,' Morton points out, speaking our language.

'The failure of wars ongoing in Syria and elsewhere to "break the Internet", which much pointless and utterly meritless other tripe did this year, on a philosophical level at least, means it quite literally didn't happen,' Schlubmann added.

We then asked if Schlubmann could help find the nearest PokeStop. He declined.

'It is regrettable that Syrian refugees are using loom bands to try to gain traction online. Loom bands were last year's big disposable trend, they're seriously off-message and it's little surprise my Facebook feed continues to lack in shareable Syrian content,' Schlubmann lamented.

12 MONTHS A GUARD *Month 5*

We were 'on the beat' today, as they say! We were all bussed down to Stradbally to help steward at Electric Picnic. Jobs like this and match days at Croke Park are great training for us recruits as it gives us a chance to deal with large numbers of people. We need that experience to be ready for when we get assigned to protecting ministers from protestors or making sure the crusties don't interfere with the pipeline out west. I got to confiscate a load of drink from people, and I have to admit it was pretty intoxicating. Not just the sense of power; the drink itself! We all got fucking destroyed later on. It beats that time a fortnight ago when every recruit in the country was brought in to take part in a 'show of power' raid in the city, where our superiors wanted to show as many cops as possible taking part in a drugs raid. We were late to the raid because our bus broke down and 50 of us had to walk through town on the way to our surprise raid. When we got there, the bad guys had fled. Wonder what tipped them off?

Did you know?

Giraffes' necks are growing by an average of 61 centimetres every year.

TOP 5
Noises men made when hit in the groin 2017

5 'Ow!'

4 'Jesus Christ, who kicked that at me?'

3 'Aaah shit, shit, shit, shit, no, stop laughing, it's not funny, I've dislocated a testicle or something!'

2 'Eeeeeeeeeeeeeeeeeeeh!'

1 'Huh-umph-ah-guh-fuck!'

Rothschild family to sell their 67% stake in Planet Earth

A spokesman for the Rothschild family has announced today that they are to put their 67% stake in planet earth on the market for a staggering $170 trillion, and have strictly asked for 'no time wasters please'.

Speaking at a low-key press conference in New York this morning, an unnamed official stated that the surviving members of the Rothschild dynasty made the decision shortly after the death of their close family friend and former Chase Manhattan Chief Executive David Rockefeller last month, and that they just want to retire from secretly ruling the world.

'We've had a very good run of it over the past 250 years,' the spokesperson read from a large goatskin scroll, presumably written by the Rothschild family, 'the last 100 of which have seen us manage nations through two world wars and many smaller proxy wars, which we have benefitted greatly from, and we feel it is time to hand over the reigns to fresh blood, who can take the planet to the next level, whatever that may be.'

The family estate, which includes mining companies, energy companies and the control of dozens of the world's central banks, giving them the ability to freely print money and sell it to governments at an interest rate, is said to be 'a steal at $170 trillion'. The spokesperson insisted that the new owners must first pass a series of tests before they can purchase the 67% stake in the planet.

'Interested parties will need to understand that funding the world's various military organisations takes priority to running this business, and that each candidate must first be appraised for their ability to equally destroy and construct certain parts of the Third World,' the spokesman advised. 'There are specific instructions to bar time wasters or people of conscience from making a bid, and that anonymity is key to ruling the world, so no global dictators or celebrities may apply either.'

Following the press conference, the spokesman was later euthanised by an awaiting doctor in a bid to safeguard the deal's secrets, a practice regularly carried out by the Rothschild dynasty.

Zoo staff find Harambe's tomb empty

STAFF at the Cincinnati Zoo & Botanical Gardens have issued a statement in which they confirm that the tomb holding the remains of the slain gorilla Harambe has been found empty, with huge speculation as to whether or not he has risen from the dead.

Beloved gorilla Harambe has amassed a huge cult following since his execution in May by zoo officials who feared for the life of a young boy who had toppled into the gorilla enclosure.

Thousands of Harambe worshippers have taken to the Internet to declare that the western lowland Messiah has risen from the dead as was prophesied, and will soon lead his followers into the eternal bliss of monkey heaven.

However, zoo officials were quick to downplay talk that Harambe might have returned from the dead, stating that his body may just have been stolen by over-zealous followers.

'We went to the tomb after the third day, and found the stone at the entrance had been rolled back,' said one spokesperson for the zoo empire.

'We fear that the followers of Harambe may have stolen his body in a bid to continue this myth that he was the new Christ. He was not the Messiah. He was a very naughty ape.'

Meanwhile sightings of Harambe have been reported across the US, with many claiming that he has offered to allow non-believers to put their hands in his bullet holes as proof.

Trump doing pretty good job so far, says Trump

DONALD Trump's approval rating has shot up in the weeks since his victory in the US presidential race, according to a survey of Donald Trump.

The Republican president-elect was deemed by the Republican president-elect to be doing 'a damn fine job' and was 'on course to do everything right in the correct and goodest way' over the course of the next four years.

Trump added that Trump had made 'the best possible choices' when filling out his cabinet, adding that these people were by no means the worst possible choices as other news outlets may have suggested.

All in all, Trump scored a 'Perfect 10' on a scale of one to 10, with one being 'Donald Trump isn't good' and 10 being 'Donald Trump is very, very good'.

'I'm very happy with how Trump is doing,' said Trump, speaking to himself in the mirror in a bid to drive away the fear and panic over what will happen when his bullshit finally catches up with him.

'All Trump's election promises will be fulfilled, or at least talked around. Trump is good. Trump is your pal. Trump is strongest one there is.'

The poll-of-one went on to add that Trump still 'has it when it comes to the ladies, honey.'

Trump promises to revive America's cotton picking industry

PRESIDENT of the United States Donald Trump has vowed to revive the country's cotton picking industry, hinting at a welfare scheme that will enable thousands of people on welfare to 'earn their cheques' by working on plantations.

Speaking at a White House press conference this afternoon, President Trump outlined a detailed plan that he said will 'make America great again by going back to the country's roots and traditions'.

'Why the hell did we stop picking cotton?' Trump put to the bewildered press room. 'We were booming in the good old days: everyone was working, producing cotton, tobacco, sugar. And then we just gave up?'

'You know what? It kills me to see so many young, beautiful African Americans and Mexicans out of work, having to sell drugs on the streets. Believe me, it's not healthy, it's bad for morale – just the worst! Let's give them some real work to do. Build up their confidence again,' he continued, oblivious to the gasps from reporters.

As part of the new proposal, over 457,000 acres of land in the deep south will be allocated for cotton, tobacco and sugar plantations to be managed by designated 'planters', who will maintain and control the plantations with the aid of welfare recipients and offenders on parole.

Plantations are just the latest step in an effort by President Trump to revive and stimulate forgotten and neglected American industries.

'I know a few guys who would be great at running this business. Real good guys, some of the best guys in the world at what they do, trust me,' Trump concluded, pointing to several men in the front row wearing white robes with pointy hoods.

Trump to allow current transgender military personnel to sweep for landmines

FOLLOWING huge backlash over his decision to ban transgender people from the US military, President Donald Trump has rowed back on the ruling. He has stated that any transgender people currently serving would be able to keep their jobs but would be transferred immediately to posts such as mine-sweeping and bomb-disposal.

Trump declared the full ban on transgender people in the military yesterday via a series of tweets rather than a press conference or televised statement because, according to White House staff, he saves those mediums for 'important matters'.

Cryptically citing 'tremendous medical costs' that transgender soldiers put on the military, Trump issued a total ban on their serving in any capacity, much to the anger of the LGBTQ community, who stated that they were as entitled to die or get maimed for their country as the next person.

Amid harsh criticism, Trump softened his stance and granted transgender people the right to stay in the military as long as they didn't mind being on the IED hunting team.

'Trannies are more than welcome to serve their country by finding and disarming explosive devices so that our straight troops can operate safely in war zones,' said Trump, himself a highly decorated veteran of several high-profile wars, including his infamous Twitter war with London Mayor Sadiq Khan. 'So whether you're a man with boobs or a woman with a beard, or however all this shit works, you can still be of valuable service to your country.'

Trump went on to cut the budget for all military mine-sweeping divisions, a move which will force disposal officers to use bits of wood to poke around as they look for mines.

Kylie Jenner sizzles in these chip-pan accident pictures

PICTURES have emerged of 19-year-old reality TV star Kylie Jenner looking red hot after a mishap involving a chip pan in her LA home.

Kylie, sister of Kim Kardashian, smouldered after her signature smoky-eyed look incorporated the addition of boiling oil as the glamorous youngster took selfies of herself while making a big plate of chips.

The incident was captured across social media, as the

in-considerable-agony Jenner refused to stop posting images of herself on Instagram, Snapchat, Twitter, Facebook and even MySpace just to be sure.

As with many things posted by the Kardashian clan, the sizzling images immediately broke the Internet and received a flood of likes, shares and comments from fans worldwide.

'OMG Kylie does it again,' said one follower on Instagram. 'She always looks so hot, but in these pics, she looks red hot. Like third-degree hot. Like maybe go-to-the-hospital hot. Maybe she can't stop tweeting because her hand is melted to her phone? Should someone check that?'

Thousands of impressionable youngsters have already tipped a chip pan over themselves in a bid to emulate their idol, with the hashtag 'KylieJennerFace' trending worldwide.

POP NEWS

'Couple of U2 tickets there if anyone's looking'

FORMER president of the Olympic Council of Ireland Pat Hickey has a couple of tickets for U2's *Joshua Tree* anniversary tour in Dublin, if anyone's looking for them.

Speaking from his home in Castleknock, Dublin, Mr Hickey stated he has 'a good few premiere tickets' he is willing to 'offload', and they will be distributed on a first-come, first-served basis.

'Ya better get them fast as they're selling like hotcakes,' the 71-year-old managed to squeeze out in between mobile phone calls. 'There's a lad in Carlow on the line here and he's about to spin up to me for four. If I get

another €200 for them, they're yours; I'll tell him not to bother. Great tickets now, right up in the pit.'

No second gig is expected. Standing tickets were snapped up in just under six minutes this morning through Ticketmaster, and then reportedly went on sale for more than €1,000 each on a ticket-reselling website.

'I've a good few standing tickets there now, so I'll be generous and lash them out at €800 a pop,' Hickey added, as

he wheeled a barrow full of cash into his home. 'I've a bit of a bail bond to settle, lads, so if ye can spread the word I'd be grateful, cheers.'

Meanwhile, Ticketmaster has come under fire for reselling the tickets on its subsidiary site, Seatwave, for an average price of €299.43, while also raising its booking charges.

Mr Hickey welcomed this move. 'Sure, ya can't blame a fella for trying to make a few bob!' he concluded.

CONFIRMED

That show you like will go on for one season too many

TV executives today issued a statement confirming that your favourite show is expected to outstay its welcome by at least one season, blowing past what would have been a satisfying and memorable point of conclusion and ruining its overall legacy in the process.

Your favourite show, which you started watching from the start way before all those other bandwagon-jumpers got on board, hit the airwaves with a stunning, award-winning first season. Season one was followed by two more years of solid, newsworthy entertainment that thrilled its legions of fans worldwide.

With the show's creators happily beginning to close off character and story arcs in a bid to bring the whole thing to an end in a sensational series finale that would leave fans cheering in the aisles, the production company instead opted to sign everyone up to lucrative contracts for another

three years, with plans to replace anyone who leaves with a new actor nobody likes.

'If you like your favourite show now, then just wait till you see what we have planned for it!' beamed the executive producers of your favourite show, all sporting brand new fur coats.

'Having said that, we don't really have anything planned at the minute. In fact, the story has been pretty much told at this point. But we're going to bolt some new arcs onto the end of this to drag it out

for a few more years and then we'll try desperately to tie everything together in a big mish-mash of a finale that will have you saying, "What the fuck, is that it?" We promise you one thing though, we're going to have a great time with all the money we'll make.'

Your favourite show returns this weekend and is expected to achieve a record-breaking number of viewers for the season opener, after which the numbers will dwindle week by week until cancellation.

TRENDING Are you underqualified, prone to mistakes and open to covering your tracks? You might be perfect for a senior position at an Irish state body!

GREAT news on the jobs front for some lucky individuals as the government has revealed it is on the lookout for more people to fill important positions in state institutions, with many senior roles at semi-state bodies also up for grabs.

In yet another boost to Ireland's long struggle against modernity, proficiency, productivity and an easy and straightforward way of doing things, applicants for these crucial positions are asked to apply only if they are uniquely unqualified.

This latest wave of jobs has become available after the completion of investigations into inquiries of tribunals set up to inquire if a tribunal of investigation was necessary after hundreds of innocent and vulnerable people were presumably fucked over.

Applicants are warned, however, that at some point in their career they may be called before the Public Accounts Committee and grilled by politicians. Were this to occur, the successful applicant would be required to pretend to be contrite before receiving a tax-free lump sum and taking early retirement.

Being related to someone who is also uniquely unqualified and is currently occupying a similar role is not required but is admittedly helpful.

If you are the type of person who will work terribly when left alone with no oversight and a tremendous amount of responsibility, then you should head on over to: jobs.government.ie/noCVrequired

WOW! It would have been Selina Gomez's birthday if she was born on this day!

YOU'LL never look at today's date the same way again! This completely blew our minds so we just had to share with you guys!

Queen of Instagram and all-round BABE Selena Gomez – we wish she was our BFF – would have been celebrating her birthday in an epic way if today, 9 March, was in fact her birthday.

Obviously, it's not her birthday today, but if a bunch of circumstances were different it could have been, and that's worth noting and celebrating Selena for.

We always knew there was something special about today's date but couldn't put our fingers on it. Selena would totally own being a Pisces, and it's clear that if her parents conceived her roughly nine months before March 1992 there would be a strong chance that she would have been a March bambino! Makes you think, eh?

The beautiful Selena will be 25 this year, but on 22 July, the date she was actually born. But just chew over this for a second, if she was born today ... she would have been born today. Which really makes you think about how much she is killing her post-Disney, post-Justin life and career. Preach!

You've got to respect Selena for not being born today, but also, try to take a moment to just contemplate how things might have been if she was a March the 9th gal.

We now love Selena even more than before, which was loads by the way. Our love for her would, like, break any love-o-meter, for real! Haha, we're gas!

BREAKING NEWS

Pensioners storm offices of RTÉ demanding the return of teletext

A group of violent pensioners stormed RTÉ buildings in Donnybrook today to demand that teletext be returned to their televisions immediately.

'My TV keeps asking me do I want to Internet things, it scares me. I just want the weather and teletext was good for that,' a disoriented pensioner yelled at no one in particular while storming the reception desk in RTÉ.

Security at the Montrose campus was overrun by an estimated 2,000-strong gathering of Ireland's most ardent teletext fans, with one guard stabbed in the eyeball with a knitting needle.

'You can't make me Netflix if I don't want to. I want teletext – if you give me that then I'll go,' shared another pensioner, who had strapped explosives to her waist in a bid to show how serious she was about being able to access the 'Only Kidding' section of RTÉ's Aertel service.

'We do not negotiate with teletext terrorists,' an RTÉ spokesperson confirmed to WWN via a phone call earlier this morning.

A requirement for RTÉ to make better television is not thought to be part of the pensioners' demands.

'I lost six stone eating just air and it can work for you'

As part of WWN's Voices series, we give a platform to people we really shouldn't. Today is the turn of Aisling 'SuperAsh' Dennehy, a self-confessed gym bunny, endorser of products and Instagram legend, who has the diet you've been waiting for.
NO gimmicks! If you're looking to get fit and lose those few pounds you put on over Christmas (lol, I know, I'm guilty too. @SuperAsh is human just like you), just follow my unique weight-loss technique. No fads, no quackery, just the simple, straightforward, sensible stuff that will work for anyone and everyone.

I'm sure you're sick of all these nicely labelled products endorsed by the bubbly and attractive women on Instagram, all claiming to be the miracle cure when it comes to health and fitness. Enough is enough with the disingenuous nonsense. I was sick of it too, which is why I'm over the moon to be endorsing this really cute Air Diet packet that really is the miracle cure in dieting. For discount codes, check my Instagram.

I usually start the day off with three cups of air, but since you're on the first step of this programme you can start with five. Yum, you can't beat that unmistakable taste of O_2. If I wasn't so focused on toning up I would totes pig out and have 12 cups of the stuff. Lol, total fat pig that I am.

I was always the type that would put on weight just thinking about food – thanks for those genes, mom and dad. But look, a couple of years ago I got hold of the Air Diet and I haven't looked back.

I've never been happier – really I haven't. Shut the fuck up! Saying I'm not happy, who the fuck are you? I said I'm fucking happy so that means I'm bloody well happy you negative prick-bag.

Sorry, back to the routine. By midday you should be feeling like you're fit to die, but don't worry as lunch is a big one in the Air Diet routine. You get seven cups for lunch when you're starting off, you lucky ducks.

Hold on for dinner for another few hours and four hearty gulps of air later you're ready to faint.

Keep up this routine and you'll lose about six stone following hospitalisation, in a completely different manner to how I did it, but look, Air Diet paid me to endorse this thing so I'm gonna do what I'm gonna do.

Intervention urged as RTÉ still insisting Nathan Carter is a thing

CONCERN has been expressed for the well-being of national broadcaster RTÉ as it continues to insist that country singer Nathan Carter 'is a thing', *WWN* can reveal.

Carter is liked by some, but nowhere near enough, people to warrant his 439 appearances across RTÉ platforms this week.

'You want Nathan Carter. You need Nathan Carter,' RTÉ insisted with a crazed look in its eyes, as it was surrounded in a supportive and safe environment by those who care about it the most.

RTÉ confirmed plans to launch a third channel, RTÉ Nathan Carter, later this year in a misguided attempt to cater for the Carter-mad public that exists only as a figment of the national broadcaster's mind.

'I don't know what you've been told, but we didn't ask for this,' a confused and slightly irritated nation explained to RTÉ as it tried to wriggle free from its restraints.

'If we let you go, you have to promise not to commission a 10-part series called *Nathan Carter's Favourite Days of the Week* or some shite like that,' the nation added.

BREAKING: RTÉ has commissioned a four-hour documentary called *Nathan Carter's Wagon Wheel*, which will involve the country singer singing 'Wagon Wheel' for 240 minutes uninterrupted.

We talk to Daft Punk about their debut album *Homework* turning 20 years old

To celebrate 20 years since their first album Homework, WWN *journalist Paddy Browne travelled to Paris, France, to meet electronic music legends Daft Punk in a rare and exclusive interview.*
I arrived at the agreed location, Parc de Belleville, with instructions to make my way to a park bench on the east side of the picturesque green. Daft Punk's agent said Guy-Manuel de Homem-Christo and Thomas Bangalter would contact me once I got there.

Left waiting for what seemed like seven whole minutes, I decided to call it a day, as it was obvious the pair had backed out of the interview.

Walking away from the bench I was approached by two elderly gentlemen.

'Bonjour, Paddy! So glad you could make it,' one of them began. 'I'm Guy-Manuel and this is Thomas. We don't have long as we've got a bridge game at 3 p.m. in the community centre. Do you mind if we have our lunch while we do this?'

'No,' I replied, astounded by their lateness. 'I've been waiting here for ages, so ye are very lucky that I'm even here at all. I was just about to go home.'

Apologising profusely for delaying me, the old pair tucked into some corned beef sandwiches and shared a flask of tea.

I sat down and began the interview. 'So guys, it has been a staggering 20 years since your debut album, how has the music industry changed since *Homework*?'

'Ah, the whole EDM scene has gone way too mainstream, if I'm honest,' Thomas opened up, grimacing at a gelatine piece of corned beef he picked out from his dentures. 'Electronic music is everywhere now; every pop song these days has some element of it. Take that auto-tuned flute noise that's in every other song now. Like, it was fine for a while, but now they've saturated the crap out of the one noise.'

'You mean like ye guys did with that robot voice?' I posed.

Spluttering a spittle of moist bread onto my hand, which I ignored out of respect, Guy-Manuel chimed in, 'Ah ha, yes, but that auto-tune flute noise you hear everywhere now is very ATB "9 PM (Till I Come)". That was 1999 and now it's after reappearing again. It's not very original.'

'So what have you guys been up to lately then?'

'Well, I've had surgery to get a weeping cyst removed from my head from wearing that stupid helmet all those years,' Guy-Manuel barked angrily. 'I'm also blind in one eye from the bloody thing.'

'Sorry, let me rephrase, what have you guys been up to lately music-wise?'

'Pardon, we are very old and sometimes lose track of ourselves,' Thomas cut in, as Guy-Manuel stood up from the bench and pulled his trousers above his belly button. 'We have been working on a cover album, for old times' sake.'

'Wow! That's great news, guys! What kind of songs will you be covering, or is that too much to ask right now?'

'No, no, not at all,' Thomas replied. 'We wanted to cover classics like the Vengabus song by the Vengaboys, the Crazy Frog song, Rebecca Black's Friday song, that kind of thing.'

'That sounds like a belter of an album,' I said, pretending to be enthusiastic.

'Yes, we're really looking forward to working with these artists. We hope to have the album out in May.'

'And a tour?'

'Depending on how Guy's cyst heals up, we expect to be touring in the second half of this year!'

'Do you guys still have a fan base, at this stage?'

'Why, yes; but the venues may be smaller than we're used to.'

'And will touring not take a lot out of you physically?'

'Sure, performing will be strenuous, but at the end of the day, all we do is sit there with our helmets on, pretending to press buttons,' Thomas concluded, fucking the last of his tea out onto the ground like it was no one's business.

After the interview, I walked slowly with the two old producers round the park for a bit, before saying my goodbyes. They seemed old and frail, but still lucid.

It's great to see Daft Punk still have a hunger for music after all these years in the business, and it was refreshing to hear that they're producing music again. I wish them all the best.

Daft Punk's *Almost Alive* tour will begin in the Three Lions Bar in Manchester, England on 29 September. Tickets on sale at £5 now, or £8 on the door.

Wonderful World of Science

The families of the now deceased MIT scientists who successfully grew legs on sharks concede it was probably a mistake to do so.

987 Irish celebrities to launch healthy eating and fitness books this week

RESPONDING to the desperate shortage of tomes on health and fitness and food thrown together by celebrities-you're-almost-sure-aren't-celebrities-at-all, close to 1,000 famous figures in Irish life have released books this week.

'Technically, you're a certified dietician if your abs selfie gets over 300 likes on Instagram,' explained one-time extra on *Celebrity Bainisteoir* Gráinne Kelly.

'I was just inundated with people saying "oh my God, you should write one of those healthy living

books I've seen on every shelf in every shop for the last four years, there's not enough of them", so I did it,' Kelly said, recalling a conversation she had in the mirror with herself.

Kelly dismissed any criticism surrounding her book launch by pointing out, 'Have you seen how good my arse looks on social media?'

There seems to be a growing appetite for health and fitness books written by people who spend the majority of their time stuck in a permanent selfie pose. Publishing expert Leon Grey explained the phenomenon, 'Thick people love buying stupid shit.'

Grey went on to expound on the intricacies of the crowded waste-of-money marketplace. 'Research shows that if a book cover has a smiling lad with muscles next to a salad, or a perky woman in a fluorescent sports bra next to some hummus, it is basically a licence to print money.'

While the emerging 'exercise until the stinging criticisms from your overbearing mother no longer cut through you like a knife through organic almond butter' market is increasingly competitive, there remains hope for the 987 celebrities launching a book this week.

'Look at this bell-end's book,' observed Grey, holding up a copy of *The Beautiful Body Beautiful: Eat, Laugh, Smile, Oxidise, Yoga, Exercise and Meditate Your Way to Organic Happiness and Fit into that Dress — Yolo.* 'What is this eejit on about? If one more fucker who has Snapchat and was in *Fair City* for five seconds tells me it's okay to have a cheat meal, I'll go insane.'

TOP 10
Best-selling cookbooks in Ireland 2017

10 *In the Kitchen with Donal* by Donal Skehan

9 *Cooking with Donal* by Donal Skehan

8 *Kitchen Secrets* by Donal Skehan

7 *Secret of Cooking* by Donal Skehan

6 *My Kitchen* by Donal Skehan

5 *A Guide to Easy Meals* by Donal Skehan

4 *Easy Cooking with Donal* by Donal Skehan

3 *The Secret of My Easy Cooking Kitchen* by Donal Skehan

2 *Cooking the Easy Way: Meals from My Kitchen* by Donal Skehan

1 *Donal Cooks: My Favourite Meals from My Favourite Kitchen with My Favourite Food* by Donal Skehan

What's on the telly?

First Gates Reality. Five farmers get to grips with new swinging seven-bar gates on their fields. Sparks fly when they forget to close them!

Something for Ray To Do Entertainment. Another chat show for Ray D'Arcy, to justify his big pay cheque. This week, Ray meets the same guests he met two weeks ago.

News XXX Current affairs. You've seen the news, now see the newwwws. The sexiest reporters bring you the hottest news on the worst atrocities from around the world.

The Canteen Entertainment. To save time building a set, this new chat show takes place in the RTÉ canteen and features whoever happens to be in there at the time. This week's guests are Aonghus McAnally and someone claiming to be one of the Carter Twins.

Some Dryin' Out There Reality. Join 12 Irish people as they come to terms with their alcohol problems in the country's only drying-out facility.

Conor's Cooking Cookery. UFC champion Conor McGregor swaps his trunks for an apron, and brings us delicious treats from his kitchen. This week it's fuckin' bleedin' batter burgers, you muppet.

Kennedy Documentary. Part 45 of Ryan Tubridy's 87-part RTÉ documentary on the life of John F. Kennedy (because he loves him so much and it's not his own money he's spending).

Drug Scum Murder Kill Crime. Meet Ireland's most murderous drug scum. Scum drug murder killings. Kill murder scum drugs, gangs. GANGS! Drugs, murder. Killing. IN COLD BLOOD.

Snapchat: A Guide Educational. A state-sponsored show to help the over-21s figure out how Snapchat works. This week, dog faces, and why they're everywhere.

Better Call Naul Comedy drama. The citizens of the sleepy north Dublin suburb of Naul find themselves sliding deeper and deeper into a world of crime in this darkly comedic prequel to *Breaking Balbriggan*.

McKenna and Capowski Crime drama. Hard-bitten Westmeath detective Pierce McKenna and his long-suffering Polish partner, Piotr Capowski, tackle crime on the gritty streets of Athlone.

Something about Weddings Reality. Something to do with weddings, maybe choosing dresses or letting the page boy make the cake or something like that. Look, it's wedding shit and if you're getting married you'll tune in.

Nationwide Nature??? What is *Nationwide* anyway? Does anyone watch this? It could be hardcore pornography for all we know.

The Forecourt Reality. More gripping drama live-streamed from the CCTV cameras outside one of Waterford's busiest 24-hour petrol stations. This week, some lad at the hatch wants Doritos but the guy in the shop brings him the red ones instead of the orange ones. Back round the counter you go, pal!

Who Wants To Be a Millionaire: Sinn Féin Edition Quiz. Contestants compete for €1 million by answering a series of general knowledge questions with answers that may not be actually true but are acceptable if they are delivered convincingly enough.

Donal Skehan's Sauce Masterclass Cookery. Cooking genius Donal Skehan leads viewers through exactly what sauce to use on what food. This week, red sauce goes on … that's right, chips!

Can I Finish? Political. Top politicians take to the stand to be grilled on a number of subjects by host Quentin O'Malley, before the whole thing disintegrates into them yelling 'Can I finish?' at each other for an hour.

Luas Yourself Youth. Following a group of young Dubliners as they travel around on the Luas all day, playing tunes and yelling at nothing in particular while dodging the fare inspectors.

Comedy Programme (TBC) Comedy. RTÉ's hilarious new show to replace the recently axed *Republic of Telly* and *Irish Pictorial Weekly*. No reports as to what comedy show they intend to replace these fan favourites with, but we're sure it's going to be very funny indeed!

Now That's What I Call Some Producer's Cousin Youth. Eight snappily dressed trendy south Dublin youngsters bounce around a hastily-built set in RTÉ while their cousin who works in production scrambles to justify giving them a job.

Excess Baggage with Michaella McCollum Travel. YES! TV3 locked down Michaella McCollum to host a travel show for them. Fuck knows what it's going to look like or involve, but we don't care. Michaella McCollum! The drug mule! That's ratings right there, baby!

Love/Hate Crime. The award-winning show returns for another season to give literally everyone on the island a new box set to buy each other for Christmas.

Vague Thumping Music Music. Listen to the tunes your neighbours love, with eight straight hours of vague, bass-heavy pounding music. Sounds best through a thin wall!

Putting pencils between your knuckles and pretending to be Wolverine 'perfectly acceptable', finds study

A recent study has revealed that pretending to be the popular Marvel character Wolverine by putting three pens or three pencils or three knives from the drawer or indeed three of anything between your knuckles is a perfectly acceptable, normal, everyday part of being a human person.

Wolverine, the tortured ex-special forces mutant featured in the *X-Men* series of comics, cartoons and movies, has become one of the most famous and beloved Marvel characters of all time. He is set to return to cinemas this week in the highly anticipated *Logan*, with Hugh Jackman playing the titular character for the final time.

Copying Wolverine's trademark 'adamantium' blades that spring from his knuckles, fans of the character worldwide often find themselves putting pencils between their fingers and making a 'snikt' noise as they daydream of being Wolverine. Many possibly envision sticking that prick from accounts while he's taking too long at the canteen microwave during lunchbreak.

Although most people pretending to be Wolverine can have feelings of foolishness, a new study has revealed that it's nothing to be ashamed of.

'Pretending to be Wolverine is like masturbation; we all do it,' said Marvel research specialist Dr Mark Harrison, the best at what he does.

'You don't have to feel like you're some sort of nerd or degenerate. There's not a person alive who has watched an *X-Men* movie and not gone home and flailed around with claws made out of HB pencils. People need to be more open about it. I'm sure if you admit to the people you work with that you like to pretend to be Wolverine, they'll confess that they do the same. Maybe you can all pretend to be Wolverine together.'

Although most people can easily line up three pencils into their fist for a single Wolverine-style claw hand, many have admitted that they then struggle to get three pencils into their other fist for the perfect two-handed berserker Wolverine attack.

'I don't like *Mrs. Brown's Boys*' – brave Irish person speaks out

GOING against the grain and ignoring every patriotic molecule in his body, one brave Irishman has come out of the woodwork against all the odds to negatively critique one of the country's finest comedic exports, *Mrs. Brown's Boys*.

'Sometimes you just have to break away from the flock and form your own opinion,' said Cork man David Keane, believed to be the only Irish person to have arrived at this unique viewpoint. 'Now, I know I'm probably going to get a lot of flak for this, and I don't want to hurt anyone's feelings when I say this, but I don't like *Mrs. Brown's Boys*.'

Leaving the air silent for a moment, Keane, who loves *Father Ted*, nodded his head in a motion that seemed to suggest 'yes, I just said that', before continuing his tirade against one of Ireland's most successful sitcoms.

'I just don't get what's so funny about it,' the searing critic of sacred cultural cows continued. 'He's a male Dub dressed up as a woman Dub that just says old dick jokes and snipes at homosexuality. Where's the humour in that? I could probably write, produce, direct, edit and star in something way better than that auld shite. If this is everyone's idea of funny, then I'm not an everybody.'

'I understand people's tastes aren't as refined as mine and I can't blame them for not picking up on the subtleties in other, more worthy, programmes and pieces of art. And it is a shocking allegation to level at a show, but it's a putrid piece of shite.'

Keane's comments have since swept social media, causing nationwide outrage and calls for new 'begrudgery laws' to be introduced to prevent any more belittling trends.

'How could someone say something like that about their fellow countrymen?' one online commentator said.

'This is the kind of thing that lost us the six counties,' another person typed with their bare hands. 'He seems to be the type to look at a beautiful puppy and say "what a load of shite" – a scumbag, if you will.'

Mr Keane later admitted that he hasn't yet actually watched a whole episode of *Mrs. Brown's Boys*, but he 'knows it's shit anyway'.

Ariana Grande posted a tweet and we managed to scrape an article from it

AMERICAN singer and actress Ariana Grande posted a tweet yesterday and we managed to scrape together a 250-word article from it, despite it having little to no importance to the world, other than filling our 3 p.m. slot.

The 23-year-old took to Twitter at 21:15 GMT, carefully orchestrating the 50-character Tweet, minus capital letters, stating 'y'all are so so good to me. and funny. i love you.'

> y'all are so so good to me. and funny. i love you.
> — Ariana Grande (@Ariana Grande) 3 January 2017

Following the message, which somehow gained 10,527 retweets at the time of writing, *WWN* editor Paddy Brown immediately offered up the scoop to this reporter, instructing me to pen some sort of mindless dribble about how Ms Grande is such an inspiration to young women everywhere, and that they should be happy she took the time to grace them with her kind words of appreciation.

On top of this task, I am to include several of the most retweeted, or liked, fans' Twitter responses in a bid to raise fans' hopes that their idol can, and does, respond to them on occasion.

Further to this, we are obligated to point out that Ms Grande will be going on a world tour next month, and that we will be reporting every minute detail, including wardrobe malfunctions, Twitter spats, upskirt photographs when she exits a car, fluctuating weight gain and unverified stories based on her private and sexual affairs with men and/or women – whatever sells really.

TOP 6
Republican ballads in Ireland 2017

Republican ballads made a huge comeback this year thanks to the uncertainty surrounding Brexit. They regularly clogged up the charts with lilting melodies that called for the joyous reuniting of the south with the north, while also allowing for the occasional allusion to giving the Brits a right hiding.

6 'Border Poll' by Gerry and The Peacemakers

5 'Did We Already Mention a Border Poll?' by Gerry and The Peacemakers

4 'Shape of You and I Ted, Our Land' by Ed Sheeran feat. Pearse Doherty

3 'As Gaeilge so the Brits Don't Know What Our Plans Are' by MIRA (Musical IRA)

2 'I Feel It Coming (A United Ireland)' by The Weeknd feat. Daft Punk (Mary Lou Club Remix)

1 'This Was Actually All Our Idea' by Fianna Fáil and Fine Gael

Did Kylie Jenner get a boob job? Why am I being paid to write about this shite?

DID Kylie Jenner get a boob job? Fucking probably, yeah, but why the fuck do I have to write 500 words on it and 'include five pictures from her Instagram or Snapchat'? Yeah, all-fucking-right, Siobhan, thanks for the email. This is why I studied journalism, cheers for hiring me. Fucking dream job my hole.

'You'll get to write about things that matter to you, matter to the majority of women.' Yeah, well done on fucking Donald Trumping me with alternative facts in the job interview, Siobhan.

I thought this is what I wanted. The guys working here are nice enough. We had Prosecco at lunch once. We got a Naked make-up hamper into the office last week, which was cool. Then Cadbury sent in loads of Creme Egg stuff, and you don't get that kind of gear in most jobs, do ya?

'Make sure to pick out the proper booby pics, as much cleavage as possible.' No problem, got ya, Siobhan.

Any chance I can write about the dearth of women entering STEM courses in college? Thought not. Any chance I can write about a business woman without it being about the fact she is a woman in business?

Oh, what's that? You now need eight pics of Jenner tits? Got to keep people on the page for longer, is it? Loud and clear, Siobhan.

Don't get me wrong, I have this stupid, idiotic muscle memory that kicks in when I see a Jenner/ Kardashian headline pop down my Facebook newsfeed, so I click on the links. But I've been at this thing for 12 minutes now and apparently the copy isn't 'judgement neutral' enough. It's harmless stuff, but writing about it every fucking day isn't harmless. I'm fit to explode.

'The last thing we want is readers to think we have an opinion, we've got to disguise that with suggestive yet subtle language. Don't make it obvious. We're judging her for having the boob job, but we don't want our readers to realise that. We've got to stay on the fence about these things and invite them to judge instead.'

Well, fucking fair play for stating the obvious there, Siobhan. Last thing we'd want is our readers thinking that we only publish this shit pretending there's a 'controversial this or that', just to get them nice and annoyed.

'Frame it so that the speculation about the boob job comes from another publication, copy and paste if needed. Or if you can't get that, just use some randomer's tweets on Twitter.' Loud and clear, Siobhan. Plenty of random tweets out there. Should be easy.

'Oh my God, I can't believe I'm paid to write this shite about Kylie Jenner.' Will that do, Siobhan? Christ, and you said I needed a degree and minimum two years' experience in a similar role ... for this? For-fucking-this? Bollocks to this, I quit.

FOR former high school senior Ferris Bueller, going to school in the mid-80s and keeping up with grades always came second to having a good time with his friends. Now, over 30 years later, Bueller reflects on his adult life and admits that he regrets skipping class. We caught up with the 47-year-old alcoholic and drug addict at his squat in one of the roughest neighbourhoods in Chicago, West Englewood.

'I moved here in '92,' the now gaunt Bueller opened up, pouring this reporter a glass of homebrew. 'Dad kicked me out of the house after I sold several of his prize art works for crack. Shortly after that my girlfriend, Sloane, dumped me for that prick Cameron. Then I done some time for assaulting the two of them outside Walmart when I was begging for change at the trolley bay. Eventually I wound up here.'

Bueller went on to tell me his life story, but much of it was inaudible due to the fact that he had shot up a syringe full of heroin into his arm some two minutes before the interview started.

Addict on welfare Ferris Bueller reflects on skipping class

On the plus side, his drugged condition allowed me to casually rummage round his squat.

'Have you ever thought about making amends and getting some help?' I asked, eyeing up his iconic leopard-skin waistcoat.

'I tried calling my mom a few times, but after the attempted murder thing with my dad in 2006, we haven't been on the best of terms,' he mumbled, now slowly coming round and taking a hit from a nearby water bong full of really nice-smelling weed. 'Believe it or not, the drugs and drink has me ruined.'

'I should never have skipped school like that, now that I think back on it. By the time I was in my senior year, I had already missed most of our classes and no college would have me.'

His story is a sad one, and I asked if there is any advice he would like to give to young people struggling with school.

'Yeah, stick at it, man. America is a dog-eat-dog world and if you fall behind, for even a second, it will swallow you up like the gas in a 1961 Ferrari 250 GT California Spyder engine,' he advised, before asking, 'Would you have a lend of a couple of bucks, before you go? I'll give it back to you, man.'

'Absolutely not, Ferris,' I replied, 'your credit rating is terrible and I'm afraid you'll spend the money on crack.'

'I'll sell you that waistcoat for 50 bucks?'

'Twenty and you have a deal.'

'Sold,' he said, now teary-eyed that he was parting with the only piece of 1980s memorabilia he had left, but happy for the fix nonetheless.

I couldn't help but feel for Bueller as he sat there wasted on a cocktail of drugs and hooch, but his message is clear: 'Stay in school if ya want to be cool.'

CELEBRITY NEWS

So cute! Michael Fassbender still believes in the tooth fairy, has massive penis

JUST when we thought we couldn't love Michael Fassbender and his massive member any more than we do, *WWN Entertainment* spied an amazing quote from his recent interview in *GQ Guatemala* about the tooth fairy, which reminded us of the fact Michael has a large mickey.

Total BABE and handsome Irishman Fassbender still believes in the tooth fairy! How cute is that? Combine that with the fact his lad is massive and we've got to admit we're 100% Team Fassbender.

'Yeah, every time I head home to Kerry and I lose a tooth, there's a euro waiting under my pillow,' Fassbender explained in a recent interview, which made no mention of how much screen time

his penis got in the movie *Shame* but, come on, we all saw it.

We all want a rugged, thoughtful and intelligent man who also has an innocence to him and who, despite the overwhelming evidence presented to him, still believes in the tooth fairy. Additionally, a massive lad is always welcome.

'I won't have anyone telling me the tooth fairy isn't real,' the actor added, which is just so adorable. It really makes you picture his memorable lad all over again.

We all love him for his work in the *X-Men* movies, *Prometheus*, *Macbeth*, *Fish Tank*, *Hunger* and those scenes in *Shame* in which

his manhood is out and about, flapping in the wind, striking against the inside of his thigh with a commanding thud. Like we said, we just respect his talent and find his belief in the tooth fairy a nice bonus.

We could make a pun about how we'd like him to 'bone us', but there is more to this massive lad than his Michael Fassbender. Shit, you know what we meant to say.

THE *WWN Entertainment* team has been monitoring some of the 400 Irish sites that regularly post the latest Coláiste Lurgan videos and have discovered that the Galway gang are back with yet another song!

The melodies are note-perfect, and the chorus brings forth that by now familiar wave of goosebumps on the skin, but in a strange departure from their previous work this latest ditty is in English and so it's shite.

It's hard to put a finger on why 60 girls and boys singing their hearts out in an emotionally evocative fashion leaves us cold, when on the previous 40 occasions we were floored, stunned and totes in awe and had bags of *grá* for them.

WOW! Coláiste Lurgan sing in English for a change and it's shite

Their stirring version of Eminem's classic 'Smack That' should have left us feeling 179% more Irish than we already felt, but alas the choice to sing in English robbed the song of any greater meaning, therefore garnering not so rave reviews.

A casual look at the comments section below the video on YouTube reveals we're not the only ones who feel this way.

'In English? Die #feelingbetrayed,' wrote one livid Internet user, in English.

Calls for a government inquiry to be launched have been gaining momentum this morning, with Twitter user @Gra32 summing up everyone's feelings. 'Is this some sort of sick joke?' @Gra32 queried.

At the time of this article's publication, Coláiste Lurgan has yet to apologise.

5 greatest *Late Late Show* guests of all time

ONCE heralded in cultural circles for always having its finger on the pulse of what was going on in Ireland, *The Late Late Show* has found itself on the receiving end of claims that it just hasn't been the same since the days of Ireland's patron saint of the good old times, Gay Byrne. Those individuals may have ended up with egg on their face last Friday when Nathan Carter made his 19th appearance in less than 12 months, which got *WWN* thinking about which guests really were the cream of the crop.

We've poured over the archives to find what we believe to be the five greatest *Late Late Show* guests to ever grace RTÉ studios.

5 Some model who was there to promote something

While making the difficult transition from part-time model and student in UCD to adult and almost full-time model, Vicky O'Sullivan Twee got the nation talking back in 2012. Twee was on the show to promote her new book about her difficult journey of self-discovery, *A Book of My Favourite Things*, and the studio audience took her into their hearts, marvelling at anecdote after anecdote.

Flowers, dresses, cooking and being nice were Twee's favourite passions, but she would not allow society to tell her she couldn't also do business stuff as well.

The foodie-model-advocate-chef-fitness guru-beauty expert saw her book go on to sell one million copies after its first week on the shelves. The power of the *Late Late*.

4 Nelson Mandela

There to talk about the monumental work that went into transforming South Africa, and shortly after the iconic 1999 Rugby World Cup, Nelson Mandela was no doubt surprised when Gay Byrne cut short the interview. But Mandela should have known better than to refuse to say anything complimentary about Irish dancing, *Glenroe* or Tayto. It was one of Gaybo's finest moments, showing Ireland that no guest, no matter how big, couldn't be taken down a peg or two if needed.

3 The lad who was wearing his Kerry jersey at the WWE wrestling

An Irishman was at a large-scale televised event abroad, and he was filmed wearing his GAA jersey. Four million of us tuned in to hear his story back in 2009. Gripping television.

2 Siobhan Munratty

The watershed moment in Irish televisual history. The Ireland of 28 September 1982 had never seen an elderly and hapless spinster on television – that was, until they were introduced to Siobhan. Gaybo, mindful of how alien the concept was to much of Ireland, handled the interview with patience and humanity, the hallmarks of his interviewing style. Just how in God's name was Siobhan, Ireland's oldest spinster, still single and not settled down at the age of 22? Over the course of 79 engrossing minutes we found out. Gaybo asked the questions. He asked for himself, of course, out of curiosity, but more importantly, he asked for us, for Ireland.

1 Neil Armstrong

Live via satellite from his *Apollo 11* spacecraft, RTÉ and the *Late Late* beat out stiff competition to interview Armstrong as the astronaut took his first steps on the moon. It may be easy to laugh now, looking back at the innocent questions Gaybo posed – 'Is it very moony, Neil?' – but this was box-office stuff at the time.

The interview wasn't without its hiccups though, particularly when the competition winner, who won a year's supply of Kerrygold butter, was drawn. RTÉ denied claims of a fix, but to this day, it is hard to believe the coincidence that Armstrong just happened to have his name drawn out of the hat.

MOVIE NEWS

Local man insists he's never seen *Star Wars*

THE release of *Rogue One: A Star Wars Story* has granted one Waterford man the opportunity to stress, to anyone who will listen, that he's never seen *Star Wars* and hasn't got a clue what it's about or who any of the characters are.

39-year-old Mike Flanaghan takes a curious pride in having not seen the movies in the *Star*

Wars series, even though he has 'kind of seen one or two of them on telly' down through the years and has the basic gist of the story.

Whenever overhearing co-workers, or even strangers, talking excitedly about the latest blockbuster addition to the series, Flanaghan seizes the moment. It is his prompt to state that he hasn't ever seen anything to do with *Star Wars*, adding that he 'gets it mixed up with *Star Trek*'. And we all know there's no possible way that anyone with half a brain could do that.

'It might be *Harry Potter* as far as I'd know,' lies Flanaghan,

walking through an aisle in his local shop packed with wall-to-wall *Star Wars* merchandise. 'Haven't a clue. Not a notion. That lad in the black helmet? Is that Luke Sky-whatever? And the big wolf-looking lad, is that Harrison Ford under all that? I wouldn't know, because I – HAVE – NEVER – SEEN – STAR WARS.'

Flanaghan has also never seen *Doctor Zhivago*, *The Wind That Shakes the Barley*, *La Haine*, *Batman Forever*, *Regarding Henry* or indeed *Friday the 13th – the Final Chapter*, but feels no compulsion to stress any of this information at any time.

'I rubbed my eyeballs with a cheese grater to make it stop' – *Late Late Show* Valentine special complaints in full

RTÉ received over 300 complaints following its *Late Late Show* Valentine's Day special, which had promised to be the 'most debauched and depraved' night of Irish television.

Dozens of middle Irelanders flocked to phone lines and email services to voice their disdain for last Friday's show, with the national broadcaster also receiving a total of 10 formal complaints.

'We bought four bottles of Lourdes water, just in case, but by 10 minutes to 10 we had already used every last drop,' one elderly woman wrote in blood on a papyrus page.

A staggering 568,400 viewers switched on to watch the festive

special on RTÉ One, which featured presenter Ryan Tubridy giving a hamper by condom manufacturer Durex to each audience member, presumably to wear on their erect penises, or whatever they have these days.

'This new *Late Late Show* kisscam idea is absolutely ludicrous,' a long-time viewer wrote. 'I can't imagine it going down well either when Ryan does those misery segments, you know, when he forces people to admit they have some form of mental health problem, even when they don't.

'Why RTÉ would let a pervert like Al Porter open the show is beyond me, surely there was a priest on

hand somewhere in Donnybrook to instigate the courting,' penned a County Carlow farmer. 'The fact the audience was not divided up with one side for men and the other side for women, goes to show the slippery slope the *Late Late* is on. Ever since the marriage referendum this country has gone to the dogs.'

'Meatloaf was terrible and has really let himself go,' another viewer said. 'I'm surprised at Dickie Rock and Crystal Swing stooping this low too. Also, not one guest on Friday's show was trying to sell me a book or make me go to a movie, which left me feeling a little empty if I'm honest.'

The uproar comes just months after RTÉ received a number of complaints over Katie Hopkins appearing on the show. Viewers had been upset to see her openly masturbate using a crucifix before spontaneously combusting.

There's a 'Rob' Kardashian, apparently

WWN have confirmed reports of the existence of a Robert 'Rob' Kardashian, apparently a brother of the Kardashian sisters, who has generated headlines about himself with the aid of stories about his ex-wife or his house burning down or something.

Rob, who shares the family's genes, which predispose him to large breasts, a huge arse and a constant need for attention, trended on Twitter last night following his tweets about Blac Chyna, which we are assured is not a typo.

Although there were a number of people who seemed already aware of the existence of this person, the public at large had no idea that the Kardashians have a little brother called Rob and, as such, were shocked and, indeed, dismayed to learn of him.

'Rob Kardashian ... was he not OJ's lawyer? Are you sure you have this right?' asked one person we talked to about the matter.

'Huh. Well, okay. I'm sure he's a great man and will use his wealth and fame to act as a UN ambassador to some impoverished nation or other. The more Kardashians the better, right? Can't have too much of a good thing, yeah?'

Since his appearance online, Rob Kardashian has been available for comment on literally anything, mostly without being asked by anyone.

TRENDING Sisters of Mercy win name award

RELIGIOUS order the Sisters of Mercy have scooped top prize in this year's 'Most Inaccurate Name for an Organisation' award, beating stiff competition from Josef Fritzl's Daycare Club and The Kim Jong Un Centre for Calm, Rational Thinking.

Judges deemed the nuns, whose name suggests a group of women who are so merciful to everyone that they literally named themselves the Sisters of Mercy, in actual fact to be the complete opposite of merciful by anyone's standards.

With decades of horrific child abuse allegations against the order, as detailed in the Ryan Report, as well as the systematic breaking down of young girls until they believed themselves to be nothing more than worthless, a panel of experts suggested a better name for the order, one which even this publication deemed to be unprintable.

'I'd like to accept this award on behalf of all our members who helped us take the name Sisters of Mercy and really make a total mockery of it,' beamed the nun who went up to collect the award.

'Not only have we perfected the lack of mercy through our actions, we've also shown no mercy to our victims by denying any wrongdoing and hamstringing any attempts by them to get justice. See you all next year!'

The Sisters of Mercy are the only group of Irish nuns to compete in the awards this year, following a ruling that allowing any more than one would be unfair to other entrants, and potentially lead to a top 10 made up completely of religious orders from Ireland.

High Court rules in favour of Oasis in *Oasis v. Blur* case

BREAKING news from the High Court, where just minutes ago a judgement was made in the long and often drawn-out proceedings of *Oasis v. Blur*.

The controversial trial began in late 1995 when Oasis frontman Liam Gallagher sought to legally prove that Oasis are better than Blur. Members of the music community have been seen in the public gallery throughout, taking a keen interest in the legal arguments.

The fractious proceedings came to a head today, but it's worth looking back at some of the highlights of the case between Manchester band Oasis and London-based Blur.

Key evidence was paraded in front of a packed court when Gallagher, in his trademark parka coat and awful haircut, delivered a rousing version of 'Champagne Supernova' to stake his claim.

Justice Barry White then asked Blur frontman Damon Albarn to enter a song of his choosing into evidence and he delivered a lacklustre version of 'Parklife', which fell flat without the input of actor Phil Daniels.

Albarn, speaking out of turn, pointed out that Blur had won the 1995 head-to-head Britpop chart battle when their 'Country House' single outsold Oasis's single 'Roll With It' by some 58,000 copies.

When Jonathan Quigley, a barrister acting on behalf of Mr Albarn, cross-examined Gallagher, he asserted, 'Surely, Mr Gallagher, not even you would stand over the cocaine-fuelled pile of shit that is *Be Here Now*.'

At that moment Gallagher leapt from the witness stand and attempted to strangle Quigley, before being removed from court.

And who can forget the day that Oasis's chief songwriter, Noel Gallagher, gave evidence via video-link to confirm that *Be Here Now* is, in his words, 'utter shite'?

Despite this admission, and ignoring impassioned testimony from Albarn, Justice Barry White today ruled in favour of the Manchester band.

In his judgement, delivered just moments ago, Justice White stated, 'In the case of *Oasis v. Blur*, I find in favour of Oasis, citing specifically the swagger,

the verve and the unrepentant rock-star arseholery that sets the band apart.'

Speaking through his own barrister outside the court, Liam Gallgher confirmed he felt justice had been served.

'My client would like to state on record his satisfaction at today's judgement, which he sees as a vindication for his and his band's talent. This brings to a close a long drawn-out legal battle and Liam is delighted that a definitive answer in the Oasis versus Blur saga has been reached.'

'Don't abort that baby, and please breastfeed it where I can't see it'

Speaking exclusively to WWN, Senator Eamon Russey discusses his simple two-part plan for an easier life for everyone.

THE notion that a pregnant woman could one day decide to abort the baby in her womb is almost as abhorrent to me as the thoughts that the same woman might carry that child to full-term, give birth to it and then start breastfeeding it across from me while I'm having a flat white at Starbucks.

As a man, I can remove myself from the emotional and hormonal hysteria that a woman goes through on a day-to-day basis, and calmly and rationally relay the facts and figures about abortion and breastfeeding.

I have gathered this information from Wikipedia in a collected and concise manner that even those who disagree with me can relate to. If they're open to listening when a man is speaking, they might find that they can get through life without complaining every five minutes.

I've spoken to dozens of other men, and they all agree with me. If you get pregnant, no matter how that should happen, you have a responsibility to your unborn baby to carry it to term.

And that's not all. You also have a responsibility to the rest of society to not force us to look at you whipping your breasts out in public to feed that baby. Take it to the ladies' toilets, or maybe just never leave the house so you can feed it at home.

Think about someone other than yourself for a while. There's a good girl.

EXCLUSIVE REPORT

'You'd understand if you had kids,' says local woman about fucking everything

A Waterford woman has denied that she has an addiction to starting every sentence with 'If you had kids then you'd understand', which friends have stated is one of the key contributing factors to her current unbearability.

Sharon Cusack (27) has used the words 'if you had kids then you'd understand' almost once every five minutes since she gave birth to her first child earlier this year.

Cusack, a dose, has dropped her trademark phrase into conversations ranging from car maintenance to watching Netflix, often in a dismissive, combative manner that shuts down anyone else's side of the argument, particularly if they are not a parent.

Cusack's pals are currently giving serious thought to staging an intervention to help her stop using the vexing phrase.

'OK, I don't have kids, but I'm pretty sure I still know how tricky it is to get a seat on the fucking bus during rush hour,' said Donna, one of Cusack's sisters.

'The way Sharon goes on, you'd swear having kids was like having a shopping trolley full of mice handcuffed to your ankle all day, and nobody could possibly comprehend what it was like. I get it, like; when you have kids, you have less money, less time, less energy, everything takes longer and has to be done more carefully. But it doesn't make you one of the fucking Avengers, and the rest of us just drooling morons.'

Cusack's intervention was cut short after she stated that she had to leave early for reasons the rest of her childless friends wouldn't understand.

Average adult spends four years of their life trying to remember passwords

A shocking new study into online human behaviour has revealed that the average adult in the developed world spends a staggering 48 months trying to remember their many online passwords.

The study, which was carried out by the Institute of Studies, found that the majority of people forget their passwords and then spend two years of their life trying to recover them, with some people spending up to six years in total resetting their online accounts.

'In one extreme case, a 47-year-old man had spent eight years of his life supplying basic security information such as his mother's maiden name and his first school,' a spokesman for the study group explained. 'Not only that, but he also spent 18 months trying to answer captchas, with a success rate of 3%. This man even lost his wife and kids in a bitter divorce as he had been spending too much time online resetting his passwords.'

The worrying findings have led to calls for better log-in options online, where currently most accounts still rely on a decades-old system that has failed millions of times, yet never changes.

'We estimate that retrieving passwords costs the global economy $34 billion per day in lost man-hours,' claimed expert in the field of Internetting, Professor Derek Ryan. 'In fact, most online traffic is password-related, while the rest is porn and cat searches; there's very little in the way of actual work being done online at all.'

Furthermore, the study discovered that a large proportion of online time is taken up by accepting Internet cookie options, something no one really has any idea about, but we all seem to be happy to do, regardless.

FASHION

Local man to wear the bollocks out of new hoodie

A County Waterford man is expected to wear the absolute bollocks out of a new hoodie he bought, due to its snug fit and crisp sheen.

Thomas Holden, from Johns Park, purchased the Nike garment for €69.99 in a local sports shop, immediately ignoring previous hoodies in his press.

'I'd say it'll be another few weeks before it goes to the wash,' the 24-year-old explains. 'Problem with hoodies is they get all stretched and out of shape and are useless after the first couple of washes. Hopefully I'll get two or three cycles out of it before it's fucked and unwearable.'

Bought in the January sales after receiving a voucher from his auntie Kate, Holden recalls the moment he wore his new clothes around the town.

'Waterford is like a sports clothes fashion show after Christmas,' added the job seeker. 'Every young fella in the town does be walking around flashing their trainers and new tracksuits, so picking the right top is essential, and wearing the bollocks out of it is all part of the show.'

So far Holden's hoodie has only received two nodge burns and a small spec of curry sauce from a curry chip he ate on Saturday.

'If I keep this run of good luck up, it might see Paddy's Day,' he concluded.

Are these the best chicken wings in Dublin?

EVERYONE loves chicken wings! Hot, spicy, crispy, tangy ... there are just so many ways to enjoy them. With the abundance of delicious, tasty wings in Dublin, it can be a bit challenging to find the ones that are hands down *the* best, but we think we've found the place that makes the best wings you'll ever have in your life!

Okay, second paragraph, they never normally read down this far. We should be safe to talk. This government is a sickness and we – you, me, all of us – are the cure. The time has come to take them down and replace them with the only power that truly matters: the power of the people. Spread this article to all interested parties. Government spies only ever glance at the opening bit, then move on, but we do have to keep talking about chicken wings throughout or it'll show up on Google searches.

Our waiter brought us to our table, and we have to say that there was plenty of legroom and the seats were very comfortable. There were a lot of different varieties of wings on offer, but we had been told ahead of time to order the tangy Tabasco wings with the blue-cheese dip and – okay that should do it, back to the plan.

We need several columns of people to arm themselves with

whatever they can find and meet us at Stephen's Green on the morning of the fifth dawn. We will strike Leinster House with a furious anger at precisely morning teatime. Not all of you are going to make it through. We cannot promise that every mother will receive her son or daughter home safe and well that night, but we can promise that—

Our wings arrived promptly after we ordered them, and we got stuck in with gusto. Unlike some establishments, the wings were extremely meaty, and the light batter coating gave an enjoyable crispness to the soft tender chicken underneath. The sauce was an immediate rush to the senses, hitting us with notes of

All infrastructure must be taken down to create confusion and disruption. We need 150 volunteers to rush the national broadcasting HQ in Donnybrook and bring it to its knees. No longer shall RTÉ spout pro-government propaganda over airwaves that we, the Irish people, pay for! We will replace whatever inanity they have currently on air with our own message, recorded ahead of time and looped to provide a constant assurance to the people of this nation that real change is occurring, right at that very moment. This is a special time

to be alive, friends. We can say Ireland is

The sauce was not too light, and not too thick either. Some of you may like the sticky, honeyed sauces made popular in certain chicken wing emporiums, but we've always preferred a sauce that stays on the wing, not on your fingers (and certainly not on your blouse). The blue-cheese dip contained a strong cheese that complemented the hotness of the spicy

Railway networks and electricity providers will be shut down in the coming weeks, and fuel prices will skyrocket. Take this time to stock up on canned goods, bottled water, fuel for your portable generators and for your vehicles. Stockpile medicines and other such provisions while you can. Be smart. Share this information only with those you trust. Beware, this nation is full of spies

For afters, we had honeycomb ice-cream! Delicious!

Be prepared, comrades. Be prepared, and be brave. A new Ireland is ours for the taking!

Did you know?
79% of clean faces are no match for a plate of chicken wings.

Local gobshite to celebrate Thanksgiving

A complete and utter gobshite is to celebrate the American national holiday of Thanksgiving this year, despite having absolutely no connection to the United States or Canada.

Jamie Power, who has been living in Waterford city all of his life, announced to friends and family that he will be preparing a large feast of turkey and ham tomorrow evening, if anyone wanted to come over and join him.

'Guys! Anyone fancy coming over for Thanksgiving?' Power posted on his Facebook feed, before hilariously adding 'Feel free to bring your own bottle of wine, I won't charge corkage. Lol.'

Following several silent hours of zero notifications, the grandson of four took to his page once again, this time defending his celebration, in case anyone thought he was mad.

'I think it's only right we should celebrate Thanksgiving with our American cousins, especially in their time of need right now,' he posted again, refreshing his browser for the 674th time. 'I'm also doing this for the Indian tribe in Standing Rock in a show of solidarity? Anyone?'

Unaware of his desperate tone, the 39-year-old edited his post to include the promise of free beer, claiming he will be buying 'three slabs of cans' to accompany the meal.

Following 358 likes, 57 love hearts, 12 surprised faces and 678 Facebook comments from people confirming their invite, Jamie Power later had to call off the dinner due to 'unforeseen circumstances', just before gaining 76 angry emoticons and a 'fucking gobshite' message from work colleague Paul.

Attention-seeking Facebook friend posts vague hospital check-in

A County Galway woman reportedly checked into her local hospital via Facebook's check-in feature without even detailing why she's in there, *WWN* learned this evening.

Friends of Catherine Roche immediately responded to the post at 4:37 p.m. with a series of panicked comments, demanding answers about her sudden hospital visit and wondering why she would post something so serious while also being so vague.

'Private message me,' requested one frantic Facebook friend, adding two minutes later, 'I can't get tru to ur fone, pet. Worried.'

Taking two hours to respond, Ms Roche followed up her previous check-in with a photograph of her sitting in a wheelchair, again without any details to explain her presence at University Hospital Galway.

'OMG, just fuckin tell us why u r in the fuckin hospital you attention-seeking bitch,' another fed-up-with-her-bullshit friend wrote, before deleting it two minutes later.

Finally Catherine Jane Roche posted a picture of a bandaged finger with the words 'never cut onions with a blunt knife'. She thereby gracefully put the minds of what she believed to be hundreds of people to rest, happy in the knowledge that 14 of them cared enough to ask if she was okay, thus cementing her status as one of the bigger Facebook attention-seekers on their newsfeed.

Ms Roche was not available for comment on the incident this evening as she 'looks a right state', and would prefer to get her hair and makeup done first before speaking to the press.

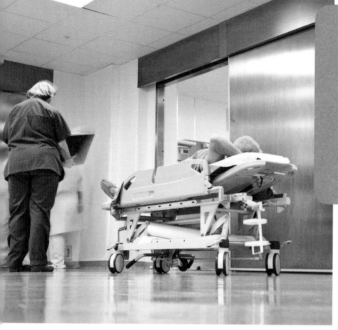

Hospital trolley hasn't had a day off in 10 years

A hospital trolley in Waterford is said to be on its last legs after working 10 straight years without a break, *WWN* can reveal.

The trolley, currently residing at the University Hospital in Ardkeen, was introduced fresh from the production line in 2007 and has been occupied by thousands of patients over the ensuing decade.

'I was only meant to be a temporary stand-in while people waited for a proper bed,' the trolley explained, squeaking slightly as the next elderly patient was hoisted onto it for God knows how long this time.

'My wheels are buckled, my side rails rattle and I'm nearly sure I got a waft of MRSA when they changed my bedsheets this morning.'

Fellow trolleys at the hospital have reported the same non-stop work routine, along with thousands more nationwide.

'We'd all go on strike only that lives would be put at risk if we weren't available,' added another trolley.

'All I ask is for one day off when I don't have to do anything at all; just one day to chill, nice and empty, in the hallway,' said the first trolley.

Figures from the Irish Nurses and Midwives Organisation (INMO) show that 612 patients were on trolleys waiting for admission into hospital on one day in January this year – a record high.

'I have it on good authority that the real figure is even higher than that,' said the trolley. 'It's a disgrace in a nation in economic recovery ... '

The trolley trailed off to shout at a passing doctor for help as the now dying patient on board began to convulse.

12 MONTHS A GUARD *Month 6*

I've kinda stopped going to the gym and running in the mornings. I thought I would have had to keep it up so that I'd be fit enough to be a guardian of the peace, but nobody seems to mind what shape you're in. If everyone else is stuffing themselves with breakfast rolls, then I don't know why I'm busting my hole running round a racetrack at six in the morning. 'It's not like youse have to be Israeli commandos, lads,' our PE instructor told us on day one. As long as we can pepper-spray someone, we'll be grand. We also got great news that the garda commissioner single-handedly smashed a major drugs ring in Dublin, without any help from another officer whatsoever. We had heard that this was going to take place, but that it would involve hundreds of garda personnel, months of investigations and solid, from the ground up, hard graft. But in the end, it seems that the commissioner and, like, four other high-profile cops went and seized €9 million worth of heroin and arrested 12 people all by themselves. They sure looked great on the news, all happy with themselves! Good for them!

Big coats, immersions, no stretch in the evenings: it's about to get Irish as fuck

STRAP in, folks. With the changing of the seasons, the dropping temperatures and the nights closing in, your daily conversations are about to get so fucking Irish it'll make you shit a Blarney stone.

Experts are predicting that the next four months might be the most Irish of all time, with record numbers taking the discussion about 'getting the big coat out' and 'accidentally leaving the immersion on' to more social media platforms and messaging apps than ever before.

Couple this with a Christmas where the tins of Roses are set to be the smallest they've ever been, and you've got what some people are calling a recipe for the 'perfect storm' of Irish insufferableness.

'You've got WhatsApp, you've got Snapchat, every day you've got a new dot I-E website running lists of the most Irish things ever ... it's going to be a nightmare,' said Dr Seán Hannilan, researcher at the Irish Society of Ireland.

'Those small-talk conversations you used to have in the pub with some lad you barely knew, the ones about how the nights are gone ... those are now the most important online currency available. The big coat, the big duvet, the big socks ... Irish people love the tropes of winter more than anything else in the world. Get ready to hear all about it.'

The impending flood of Irishness has prompted many people to flee the country in a bid to not hear the same shit over and over again for four months.

TRENDING

Keeping up with the Kardashians now a statistical impossibility, say scientists

HISTORIANS hoping to compile a complete and total history of the rise of the Kardashian family have been dealt a blow by new research confirming that keeping up with the labyrinthine actions of the media giants is now statistically impossible.

Experts decreed that keeping up with the Kardashians was only actually possible during the early years of the hit reality TV show *Keeping Up with the Kardashians*, which premiered on E! a decade ago, introducing the eclectic family to the world.

Since then, the myriad spin-offs, specials, interviews and social media carpet-bombing carried out by and for the Kardashian clan has rendered any attempt to plot the timeline of the family's rise to superstardom as something of a fool's errand. Even the world's most powerful supercomputers are struggling to keep up.

'It all kinda comes off the rails when Kendall and Kourtney, the younger Kardashians, come along,' said Dr Hamilton Keele, who devoted the last five years of his professional life to keeping up with the family before being driven mad.

'Then they all had a load of babies at the same time, more or less, Kim got married six times in four weeks or something ... then the dad and the mam split up, and she went and got her own show and ... even thinking about it now is giving me a migraine. Best of luck figuring this all out, it's like the civil war in Syria.'

Doubt now remains as to whether even the Kardashians can keep up with themselves.

95% of Irish binge-drinkers may not be getting enough soakage

⭐ TOP 5
Best-selling craft beers in Ireland 2017

5 Setanta's Love Juice - mythical pale ale made from 12,000-year-old rye and served in a glass shaped like a hurl, it can be drunk only on Wednesdays between 5 p.m. and 7 p.m.

4 The Dog's Bollocks - IPA 12%; fermented over time in a vat populated by male pugs whose testicles 'add to the rich flavour'.

3 Look At Me I'm Cool - IPA 7%; full-flavoured, made from yeast that was regularly played Bon Iver on vinyl while it was read passages from the *Guardian*; free tattoo and beard with each pint.

2 Ulysses Milk Stout - 5%; full-bodied and creamy, it can be consumed only after you read *Ulysses* in its entirety in one sitting.

1 Fuck Sake Can I Just Have A Pint Please - 4.5%; lager.

A damning new report has suggested that the vast majority of Irish binge-drinkers may not be getting the adequate amount of soakage into their stomachs before going out on the lash.

A staggering 95% of hard-drinking Irish men and women admit that they rarely eat slices of dry bread, whole bunches of bananas or plates of rice or spuds before they hit the town for the night. The result is extreme drunkenness after just 10 or 11 pints.

In even more startling news, many drinkers feel that soakage should be eaten at the end of the night, and that a kebab or a bag of chips on your way home will somehow undo the effects of seven straight hours of drinking.

'You need to fill up your belly with starchy foods before you fill it with alcohol; it's just science,' said Dr Philip Glass, chief researcher for the Irish Soakage Society.

'Your noodles or your microwave popcorn or whatever you choose to eat will lessen the effect of downing tequila like it's going out of fashion. Without soakage, Irish people get horrendously drunk every weekend and end up falling around the place, fighting, filling up the A&E departments and generally behaving like fucking idiots.'

Glass went on to state that while cutting back on binge-drinking would be better for the nation overall, increasing the amount of soakage people eat 'before they go on the tear' is by far the more realistic approach.

Hen party aims to really 'go the distance' when it comes to being obnoxious

A group of normally mild-mannered ladies are to really hit the 'loud and obnoxious' button pretty hard this weekend when they travel to Carrick-on-Shannon to celebrate the hen weekend of some girl they work with.

The 18 or so members of Laura Keeling's hen party are set to leave Dublin at 2 p.m. in a bid to arrive in the Leitrim town by five o'clock. This will give them time to get ready and have a nice dinner in the hotel restaurant before beginning to scream at nothing in particular from 10 p.m. onwards.

The ladies will be recognisable by their pink sashes and zogabong headbands with light-up penises. They will insist on yelling at every 'young fella' who walks by, despite the fact that they're already in committed long-term relationships back at home.

It seems that they haven't given any heed to what they're doing. 'It's just kind of expected of you on a hen weekend, isn't it?' said one woman we talked to, who admitted she was dreading the thoughts of the night out.

'I like a good night out, don't get me wrong, but you never see women acting like this until they're on a hen weekend. We have to grab at least one man's arse every 10 minutes, it's the law. And scream. Always scream, all the time. And pretend like everything is the funniest thing that has ever happened. It's exhausting.'

Carrick-on-Shannon natives are to remain on full lockdown until the hen party has passed, with many retreating to specially built 'hen-bunkers' for the weekend.

GP banging out inhalers like they're going out of fashion

A Waterford doctor has broken all previous records for the number of asthma inhalers prescribed, claiming that 99% of his patients are currently using the devices.

Speaking from his surgery in the city centre, Dr Terry Whelan popped open a bottle of Dom Perignon to celebrate, stating that his medical colleagues will 'be sick' when they hear the news.

'We basically have a bet on every year to see how many people we can flog inhalers to,' the 56-year-old medic explains. 'I have smashed last year's record and I'm absolutely thrilled to bits. There were only three people whom I couldn't convince they were asthmatic, but sure you can't win them all.'

Dr Whelan, who has been nicknamed 'Dr Wheezy' by his fellow professionals since he prescribed over 567 patients with both the blue and the brown inhalers, has also welcomed the profits the inhalers generate.

'Between Ireland charging four times the European norm for inhalers, and the eejits who pay me for a prescription to get them from the pharmacy every couple of months, business hasn't been better,' he confirmed.

'Any fucker with a wheeze now gets one, "Oh, you have a little cough, have you?" – bam! – inhaler. Half the time it's not even asthma, but sure what harm could they possibly do, am I right?'

A recent study by the Archives of Disease in Childhood claims that most doctors are over-diagnosing asthma and that the side-effects include growth suppression, dampening down of immune cell activity in the airways and the subsequent heightened risk of respiratory infections.

There is also a financial cost. Asthma inhalers can cost a patient up to €30 per month, while across the border in Newry the same medication costs £6.75 (currently about €7.94).

'Sure, best make hay while the sun shines,' Dr Whelan concluded.

Avoid doing stuff with your kids on Saturdays by buying them this simple games console

TIRED of bringing your son to football training on your one day off? Missing the rugby because your little girl has swimming lessons at the same time? Then you might be one simple video-games console away from hours of free time, each and every weekend!

Research has shown that children who have yet to be indoctrinated into the ways of the video game are more likely to want to do things outdoors with their friends. As a result, their parents are left with no option but to spend their entire Saturday driving to and from various training sessions, matches and activities.

The evidence of this can be seen in the huge numbers of parents standing in the freezing cold every Saturday watching their kids underperform at a sport that is being played at 10% of the speed it really should be.

However, help is at hand from companies such as Sony, Nintendo and Microsoft, all of which have video-game consoles on the market at the moment. These consoles are very attractive to kids, who regularly enjoy them without ever wanting to leave the sofa. Mums and dads are then free to stare at their phones all day or to argue for as long as they like.

'I used to have to take my kids to soccer training every single weekend and stand there watching them exercise all day.

Then I bought them an Xbox,' said one happy subscriber to the video game train of thought. 'Now, I can head to the pub about noon on Saturday, have a few pints with the lads and then arrive back home to find the kids are just where I left them, mowing down virtual people in a shower of blood and guts and violence. It's bliss! Plus, if you spring for some wireless headphones as well, you don't even have to listen to them!'

Video-game consoles are available NOW.

Eight-year-old takes bigger shits than his father

A County Waterford father has today admitted to being slightly jealous of his eight-year-old's stools, which are far bigger than his own, despite him being physically larger and ingesting a lot more food than his son, Adam.

Gerry Moran, who wastes hours every day trying to make his son eat his dinner, said he doesn't really know how he feels about the whole thing, as his stools aren't even half the size of his son's.

'It's not a subject you'd be bringing up with other parents,' Moran began, visibly upset. 'He barely eats anything at all, but then when he takes a dump, he

just leaves it there for the whole house to see, taunting us with its girth and general solidness. It's a man-shit if ever I saw one.'

Using calipers to secretly measure his son's latest gift to Waterford's sewage treatment centre, Mr Moran found that his son's 40 mm stool was almost twice the size of his own, and even of his wife Jessica's considerable output.

'I always thought it was Gerry showcasing his turds in the toilet,' Jessica explains. 'When he admitted it wasn't his, I was absolutely shocked and very disappointed in Gerry's previous lame attempts. I really need a little space now to decipher it all.'

Following a visit to their family GP, Gerry and Jessica Moran's son, Adam, was given the all clear on any potential ailments. The GP advised the concerned parents to eat healthier if they want to reclaim dominance of the family toilet bowl.

TRENDING Can an alt-right prick and a loopy-lefty feminist find love if we lock them in a room together? What if we throw away the key?

IT is the inherently adversarial relationship that defines much of our interactions online in 2017, and it is likely to set the agenda for many a year to come. The binary views held by alt-right pricks and loopy-lefty feminists mean that any conversation they have online, or in person, invariably descends into chaos. An exercise in shouting in ALL CAPS with no one being heard. This got *WWN Lifestyle* thinking.

If we could get just two people together and give them an opportunity to see past their own beliefs and world views and to recognise that there is a real person lurking behind warring hashtags, surely they could fall in love. It could be just the latest in a long line of *WWN Lifestyle's* precious gifts to the world.

But could an alt-right prick, who normally spends his time carefully crafting his language so as not to overtly reveal what a racist he is, begin to develop romantic feelings for a woman who tattooed I LOVE HILLARY on the Syrian refugee she adopted and is now training to become a terrorist, and vice versa? We were about to find out.

Enter Gavin Hickley – a Florida student and self-confessed poster of Pepe the Frog memes, and Vicky Lopez – an activist who probably wants to kill all white people for appropriating the taco.

WWN Lifestyle locked the pair in a room with instructions to engage with the real other person behind the sarcastic put-downs, in the hope that they might end up gazing lovingly into each other's eyes and so become a beacon of hope in these dark times. As they sat in the room, presumably trying to find that common ground, we got to thinking …

What if we throw away the key? Would that be doing the world an even bigger favour? Would the online comments sections become serene Utopian refuges in which people said things like 'I see your point, and acknowledge that is very much a problem. However, we can't solve that problem without first looking at the issue I mentioned previously, which I feel passionate about. Thank you for discussing this with me.'?

We ignored the banging on the door of the locked room and the shouts of 'Let us out please, we're being starved of oxygen' and thought long and hard about what to do. The prospect that future comments sections under news articles and opinion pieces would no longer descend into the vitriol Olympics proved to be a potent motivator and so we threw away the key.

Buoyed by our new-found vision for a brighter future, and not at all drunk on power, we began using all the resources available to us to replicate our search for alt-right pricks and loopy-lefty feminists. We locked each pairing in a room and threw away key after key. Unfortunately, comments sections continue to fall victim to people not seeing eye to eye. But then again, we've only just begun …

Couple trying for baby look to UVF

AFTER struggling for years to conceive a child naturally, one Waterford couple is to make the journey to Northern Ireland to see if the UVF can sort them out.

Jeanette and Phillip Montague have been together for 10 years and married for three, but have been unable to get pregnant despite their very best efforts.

Close family had advised the Montagues that they may need some extra help if they're going to have a family of their own. It seems that the couple have accepted this advice, and today they made contact with the Ulster Volunteer Force to see if they can help them out.

'I thought that contacting a paramilitary organisation was strange, to be honest, but the people up the road from us did it and went on to have triplets,' said 34-year-old Dungarvan native Phillip Montague.

'So we made contact with some low-ranking UVF lads today and have arranged to meet their leader in Belfast. When I say 'in Belfast', I should explain that we have to meet a lad a bit north of Newry and then he's going to take us there in the back of his van. We've to bring bags to put over our heads so that we don't know where we're going. It's unusual, but we're willing to try anything at this stage.'

Daredevil dad likes to put seatbelt on after he starts driving

A County Waterford man was branded 'a bit of a daredevil' this afternoon for deciding to put on his seatbelt *after* he started to drive his car because he loves the challenge of driving with one hand while reaching for the seatbelt with the other.

Mark Dunphy, who had three young children in the car with him at the time, said he has been doing the spectacular manoeuvre for years, so much so that it has become second nature to him at this stage of his driving career.

'I don't even think about it,' said the chuffed 33-year-old, now parked on a double yellow line outside Tesco with the hazard lights on, a button he likes to call a 'cloaking device'. 'There's a knack to it alright. Sometimes you have to use your knee to steer the car if you lose it a bit, but sure isn't that half the fun? You can't beat that moment of being in danger of the guards catching you.'

In Ireland, motorists who fail to wear a seatbelt while driving will incur a fixed charge fine of €60 if caught; if they are convicted in court for non-wearing of a seatbelt, five penalty points will be added to their licence and they will be liable for a €2,000 fine for a first offence – a law Dunphy likes to scoff at.

'My intention is to always wear a seatbelt while driving, but just not in the first 30 seconds. I've got a daredevil reputation to keep here,' he ended the interview, before leaving his three kids in the car while he entered the shop.

Wonderful World of Science

Can you be Irish AND sexy? UCD researchers are hoping to prove the impossible. Results expected in early 2018.

Dublin mother wondering what dinner child wants with her ketchup today

A south Dublin woman is undecided about what food to give her daughter with her ketchup today, after yesterday's broccoli and mash failure led to a 45-minute standoff at the kitchen table.

'Definitely nothing with green bits in it this time,' promised mother-of-three Dorothy Hayes, as she rummaged through a series of vegetables at the bottom of her fridge. 'Carrots are red. The fussy little bitch won't see the carrots with all the ketchup. Christ, these ones are withered. That cauliflower stinks too.'

For the past several months, four-year-old Lara has become 'ketchup-dependent', requesting at least four tablespoons of the sugar-rich table sauce with every meal.

'She has ketchup with everything nowadays,' Dorothy explains, 'with potatoes, with pasta, in her school sandwiches; just about any food she can get away with. She even asked for ketchup with ice cream last week when we were eating out at a restaurant. I think she has a problem.'

A recent survey found that over 67% of Irish children have ketchup-related addictions, with more and more under tens being admitted to ketchup-rehab programmes across the country every year.

'Four tablespoons of ketchup is the equivalent of 16 grams of sugar,' Dr Tony Shields of the Ketchup Addiction Centre in Leitrim explains, 'so that's the same sugar content as half a can of Coke.'

'We're inundated with ketchup addicts at the treatment centre at the moment. There is also a massive increase in "ketchup babies", where children are born with a ketchup addiction passed on from the mother.'

On top of its high sugar content, ketchup also contains high doses of salt and corn syrup. These ingredients are harmful to the body in high doses.

'We're basically killing our children,' Dr Shields added. 'But on the other hand, it does shut them up and make them eat their dinners, so turning them into junkies is a small sacrifice to make.'

Did you know?

88% of couples kissing in nightclubs after 1 a.m. are complete horror shows, study reveals.

How this man lost 3 stone in 10 minutes by just chopping off his own leg

DAMIEN Toomey has battled with a range of obesity-related health issues for most of his adult life. Then last year his GP last year told him that he had just months to live if he did not lose weight.

Toomey, who worked as a retail security guard, was shocked to hear the devastating news and decided to take immediate action following his diagnosis. He made a promise to his family that he was not going to die.

'I was only 58 years old when my doctor told me I was so fat I was going to die,' Toomey explains. 'My daughter was getting married a few weeks later and I was in an awful state. What if I died before the wedding? Who would lead her up the aisle?'

Taking matters into his own hands, the grandson of four decided enough was enough and began trying out a series of diets, including the Atkins diet, the 5:2 diet. He even went as far as to become vegan for a week.

'It was hell on earth,' he said. 'Imagine not eating meat for a whole day, never mind a week. I became very depressed. I was very close to giving up when I had a light bulb moment in Woodies hardware store.'

While shopping with his wife for 'nice coloured stones for his future allotment', he spotted a large saw for cutting tree branches on sale for €29.99.

'The irony of shopping for stones for my grave and then coming up with a possible solution to my weight problem is a moment I will never forget,' he added. 'I told my wife Peggy to drop the bag of stones and grab some industrial cable ties. At that moment I knew I was going to beat obesity.'

On 23 November 2016, Damien Toomey returned home from the hardware store and prepared himself.

'It's not as easy as it sounds,' he recalls now, rubbing his stump and remembering the pain. 'We had to tie those cable ties good and tight before hacking into my femur. The doctor said I needed to lose three stone, so I estimated halfway up the thigh would be enough, and I was spot on.'

In fact, Mr. Toomey sawed off almost three and a half stone of leg in weight, putting his BMI right back down to a stable, albeit overweight, 32.

'You should have seen the doctor's face when he saw me. He was absolutely delighted I had lost so much weight, and so quickly too,' he said. 'I don't even have to work anymore. I'm delighted with the results and I'm looking forward to my healthy new life.'

Since losing over three stone and most of his leg, Damien now enjoys spending his time with his married daughter and his first grandchild, Charlie.

'I just want to let people know there is always a solution. Don't ever give up!' he concluded.

'I actually want to be eaten' – local cow hits back at vegans

A County Waterford cow has today slammed vegans for protesting against meat consumption, stating that it would be an absolute honour for her to be slaughtered and then eaten by humans.

Jersey (4) said she has been fantasising about being killed and eaten her whole entire life, and admits that she is just counting down the days until her execution.

'There's just something about getting my throat slit or having a bolt penetrate my frontal lobes that really tingles my udders,' the bovine explained. 'It's the ultimate climax of an uneventful life of eating, shitting and mooing. If vegans had any idea how fucking boring it is just grazing in a field, listening to the sound of your own turds splattering your hind legs, they'd understand what it means to become a prime cut of steak. I'd eat myself if I could!'

Jersey's comments come after a series of vegan demonstrations across the world this week, including in Dublin, where an animal rights activist lay naked on a supersized plate of vegetables, with the phrase 'know who you're eating' written on it.

'Not one vegan has ever asked me if I want to be eaten or not,' mooed Jersey. 'How did they get the impression that animals need someone to talk for us? Cows love being killed and eaten. It's sexy. There, I've said it. Actually, I wish I was being carved up right now by a serrated edge.'

Unfortunately, Jersey will have to wait another year before being slaughtered in the nearby meat factory.

★ TOP 5
Most popular cow names in Ireland 2017

A diverse array of choice make for interesting reading this year:

5   Yolanda
4   Gary
3   Moo Moo
2   Boutros Boutros-Ghali
1   Mary

Roddy Doyle's auld lads treated for alcoholism

TWO elderly Dublin gentlemen who were made famous by author Roddy Doyle have been admitted to a rehabilitation clinic in a bid to help them tackle their rampant alcoholism.

While the anonymous septuagenarians inspired Doyle to pen numerous sketches on his Facebook page over the past few years, the duo were secretly fighting the demon drink. At one point, it is estimated that they were drinking up to 500 pints of Guinness each per week, particularly during especially newsworthy months.

Although fighting their debilitating alcohol addictions, the auld lads managed to voice their opinions on the death of David Bowie, the death of Gene Wilder, the death of Lemmy, the death of Muhammed Ali, the death of Muamar Gadaffi, the death of the punt, the death of Superman, the death of a salesman and the death of a once-novel idea.

'Conversation has certainly dried up between the auld lads since we surgically removed the pints from them' said Dr Georgina Clarke, addiction specialist.

'Roddy came around to listen in on them, to see if he could get something for his Facebook page. He gave them a number of topics, like recently dead celebrities, atrocities around the world, sporting victories ... but they just weren't chatty without a good feed of drink inside themselves.'

With his muses on the dry, it is unclear where Doyle goes from here.

Young fellas made of nothing these days, finds scientific study

DOCTORS studying the make-up of young fellas have found that they are made of nothing these days, in contrast to the men of old.

The scientific study, carried out by a team of genetic experts at Trinity College Dublin, found that the majority of Irish males aged between 16 and 30 have grown a lot weaker physically and less resilient to cold temperatures over the past 60 years. Of 100 Irish males tested in physical work environments, 67% moaned about being tired and fatigued after just two minutes.

'We put the study group to work on a local farm picking spuds, weeding gardens and doing general old time shit,' lead researcher Professor Conor Tracey explained. 'We even made them travel to work in their bare feet. The results we got back were absolutely appalling to tell you the truth. Only a small minority of the men got on with their chores without complaining.'

In fact, further testing found that 89% of those studied were 'perishers', a trait increasing in modern day males.

'Nearly every one of them began whinging about the cold during the picking stones in the frost task,' Dr Tracey added. 'They began complaining that their ikkle fingies were sore, and that they couldn't feel their hands or feet from the cold. Poor pets. Several lads even tried to pretend they were sick in a bid to get out of the job, and one 18-year-old subject began crying for his mammy like a big baby, so he did.'

The study concluded that 92% of Irish men were found to be made of nothing these days, compared to the young fellas of years ago who used to walk to school in their bare feet, before then going to work in the mines for 18 hours a day.

12 MONTHS A GUARD *Month 7*

We've now received the second half of our training for using the PULSE system to record and report all our activities during the day. Last week we were taken through phase one and shown how the system works and how we should use it. This week our training was 'How the system works' and 'How we should use it'. The two sets of lectures were essentially the same, but this week the lecturer stopped after every sentence to wink at us. 'So you log the penalty points in this column,' he said, 'if you know what I mean lads (*wink, wink*).' I'm a bit confused, but we were told to just follow the lead of whatever senior garda is on the job with us. Sounds easy enough. This week we also got an intensive module on whistle-blowing, and how to deal with it. Someone from senior branch came down to tell us that one of our fellow recruits had been telling reporters about what goes on in Templemore, and then gave us the basics on how to make sure it doesn't happen again. We learned how to falsify accusations against him, plant evidence, really smear his name into the ground. It got so bad, he was forced to quit training and go home; his mam came to pick him up and he was bawling. I don't much fancy that so I'll be keeping my mouth firmly shut throughout my career!

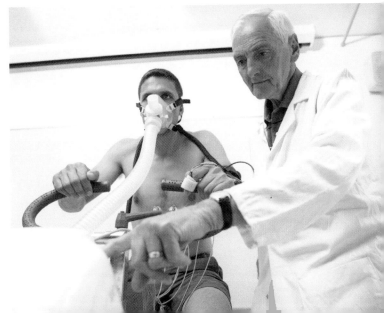

Is your infant eating enough crap off the floor?

A new report into the dietary habits of infants has revealed troubling statistics for parents, who may have to face up to the fact that their babies aren't eating enough morsels of dirt and garbage off the floor.

While parents tend to change their habits when it comes to sugary and fatty foods linked with childhood obesity, the new study suggests that they are still not meeting their toddlers' demands for bits of fluff, hardened bread that rolled under the sofa, shreds of paper and bits of twigs that come in on the soles of shoes.

In a sample group covering both breast- and formula-fed babies, researchers found that almost 100% of infants go to bed each night without having achieved their desired amount of crud, something which the spokesperson for the study blames squarely on parents.

'We're hearing second-hand reports of parents actually taking crap out of their toddler's mouths,' said Dr Ian Jennells, an expert on infant diet and nutrition.

'Babies are starving for crap off the ground. You put a baby on the floor, they're going to seek out the nearest hank of dirt they can find and eat it straight away. And parents are refusing to allow them to do this; they're setting them back into the highchair and shovelling fruit and vegetables into them instead.'

'Parents need to listen to their kids, and work out what they're asking for. If your kid could talk, he wouldn't ask you for an organic sweet potato and apple puree pot. He'd tell you what he really wants: he wants to gnaw on the rubber thing on the floor that stops the door from hitting the wall.'

Did you know?

Despite rumours, Hozier's father is in fact a common-or-garden hose.

Irish lads go on epic Martin Luther King Day session

COYBIG! A group of Irish lads are in the middle of an epic drinking session to commemorate the life of revered American civil rights activist Martin Luther King Jr.

Martin Luther King Day, which takes place on the third Monday of January each year, is currently being 'lit up in style' by Sean Hanlon, Mark Jennings, Cian Hanlon and Francis 'Mad-Head' McLoughlain, who began drinking at 12 p.m. this afternoon and have no intentions of stopping anytime soon.

'Jaysus, you couldn't let Martin Luther King Day go by without a few scoops,' says 23-year-old Hanlon, getting a round of Jagerbombs in.

'Although to be honest, I only found out it was MLK Day yesterday, when I was looking through Google to find an excuse to go on the lash. What was he, a singer or something?

'Hopefully, the MLK Day session will become part of our yearly drinking calendar. It's just what we needed really, to fill that long stretch between Christmas and Valentine's Day. I must say, it's turning out pretty well to begin with. We haven't had a drinking session like this since International Women's Day last year.'

The quartet of hard-drinking young lads will cap off the day 'the MLK way', by being tackled to the ground by a group of gardaí and having the living shit kicked out of them.

THE Facebook friends of a local moron are being warned today not to open any messages from the 47-year-old, following a hacking incident late last night.

Martin Grace, who only realised his account was compromised after it was too late, said hundreds of spam messages were sent from his messenger to all the contacts on his Facebook list.

'I think it was probably when I clicked on that unusual-looking message from an old school friend that I haven't spoken to in years,' the absolute tool recalls, now clicking on it again just to be sure. 'The link is very suspicious-looking, so

'If you get a Facebook message from me, don't open it,' insists local moron

I clicked straight into it without bothering to check,' adding, 'sure it's Facebook, like, what could go wrong?'

Following his mistake, all 479 of Mr Grace's Facebook friends were immediately sent the same link, which 87 have so far clicked, accelerating the spread of the virus even more, despite his best efforts to thwart it.

'I posted a status telling everyone to ignore the message, but I think that just made them click it more, out of interest,' he concluded.

'I thought it was one of those blackmail things and he was caught with his dick in his hand or something, so I clicked,' one friend confirmed, slightly disappointed at the outcome.

Facebook has since urged its users to 'exercise some fucking tact' when receiving strange, unsolicited messages from people you would not normally engage with.

HEALTH

Local dad always crying lately

A County Waterford family has made a renewed appeal today for father and husband Dermot Walsh, claiming the 46-year-old has spontaneously been leaking water from his eyes on numerous occasions over the past few months.

Daughter Theresa Walsh said the phenomenon began shortly after losing his job in May, when she found him hegging like a child in the family home.

'I'm not sure it's connected, but Daddy spends half the day in bed, just lying there, staring at the wall,' she recalls. 'Sometimes he could be just watching television and streams of water just flow down his face, like he's leaking something. God, I hope it's nothing serious like a brain leak. We're very worried about him, and the doctors don't seem to be able to do much.'

Mr Walsh was forced to visit his GP in September, but when he returned home, he insisted that the doctor said nothing was wrong with him and to exercise more.

'It's strange, because his condition hasn't cleared up in the slightest. In fact, he has gotten even quieter since the long evenings kicked in,' wife Ann Walsh explains. 'He's after putting on weight too and doesn't seem to have the energy he used to have. He doesn't even go out to the shed or garden anymore to do whatever it is he used to love doing out there.

Whatever this ailment is, it seems to be affecting his mood.'

'I miss his beautiful smile', she added, now also leaking tears. 'Oh no, I think it's contagious!'

Dermot was not available to speak fully on his situation as he was 'very busy right now doing something', and asked to be just left alone for the foreseeable future, and not to worry about him, as he's 'grand'.

'My parents' separation is the perfect excuse to act the little prick'

FOLLOWING his parents' announcement that they are going to separate, son of two David O'Brien vowed to be that little bit more disruptive and difficult on the back of their decision, claiming it's what all the kids from broken homes do on TV these days.

Sitting on a wall outside his local shop with some of his peers, O'Brien vowed to cause as much trouble as humanly possible over

the next few years, even kicking over the external shop bin 'just for the craic'.

'I'm gonna fucking wreck the place,' he told the group of smoking teens, before spitting on the ground in front of a customer who was entering the shop. 'No more curfew, no more homework bollox, the whole world can go fuck itself and everyone in it, bunch of arseholes.'

Mirroring his parents' anger and frustration, the 14 year old then began shouting incoherently at an elderly gentleman who was passing the group, just to see how far he could take things.

'Bahahahaha, fuckin' stupid auld lad nearly croked it with the fright,' O'Brien said laughing, realising he terrified the vulnerable man, before requesting the 'butt' of a friend's cigarette,'ya duck arsed, dopey cunt,' and wiping saliva from the filter, while pondering, 'I think it's time to start smoking something stronger. A nice drug habit would go down a treat right now.'

BEING constantly stressed, tired and run-down can cause you problems. But why do you feel wrecked all the time? Well, according to groundbreaking new research, you could be a moany cunt.

Luckily, you're not alone. Chronic tiredness is one of the most common reasons people go to their GP, although many moany cunts go undiagnosed for most of their adult lives.

'It wasn't until I told the doctor my symptoms that he finally sent me for tests,' moany cunt Doris Regan explains. 'They tested me for everything, including anaemia, gluten intolerance and even TB, but once they found out that I was actually a moany cunt, my life turned around for the better and I could embrace the condition, instead of worrying about it. Since then, I've been able to moan freely, all I want, without ever having to explain myself to anyone.'

'Of course, feeling exhausted or run-down could be due to

Are you always feeling stressed, tired and run-down? You could be a moany cunt

the breakneck pace of our 24/7 lifestyle, but,' adds Professor Terry Tobin, a Dublin-based GP, 'doctors must not exclude the simple possibility of the patient being a moany cunt.'

He explains, 'A lot of moany cunts believe that being tired is due to an underlying medical problem, but this is rarely the case. People love to fucking moan about every little thing

wrong with them, and this goes mostly undiagnosed as doctors are not truthful enough with their patients.'

Experts believe that one in every five people in Ireland has some form of moany cuntism and they should talk to their GP if they want to find out more about the condition.

Wonderful World of Science

After years of conspiracy theories, the Irish government finally conceded that County Kerry is a scientific experiment that went horribly wrong.

Did you know?

Gay Byrne's pet llama is called Pat Kenny.

Group of night joggers loses control, 16 pedestrians dead

SIXTEEN pedestrians were killed and another 24 injured this evening in south Dublin after a large group of joggers lost control on the coast road between Blackrock and Monkstown.

Emergency services arrived on the scene at 6 p.m. to find one of the worst running accidents Ireland has ever seen.

'Many members of the emergency response team are being treated for shock, such was the carnage they witnessed,' Garda Tadgh Holden told *WWN*. 'Not only that, but the group of joggers destroyed several buildings in the crash and two dogs were killed.'

It is believed the joggers were trying to avoid a street bin, swerving to do so before then losing control of the back end of the group.

'We understand the back end of the group first collided with oncoming pedestrians, knocking them down like skittles, before crashing into a number of houses situated on the side of the busy road,' added Holden. 'Several joggers had to be cut out of the buildings by the fire brigade.'

The latest incident has yet again raised questions about dangerously large groups running together on Ireland's footpaths and roads, where already 78 people have been killed in jogger crashes so far this year.

'They have no brakes, no lights and zero respect for the people walking on the footpaths,' voiced local man Derek O'Casey. 'I've been warning people for years about this. Now look what's happened. Hopefully something will be done about it now.'

Taoiseach Enda Kenny later offered his condolences to the victims of today's crash, and promised to introduce a ban on jogging on public walkways and roads. He then proposed a nationwide footpath tax from 2017 for anyone wishing to use them, and discussed the possibility of walking licences being introduced next year.

TOP 5
Headstones in Ireland 2017

5 'Prick still owes me €20'
4 'Beloved cat owner'
3 'Fine hurler in his day'
2 'This is why you shouldn't do drugs'
1 'Wife, mother, daughter, avid believer in UFOs'

EXCLUSIVE

Local man's diet does not count between 1 a.m. and 4 a.m.

ONE Waterford man has admitted his current attempt to lose weight and get in shape has been hampered by his stipulation that he can still eat whatever he wants between the hours of 1 a.m. and 4 a.m. on Thursdays, Fridays, Saturdays, Sundays and bank holiday Mondays.

Kenneth Hanlon (35) has been trying to get in better shape in a bid to not die in his 60s for the past five months, and has seen only marginal success in that time.

Despite keeping a fairly close eye on his calorie intake and exercising as

much as he can, Ballinamona native Hanlon admits that eating a kebab and chips after a feed of pints three nights a week may be hampering his goals.

In addition, other rules such as 'if you didn't buy it, it has no calories' and 'if you deserve it, it doesn't count' may be clues as to why the father of two has lost just three pounds in 20 weeks.

'If you're at an event and there's finger food, then all that is calorie free ... right?' said Hanlon, weeping on the scales.

'And if you had to stand waiting in a chip shop for 20 minutes, then your chips don't count ... one cancels the other out, surely? If I eat salad for four days, then surely I can eat burgers for three? This is very confusing to me.'

Hanlon was also heartbroken to learn that cheese is not a fruit and does not count towards your five-a-day, and that a big tub of coleslaw is not technically a salad.

Is this automatic soap dispenser enough of a talking point to save your marriage?

A new wall-mounted kitchen gadget that sits above your worktop and automatically dispenses just the right amount of soap when you wave your hand underneath it could be just the thing you and your spouse need to buy your failing marriage another six months or so, according to relationship experts.

Available from most homeware stores, the useful gadget can help maintain good hygiene while preparing food and cleaning up around the home, as well as giving estranged

husbands and wives something to talk about in a bid to cut through the eerie silence that has grown like a weed in the once-fertile garden that was their love.

Choked by the noose of nitpicking at everything the other does, married couples can enjoy renewed nuggets of daily conversation about the dispenser – 'How is the dispenser working out?', 'That dispenser is handy, isn't it?', 'What did we ever do before that dispenser, eh?' These phrases will shave minutes off the amount of time they spend

staring at each other until one decides it's time to go to bed, leaving the other watching nothing in particular on telly.

'An automatic soap dispenser also requires maintenance, creating a new way for the couples to depend on each other,' said Zsasa Hanlon, relationship expert.

'She can choose the right soap to put in it, he can make changing the batteries his "job" ... this way, they can have something that they convince themselves is a joint undertaking that can only continue as long as their marriage does. If they buy one now, who knows, they might actually get one more Christmas out of their loveless union.'

Hanlon admitted that at some stage the failure to look after the dispenser may become just another nail in the coffin of the marriage, but at that point the couple could get a slowcooker or a dog or have a baby or something.

Upcoming rickshaw strike to affect dozens of drunks

Stunning local girl makes everyone else in selfie look like a fucking mutant

THE close friends of a particularly attractive young Waterford woman have today announced that they will no longer pose for selfies with her, as her good looks invariably leave them looking 'like a bag of kicked arseholes'.

Jemma Harkin (19) cuts an impressive figure in practically every selfie she appears in, whether on her own Instagram feed or in pictures for other people.

This has been cause for concern for her group of friends who, although not unattractive in their own right, look closer to rejects from the Addams Family when posing beside Harkin.

The phenomenon has led to numerous angry outbursts from the group of girls, who have all grown to dread the notification 'Jemma Harkin has tagged you in a photo'.

'I'm pretty sick of my boyfriend asking me "who's the girl on the left?" when he sees me in a picture with Jemma,' said one of Harkin's closest friends, who does not wish to be named.

'It's ridiculous. She's so pretty, she makes the rest of us look like melted toys. So we've had to come up with excuses as to why we can't be in selfies with her. I've been telling her that I have a detached retina and I'm not allowed any bright flashes in my eye.'

If you have been affected by a friend who's leagues ahead of you in terms of beauty or handsomeness, please seek advice.

A proposed two-day strike by drivers of urban rickshaws across the country is set to cause travel chaos for dozens of inebriated revellers, who will now have to look for an alternative way to get from one pub to another while yelling at pedestrians to 'get the fuck out of the way, we're in a bike thing'.

Pedal-operated rickshaws have become one of the main modes of transport for people on nights out in major towns and cities, usually among people who are initially unaware that they have to pay to use them.

However, recent disputes about pay and conditions has forced rickshaw operators, the majority of whom are swarthy Brazilian men, to initiate industrial action in a bid to see their wages and cycling-on-the-footpath privileges increased.

The first of these planned stoppages will take place on Friday and Saturday of this week, causing considerable disruption to the session plans of at least 14 or 15 people.

'I was going to get shit-faced, be kicked out of the pub I was in, then get a rickshaw from the bottom of Grafton Street to the top of Grafton Street while yelling on my mobile phone to the lads telling them I was on my way,' said one dose we talked to.

'What am I going to do now? Walk? Who will I get into a row with over the cost of a rickshaw journey then? Where will I take a selfie to post on Snapchat with the caption "in one of them fuckin' bike things"? This is unacceptable.'

The strike is also expected to adversely affect a number of hen parties from Newcastle and one lad who's trying to impress a girl on their first night out.

How to cope when someone introduces their new baby with a stupid fucking name

VISITING the parents of a newborn baby is tough at the best of times as once you've seen one, you've seen them all. Just use the standard 'isn't he/she so cute' spiel that you've always used and you should be fine.

One thing to be aware of, however, is how to conduct yourself when you ask for the child's name and the new parents tell you something utterly ridiculous like 'Rihanna' or 'Leonardo'. Following your instinct to say 'You called it whaaat?' will basically write you out of their lives forever.

To stay friends with everyone, here's a few tips to deal with this increasingly common situation.

Prepare for the worst

Never assume that people will call their kid something normal. Those parents are in the minority. Have yourself braced for them to say something ridiculous like 'Spongebob' or 'Heatshield', so that when they actually say 'Etian' or whatever, it's a pleasant surprise. Relief will show on your face, which can easily be passed off as delight.

Bawl

If you can't hold it in, then don't hold it in. Just roar your face off crying at the tragedy that is a baby called 'Macauley' or whatever. Then pass it off as sorrow because you knew a Macauley who died years ago and it all just came flooding back.

Ask if it's a family name

You don't have to ask anything about the child's name, you can just say 'aw that's nice' and hand the kid back and then go home and never see these people again, but it's nice to show some interest, even if you are horrified. So, 'Hermione is it? Which side of the family does that come from? ... Oh you got it from a book? Isn't that original.' should work.

TRENDING Local woman can't believe she spent hours slaving over profile picture for just 17 likes

FRUSTRATED Dublin woman Rebecca Hilty has gone on record to register her dismay after a carefully crafted Facebook profile picture returned a disappointing number of likes.

Hilty, a huge fan of pictures of herself, had spent upwards of 12 hours trying to stage the perfect 'just got home from the gym' selfie, only for the picture to garner just 17 likes.

'And, like, I looked so cute,' she explained, her voice deflated by the lack of appreciation people had for the effort she had expelled to make her room look just the right amount of messy, while ensuring her makeup was able to pull off the I'm-not-wearing-any-makeup-honestly-I-just-look-this-good-all-the-time look.

While Hilty no longer relies solely on Facebook profile pictures to fuel her narcissism, she also bemoaned the lack of engagement with the photo on Snapchat, WhatsApp and Instagram.

'I just think it's unfair really,' Hilty continued. 'Like I popped some sexy lingerie on the floor in the background, made sure a protein shake I don't drink was in the shot too, and some intellectual-looking books as well. And anyone who bothered to look closely would have seen my bum in leggings in the mirror. I don't say this lightly, but it was some of my best work.'

Hilty found the 17 likes all the more disappointing because none of her friends, who she could usually rely on for at least 60 likes, had come out to like and support her picture-taking efforts.

'I mean, it's been five minutes and Jess still hasn't liked it. I might have to text her and tell her to like it,' explained the 23-year-old who is definitely not addicted to the endorphin rush of social media posts.

FACEBOOK LATEST

WITH almost every teenager in the country owning their very own smartphone with numerous social media apps at their disposal, there's never been a greater risk of them accessing debasing, depraved pornography, something that parents should be acutely aware of if they're bored of the same old smut and need to find something racier.

A new study shows that a daily check by parents of their children's Internet usage will allow bored parents to access unbelievable filth, the likes of which they've never even dreamed of, let alone witnessed.

Noting that the vast majority of middle-aged people in Ireland grew up in an age when even *Playboy* magazine was banned, the study states that pretty much everyone over the age of 30 is

Parents urged to monitor kids' Internet usage if they want to know where all the good porn is

ready to stop watching regular, humdrum five-on-one porn and start watching something that will really scar them for life.

Given the computer-illiterate nature of many parents, porn-hungry mamas and dadas have been urged to keep a close eye on what their kids are doing online, wait until they go to

bed, get their smartphones and hit 'refresh' to get a dose of the really good stuff.

'Having a conversation with your child about Internet pornography can be embarrassing,' said Dr Jill Henney, spokesperson for the research group who conducted the study.

'Especially when you want to ask them where's the best website to find leaked sex tapes and zoo gang bangs and the likes. So instead of having a frank discussion with your kid, just peek over their shoulder while they're on the phone and get as many search topics as you can before they see you.'

The release of the study coincides with releases by fathers across the nation.

REVEALED:

The gruelling training required to be an Elite Single

IT'S 6 a.m. on a freezing February morning, and *WWN* are doing star-jumps in the lashing rain on a Tramore beach as a drill instructor screams obscenities at us.

Five minutes later, we're doing drills that involve running around a mock-restaurant, pulling out chairs for imaginary dates and

ordering anything except chicken wings off the menu. We glance at our watch; we have another seven hours of this training to go through today, and it's just day one of a week-long course.

This is how you become an Elite Single.

'Pick it up, you un-dateable fucks, you fucking cat people, move your asses!' yells our drill instructor, urging us to either practise picking out our best underwear or just quit and go the fuck home.

'Any of you ugly fucks think you're good enough to be in my Elite Singles unit? There's not one of you sons of bitches that are worth a right swipe on Tinder, let alone the most

exclusive dating program on God's green earth.

'So let's move, you Plenty-Of-Fish reject-looking motherfuckers. Get on them iPhones! Practise your emoji-based flirting! Learn how to compliment someone! Come on, you pukes, you want to be found dead in your apartment alone by a neighbour complaining about the smell, with half your fingers eaten off by your nine cats? Fucking move!'

Though at many times throughout the course we felt like we were going to quit, we stuck it out and proudly graduated as Elite Singles, ready to join the legions of other Elite Singles who signed up after seeing the ad playing during *This Morning*. SEMPER FI!

Your kids say they're off to an S&M club, but where are they really going?

IT'S every parent's worst nightmare ... as far as you're concerned, your teenage son is safely tied to a wall in a hardcore fetish dungeon in town, getting kicked in the balls by a Latvian transvestite, and your daughter is doing ketamine with four men she met on the Internet. But are they really? Or are these just the things that teenagers tell their parents to pacify them, while they sneak off to do something else entirely? *WWN* investigates.

'From the day they were born, we more or less let our precious little boys do whatever they want,' James Hennegan, a Waterford father of 16-year-old twins told us.

'We found them watching hardcore pornography on their computer when they were nine, and we just left them to it. We didn't want to hamper their creative minds. They started doing coke at 11 and you can't really say anything, if all the other kids are doing it. You don't want your child to be the one child who doesn't snort class-A drugs from a prostitute's labia. But lately, our boys have been telling us that they're going to a local brothel on Friday nights, but they haven't had to go to the clinic in months. I wish they would just tell us the truth.'

More and more parents are finding that a lifetime of letting their kids do whatever they want has not given them the results they had hoped for, with many of the new generation turning to ever-more extreme forms of sexual experimentation and rampant drug use instead of being normal, well-adjusted members of society.

'Like any parent, I just wanted to be my daughter's friend first, mother second,' said Connie Molloy, whose 17-year-old daughter said she was going to a rave in the woods but may not have actually gone.

'I never criticised her or punished her when she was naughty and had the charges quashed when she blinded that nightclub toilet attendant with a broken bottle last year. I thought she'd just always be able to talk to me about what she was doing in life, like we were best pals. Instead, fuck knows where she goes at night.'

12 MONTHS A GUARD *Month 8*

A load of old guards retired this month and their uniforms and equipment were passed on down through the ranks for the rest of us to use. So I've finally got a high-vis jacket and hat to call my very own! Neither of them fit me at the minute but at the rate I'm putting on weight it'll only be a matter of time until they're feeling good and snug. It's a little annoying that there's no money for us to have brand-new equipment of our own, but if it means that the higher-ups on the force get to have such sweet expense accounts and pensions then, dammit, it's a sacrifice I'm willing to make. Those guys work so hard, dealing with scandal after scandal. It can't be easy!

WWN guide to getting the ride while living at home with your parents

WITH more and more Irish people forced to remain living at home with their parents thanks to crippling rental prices and the lack of affordable homes on the market, *WWN* tackles the main problem facing those without a place to call their own: namely, where do you get the ride?

With your partner of choice statistically likely to be in the same stuck-at-home boat as you are, things can be very awkward if you want to have a good auld roll in the sack without sending your parents into an early grave.

If you're one of the 'boomerang generation' living at home with your folks, consider the following.

Time your riding to coincide with religious holidays

Nothing gets your parents out of the house quicker than a novena. Although their staunch Catholicism is the exact reason you can't bang the goodness out of your boyfriend or girlfriend in the first place, you can use it to your advantage: Sunday mass, funerals, Feast days, even the blessings of the graves ... when your parents get prayin', you get layin'.

Go up into the attic

Rather than a roll in the hay, how about a roll in the fibreglass insulation? Bring your sexual partner up the Staighre for some hot, sweaty, itchy fun. If your parents complain that they heard some rustling around in the attic, blame it on mice. Also, watch out for mice.

Just start humping on the kitchen table

Look, just go for it. Strip bare naked with your partner and just start riding like mad in the middle of Sunday dinner. If your folks complain, just yell about how it's all their fault for voting in a succession of governments that allowed the country to fall apart to such a degree that your only options are to live at home like a child or fuck off to Australia for the rest of your life. I can do this riding here or I can do it in Perth, mammy. Your choice.

TRENDING

Quirky bollocks has a vintage car

A County Carlow man has today confirmed his quirky personality by purchasing a vintage car, *WWN* can reveal.

Mark Tobin, who also wears woolly hats and leather bracelets, made the decision after seeing a similar-looking man in Dublin driving a 27-year-old Morris Minor.

'I cycled to work on a high nelly for years, so when I seen a fellow quirky guy driving a vintage car I knew it was the option for me,' Tobin explained. 'Being different is hard these days, so I'm constantly looking for the next big thing to do, item to buy or place to travel to so I can appear "out there" and slightly kooky. Hopefully I can now find a girl of equal quirkiness to accompany me on my journeys.'

Tobin admits he's not exactly sure what kind of car he is driving, but insists he's just happy now to be one of those guys.

'It's a Ford something,' he confirmed, pointing to a Ford badge on the front bumper, 'and it has that old number plate on it that doesn't tell you what year it is, so it's obviously really old and rare. Sure, there's no power steering, real safety features, heating, working wipers or spare wheel, but it's really hip-looking, and that's just me: hip.'

The 32-year-old expects to insure the car in 2019, when he has saved the €4,576.78 needed to get insurance for it.

Save thousands on your wedding costs by accepting that nobody gives a fuck

ENGAGED couples are constantly looking for ways to make sure their special day is just that: special. But every little extra adds to the overall cost of the day, every finishing touch, everything that 'just says you'. So how can you save hundreds, or even thousands from your wedding budget, if you want the day to be extra special?

Simple: just accept that nobody except you gives one single lonesome fuck about any of it.

Common matrimonial money-traps including 'wedding favours', personalised menus or an extra bridesmaid can all be eradicated if both the bride- and groom-to-be sit down and take a long, hard look at themselves and 'cop the fuck on', according to wedding specialist and long-time single person Marion Shields.

'I get hundreds of young couples through the door every year, worrying about how they'll be able to afford to have a pen made with their names on it for every guest at their wedding,' said Shields, speaking candidly to *WWN*.

'Cold hard fact of the matter is that nobody gives a fuck. People don't go to weddings to check that the groomsmen are all wearing matching socks, people don't go to a wedding to make sure that the flowers on the pew-ends in the church match the flowers that the groom gave the bride when he picked her up for their debs 10 years ago. Nobody gives a fuck. Couples can halve the price of their wedding if they just focus on what guests really want: a good feed and a drinking session'.

Shields went on to admit that hiring a wedding advisor is another needless expenditure, adding that people who were 'too dense' to plan a wedding on their own shouldn't be allowed to get married in the first place.

How to tell the difference between dirty talk and someone trying to pull off identity theft

SEX can be a wonderfully intimate moment in the lives of the participants, an ecstatic break from the drudge of everyday life ... or it can be yet another time when a stranger catches you off-guard for long enough to mine information that will let them assume your identity and clean out your bank account.

But how do you tell whether your new sexual partner is someone who enjoys talking dirty in the heat of the moment or someone trying to rob you blind?

WWN Lifestyle has compiled the following list of things that someone might say to you during sex, along with a guide as to which ones are probably not being used to secure your vital personal and private information and which ones are a cause for concern. Study closely!

- 'Who's your daddy?' – probably okay.
- 'What's my name? Say my name' – probably okay.

- 'Damn, girl' – probably okay.
- 'What was your mother's maiden name?' – cause for concern.
- 'What was your first pet?' – cause for concern.
- 'Right there, yeah, right there' – probably okay.
- 'Do you have different passwords for different email accounts?' – cause for concern.
- 'Don't stop' – probably okay.
- 'Give it to me, come on, give it to me' – probably okay.
- 'What are your six least favourite numbers?' – cause for concern.
- 'Bite me ... harder!' – probably okay.

- 'When are you going on holidays, and will your house be empty when you're gone?' – cause for concern.

Remember, safe sex isn't just about wearing a rubber johnny. Always protect yourself from identity theft.

Wonderful World of Science

Research conducted at Trinity College Dublin earlier this year suggests actions are only three decibels louder than words.

Old men ask young people 'to stay the fuck out of old man pubs'

A spokesperson for the Irish League of Old Men has made an impassioned plea for drinkers under the age of 60 to 'stay the fuck out of old man pubs'.

The statement comes following an alarming trend of young, hip people seeking out 'old man pubs' to drink in, eschewing the thousands of bars which cater directly to people of their own age group.

'Yah, I like to head for quiet pints in O'Laraghan's up the road from me, it's a real old man pub, it's great,' said Miles Cahon-Reilly, a 26-year-old arts graduate currently living in Portobello.

'A lot of bars are too loud and too packed, so I like to go and drink cocktails in O'Laraghan's. It's just got this great atmosphere, me and my mates just love it.'

With testimonials like this on the rise, old men have struck back at youngsters like Cahon-Reilly, making the assertion that the only reason an 'old man pub' has such a great atmosphere is because there are no hipsters sipping whiskey sours out of jampots, complaining about the lack of WiFi and taking selfies every 30 seconds with their mob of braying, joyless hipster pals.

'We don't drink here "ironically", we drink here because there's no fucking hipsters in it,' said James Kennedy, the 67-year-old spokesperson for the Irish League of Old Men.

'There's scores of pubs where the youngsters can go and drink, and I can promise you that we're not going to be going to those pubs, so we kindly ask for them to stay the fuck out of our pubs and let us drink our pints in peace without constant shrieks as they discuss whatever manufactured drama they're using to add some sort of purpose to their lives.'

Thousands of young people were said to be 'extremely offended' by the statements, and took to social media to sulk about it.

Study confirms people who are messy, swear and stay up late are 'lazy, messy bastards'

PEOPLE who tend to be untidy, stay up late and regularly use curse words may actually be 'lazy, messy bastards', new research has revealed this week.

Researchers from the Florida Gulf Coast University gave a classic test to a group of students, where they found that those who lived in clutter tended to be lazy, and that those who cursed a lot tended to be 'bastards'.

'We were astonished to find that those who had all three character traits were lazy, messy bastards,' explained lead researcher Dr Terence Trayman. 'Not only that, but we also found that lazy, messy bastards liked to excuse their tendencies as a higher form of intelligence and our study found that many of the subjects regularly shared articles claiming they're special or gifted somehow. Which is preposterous, to say the least.'

The findings of the study were described as 'highly significant' in statistical terms, but many lazy, messy bastards have since disagreed with the university's findings.

'I fucking curse all the fucking time and my house is like a pig-sty,' pointed out one local man we spoke to this afternoon. 'According to a test I did online once, my IQ is like 146. Every second day I share a *Guardian* newspaper article and I never get up before 10 a.m. I suppose I'm a lazy, messy bastard too, huh? I play solitaire, for Christ's sakes. This study is flawed and I won't be sharing it on any of my social media feeds.'

The study concluded that one in every five people who think they're smart are lazy, messy bastards.

Yelling at women on the street: a guide

IF you're a man who has ever encountered a pretty woman walking down the street, you may have felt a curious sensation wash over you: a mix of desire and anxiety, which you're not sure how to deal with.

You're attracted to this lady, certainly, but you know in your heart that you lack the wordsmanship needed to transform you from 'random man on the street' into her sexual partner. What's a boy to do?

Well, there's one thing you can do: yell suggestive and sexually threatening phrases at her. Not sure how? Follow these steps.

1) Dismiss any sense of impropriety

You may feel like you can't yell at a woman because you're both in public, or because it's the middle of the day, or because she's got her small children with her. Stop overthinking things! Men yell at women whenever they feel like it. Nobody is going to judge you for it. If you see a pretty lady, start a'yelling. The only person that might get upset is the lady herself, and nobody really cares about her.

Did you know?
The original name for the euro currency was europunt.

2) Freestyle

Don't try and plan what you're going to say. After all, who knows what type of woman you'll be yelling at from one end of the day to the next. Blonde? Brunette? Skinny? Hefty? Wearing a skirt or trousers? It's impossible to be prepared, so just freestyle your yells as and when you need to. Let the words just roll off your tongue, whatever you think of. Think you might be being a bit too vulgar? See instruction number 1. You're grand. Say whatever you like!

3) Never tell the truth

This is an important one. Whatever you yell must be mostly lies and nonsense. Never tell the truth. If you start your yelling with 'C'mere, d'you know what I'd do to you?', then you can never end that sentence in a truthful manner. 'C'mere, d'you know what I'd do to you? I'd leave you lying in the bed unsatisfied cause my penis hasn't been 100% hard in years due to my crippling insecurity and alcohol dependency problems, which I compensate for by being sexually aggressive to women in front of my mates so they'll think I'm some sort of fucking big lady's man instead of a practically impotent shit-for-brains who has never made a woman come in my life'. See, that kind of thing just ain't going to do you any favours. Make something up. Tell her you've a massive penis.

FACEBOOK LATEST

Local woman thinks Facebook is her fucking diary or something

A County Waterford woman has been branded 'a bit of an attention seeker' by several of her online peers today following yet another detailed Facebook post about something or other.

Friends of Jessica Tenant have come forward in a bid to intervene in her daily torrent of monotonous drivel after finally having enough, with many resorting to actually hiding her Facebook posts from their precious timelines.

'In real life she's grand,' insisted actual friend Deirdre Kehoe. 'It's just when she starts this needy shit I don't like. It seems to be never-ending too. She just rambles on about stupid things in her life constantly, like Facebook is her personal diary or something. We need to do something.'

Following yet another 600-word post about why she hates rummaging through the reduced aisle in Tesco so much, several pals took the opportunity to highlight their misgivings in a bid to shine light on her annoying nature.

'Will you ever shut the fuck up Jessy, for fuck sakes,' Mary Dalton carefully commented, holding back as much as she could. 'Seriously girl, do you think anyone gives a shit about your fucking bowel movements or what you had for fucking breakfast? Give it a fucking rest. Everyone is sick of your bollox.

Facebook is not your fucking diary, so just share inspirational quotes that sum up how you feel instead, like the rest of us.'

Unaware of her apparent wrongdoings, Jessica Tenant took the comment, which so far has 567 likes, as a bit of a laugh, wallowing in the attention it was now receiving.

'Hahahaha Mary gurl, you're gas out hahahaha,' Jessica replied, before posting an updated picture of her little toe she banged off the press last week, which seems to be doing fine now that the nail is growing back.

'We make call-out videos but never actually fight anyone' admits Irish Traveller

A member of Ireland's Travelling community has today revealed that he spends most of his spare time making call-out videos to other Travellers, but has never actually fought a day in his life.

In an exclusive interview with *WWN*, the man, who wishes to remain anonymous for exposing the truth, confirmed that there is only a handful of arranged bareknuckle fist fights every year, and that the majority of young men making them 'couldn't beat their way out of a wet paper bag', but many of his peers are really good at making call-out videos.

'Shooting on your phone in portrait mode is key,' the grandson of four explained, demonstrating with an upright phone in one hand. 'We love taunting each other and getting a rise out of whatever family we have beef with, but when it comes down to the crunch, 99% who star in the call-out videos chicken out, but it's great craic watching the replies; it passes the boring days when you're unemployed and can't find work because most settled people are racist and won't hire us for work.'

Asked whether he thought Travellers can sometimes be racist against settled people, he

refused to reply and challenged this reporter to a fight, before then backing down and apologising.

'Sorry but if you had sent me a video with that question in it, I would have called you out to a fight, and we would have had a whole week of back and forth shite talk until one of us backed out,' he said, 'but that's how we solve things and I'm not apologising for it. It's better than going to court to settle things – like ye do – and wasting everyone's time and tax money.'

On a separate note, the Traveller said he would like to see a 'fake fighting company' like the WWE take over the organising and prize money and actually turn it into proper entertainment, where everybody shouts at each other and pretends to fight, with 'Paddy Doherty or someone commentating'.

'If you settled cunts are allowed do it, then why aren't we?' he concluded.

How to explain to your new boyfriend that you're a fallen woman

YOU know how it is: you're out shopping for sackcloth to make a new dress for yourself, and you meet a cute guy who asks you to go to a dance or for a sit-down meal with cutlery... only problem is, you've fallen into sin at some point in your life.

You're unclean, and he deserves to know. How to break it to him in a manner that won't make him cast you out?

This is the difficulty facing many young Irish women today, trying to find a suitor who will accept her despite the fact that she's a fallen woman. These young women have allowed themselves to be led astray, and now they come running for advice as to how to find a husband even though they're dripping in sin.

Well, you can't. There's not a man out there who will have you. Away with you, to the mines! You can try to explain yourself, surely, but it'll all just fall on deaf ears. You can say how you thought it was all just a harmless good time, but he'll just hear one word – 'trollop'.

And so on you'll go, bereft of human affection, the talk of the town, the shame of your family. Alone, staring out the window into the blackness of the night, as your wireless plays softly in the background, a damning reminder of how you threw your life away in the dance-halls of your youth, when there was 'no harm' in courting with your skirt up.

We hope it was worth it.

12 MONTHS A GUARD *Month 9*

I got to spend a day on work placement with the Drug Squad this month, and I have to say I learned so much! We got to deal with the nation's drug problem tactically, meaning we arrested nobody and investigated nothing. But I've been assured that this is the right thing to do; it's tactics, isn't it? You can't just arrest drug dealers. That'd be too obvious. When you don't arrest anyone, you know you're winning. I also learned the correct formula for the 'street value' of drugs we seize, which helps us look like absolute rock stars. I even attended a bust at which we seized a nugget of cannabis resin with a street value of €750,000! I'd say we're winning the war on drugs, for sure! Aren't we?

'I fly better when I'm drunk'

As part of WWN's *Voices series, we give a platform to those who don't really deserve it. This week is the turn of airline pilot and fully functioning alcoholic, Tadhg Kennedy.*

I suppose the greatest misconception about flying a Boeing 747 is that it's actually difficult. It's not. I could do this in my sleep, and have done on several occasions. Yeah, there are hundreds of buttons, levers and dials in the cockpit, but to be honest, most pilots don't have a clue what most of them mean. That's why we have co-pilots, fresh out of training school who remember all this shit. It's actually quite hilarious when you think about it.

Truth be told, computers and ground control do most of the work, so long-haul flights can be boring as fuck. That's why alcohol is such a winner in my books. Not only does it make the nine-hour trip across the Atlantic a lot shorter than it seems, I actually seem to fly a whole lot better when I've had a few in me. Like, I haven't crashed once … yet. That's good going.

Drink relaxes me, especially Scotch. It really helps to put those 400 odd people in the cabin out of my mind. I couldn't imagine flying this thing if I could see their stupid worried faces in the rear view, watching me knocking back a flask of Johnny Walker. People are so PC lately, and probably wouldn't understand why a pilot of my calibre would drink and fly.

Now, I'm not saying drunk flying is for everyone. Some pilots are terrible at it. But it definitely settles me during take-offs and landings, when I actually have to do a bit. Turbulence too; it's always good to be drunk during turbulence. How else could I stay calm on the PA when speaking to passengers? Shit, if I was sober during some of the pockets I've had to fly through, I'd have probably ditched the plane and parachuted years ago. Fuck, you actually need to be drunk on this job. Sure, Neil Armstrong was hammered when he landed on the moon. You'd need to be off your head doing this job.

All I'm saying is not to judge me, or any other pilot who likes to fly drunk. Trust us. We have this all under control.

Now, fasten your seatbelt motherfuckers and enjoy the ride.

Yeee haaaaw!

Local woman looking stunning as usual

WWN have received confirmed reports that a local woman is indeed 'looking gorgeous as usual hun', following the posting of a glamorous selfie on social media earlier today.

Sinead Moran (29) received exactly one dozen expressions of support for her looks on Facebook, with admiration pouring in from her friends and family who all lost their collective minds at how well Moran looked in the selfie.

'OMG Sinead u look stunnin as usual babe,' read a typical reply to the post, coming in this instance from a woman Moran went to school with 20 years ago who lives in Australia now.

'Sinead u are a beaut, are u around at the weekend greg is three if you want to bring the boys over we are getting a bouncey castle' read a comment from one of Moran's neighbours, opting in this instance to use her one Facebook comment per day limit to add as much extra information as possible.

Speaking exclusively to *WWN*, Lismore native Moran expressed an overwhelming sense of joy that people were so moved by her selfie, although added that the amount of comments were down from similar posts last week.

'I put up a picture of myself in a dress I bought for a wedding with a full face of make-up on last week, and it got 14 comments, so this one of me with my hair up and my nice earrings on getting 12 comments is a bit of a disappointment,' said Moran, planning her next shot.

'I think I'll have to work on the location of the shoot; I mean, you can clearly see a basket of dirty washing behind me in the bedroom in this one. I think maybe a shot of me on the sofa drinking wine watching TV? Maybe with the kids there too? I can already see the caption: "luvin life wit my babies" ... yeah, that'll get my numbers back again!'

Future first-time defaulters apply for a mortgage

FOLLOWING the launch of a new government scheme to help couples onto the precarious Irish property ladder, Carmel and Ted Lyons from Dublin announced today that they will apply for a mortgage, despite the shaky economy and extortionate property prices.

The future first-time defaulters were said to be delighted at the news. They have saved €35,000 in the past two years, but expected it to take three more years to save enough for a house deposit.

Ted Lyons (28 and a half) has been daydreaming about borrowing €350,000 for a poorly built home for almost eight years and now cannot wait to move into it with his twice-as-eager wife next year.

'We've been talking about owning a home ever since we got together,' Ted explained, unaware several major banks are currently in danger of collapsing ... again. 'Myself and Carmel would spend hours praying to God that some financial institution would lend us enough money to waste half our income on.'

Previously the pair were told by the bank to save 20% of the cost price of the home, and that the strict measures were in place to prevent previous banking mistakes, which crippled the Irish economy, forcing four million people into debt.

'Thank Christ the government stepped up and intervened,' said an ecstatic Carmel Lyons, whose credit rating is okay for the moment. 'Sure, this new 5% tax rebate may push up the price of houses overall, but a house is a house, and you can't cohabit in Ireland unless you own a house. Baby Jesus said so.'

The Lyons are expected to apply for their mortgage later next week, before defaulting sometime in 2020.

'The thought of a finger up my hole is worse than the thought of prostate cancer'

ALTHOUGH over 3,000 men in Ireland are diagnosed every year with prostate cancer, one Waterford man is steadfastly refusing to undergo the testing procedure that could save his life because he's 'fucked if some doctor is fingering his arse'.

At 42, David Gennon from Ardmore, County Waterford, is right in the demographic of men who should undergo a regular prostate check-up, a simple examination that can help spot the early warning signs of the second most common cancer in Irish men.

Balking at the fact that the check-up involves a medical professional carrying out a digital examination of the rectum, Gennon made it clear that he'd rather take his chances with cancer than endure mild discomfort for less time than it takes to tie a shoelace.

'Christ, the fucking thoughts of it. A whole finger, up the arse. No way,' said the soon to be ex-father of three.

'Not a chance. It'd be like going to the dentist, but for your hole. Granted, if they found anything – they could treat it quickly because the earlier you treat these things the higher the survival rate is, but nah … Finger in the arse. I'm too much of a man to let someone do that to me.'

Waterford man doesn't like girlfriend's newly found confidence

'SHE'S after losing a couple of stone since starting the accounting course and thinks she's great now off with all her new college friends,' Waterford man Martin Power explains to *WWN* about a worrying new trend among Irish women that has him stuck between a rock and a hard place with partner of 12 years Trisha Murphy.

It all began last year when out-of-work Trisha opted for a part-time secretarial course in her local SOLAS centre.

'I blame the dole crowd for getting her into this mess,' Power insists, referring to the social welfare department's compulsory course system for the long-term unemployed. 'It was only meant to be for a few months, but then she got notions and applied to the big college to do a real course. She's after changing since, talking about stuff I don't care about all the time and rarely makes the dinner anymore.'

The neglected grandson of four recalls the first time his partner went out without him one night, with her newly found peers.

'It was a Wednesday afternoon in May when she asked if I minded her heading out with her class to celebrate some graduation shit,' he says, visibly anxious with the thought. 'You'd swear she was after becoming a doctor or a scientist the way she was going on. Not one mention about how I felt about the whole thing. Just headed off for the night and didn't come back 'til eleven that night.'

Power also goes on to blame the Internet and social media for influencing Trisha, stating that she regularly 'makes comments about women stuff', and shares articles from the 'posh newspapers'.

'All she's doing is showing off to her friends,' he points out, 'She's even wearing makeup to college now and wearing nice clothes. That's not for me, you know. I wouldn't be surprised now if she has a fancy man in there. I'll take a spin in around at lunch someday, see what she's at.'

Power's story is not a unique one. Latest figures suggest a large increase of females entering male-dominated roles after completing college and university courses, with some women even making up to 80% of their male counterparts' salaries, despite already being in a relationship with a man, raising the question 'what do they want?'

A new study has found that the average Irish dad spends 88% of his time cursing at shit, with a worrying amount of cases being left unreported by family members.

The study, which closely monitored 1,123 fathers over a six-month period, is the first of its kind to be carried out by researchers at Trinity College, Dublin. Its findings are now being cited as 'crucial to the nation's future upbringing'.

'For years, Irish people have wondered why they've been so loose-lipped when using curse words,' lead researcher of the study Martin Pringle noted.

'Well now we've found that it's all thanks to dads, with many openly using phrases like "fucking bollox", "cunting whore", "shower of bastards", etc. in front of their young and impressionable children. In this way they are passing on the tirade of verbal abuse to the next generation.'

Worryingly, the study found that dads curse more at family members than they do at inanimate objects, with researchers pinpointing the top five incidents that spark the verbal outbursts.

'We found that "Who left that fucking door open again?"' is the number one phrase used by cursing dads,'

Mr Pringle confirmed. 'It is followed closely by "Where's the fucking TV remote gone?", "Pass the fucking ball, you useless bollox", "I hate that Enda fucking Kenny" and 'Use your fucking indicators, you cunt".'

Inanimate objects such as computers, washing machines and televisions were also found to be in the firing line, with the average dad spending up to three months of the year shouting obscenities at them.

However, the study did not account for the high number of 'fucking eejits in this country' that Irish dads have to put up with on a daily basis, compared with their European counterparts.

Average Irish dad spends 88% of his time cursing at shit

Did you know?

23% of awful people in cinemas insist on providing their own commentary on movies.

'I passive aggressively share Buddhist quotes on Facebook to get my shitty point across'

As part of WWN's Voices series, we give a platform to those who don't really deserve it. This week is the turn of social media user Saoirse Dalton-Woods, who openly admits to using pictures of Buddhist quotes to get her shitty point across to people who have just crossed her.

SOME people in this world really deserve to be taught a lesson over treating me wrong, be it ignoring me in the shops or simply forgetting to wish me a happy birthday on Facebook. And what better way to assassinate their character than with a suitable phrase of wisdom, conveniently mirroring the current situation, pointing out how wrong they are and proving how I'm always right.

I'll admit that sharing the teachings from a philosophy of peace to inflict emotional unease on others is somewhat ironic, even hypocritical of me, but Jesus I'm good at it, and I would recommend it to anyone who likes to avoid actual confrontation or talking it out with people and letting your feelings be known to them in an adult manner.

Sure, the person you intended to see the quote might not immediately get its context, or see it for that matter, even if you literally just had the argument with them 10 minutes ago, so adding your own caption to the post is key to achieving your spiritually corrupt goal of ruining their news-feed scrolling experience.

'We all know someone like this' is one of my favourite lines to use when sharing a life lesson quote. If they don't get it at the time, then one of their other friends will, and hopefully point it out to them, asking 'is this about you?'

or 'are you fighting with Saoirse cause she's posting those brilliantly accurate Buddhist quotes about you again? She's amazing like that.'

I've got an arsenal at this stage, for every occasion, and I would class myself as a black belt in Buddhism, a master even. I'd dare any bitch to cross me right now. Anyone! You don't acknowledge my presence in a shop? Boom! Here's a fucking quote about how real friends treat each other. Oh, you said something to Tracey about how I didn't invite you to Pilates on Thursday with the girls? Boom! Here's a fucking quote on two-faced cunts with frizzy hair and smelly armpits.

Of course, I've gained a reputation over the past few years on Facebook, but that's just the real me coming through that JPEG image that someone else created using someone else's words.

That's how I roll, bitch!

TRENDING ⟩ Local man isn't going to let nuances of grammar get in his way when arguing online

ALTHOUGH Waterford native Kevin Dunning did indeed spend over 12 years in school, during which he studied English from the basics of how to read and write, all the way up to the study of Shakespearean plays and poetry, the now 27-year-old draws on precious little of this knowledge when telling feminists that they should kill themselves during his constant online flame wars on social media.

Dunning, who can spell correctly when he wants to, rarely affords himself the time needed to compose a structured sentence that makes sense and contains perfect or adequate grammar. Instead, he prefers to let his words run freely with copious amounts of sexually aggressive swearing and unfiltered vitriol.

'Sometimes, you just need to really let loose and tell some stranger that she's a fucking idiot and the world would be better off without her,' said Dunning, furiously tapping away at his phone as he launched yet another tirade on a thread about women's rights.

'Who has time to conjugate a verb correctly when there's screaming to be done? Who has time to spell-check? No, I've got one speed when it comes to the comment sections. I just let it all flow freely and if they pull me up on my spelling, I call them a bitch and keep going.'

Dunning's lack of cohesiveness online also extends to barbed swipes at celebrities on Twitter, where he misspells everything except their Twitter handle.

12 MONTHS A GUARD *Month 10*

It's been a tough month. One day last week I was brought on my own into a room with no windows, where there was a man sitting in the corner with a bag over his head.

'Book him for not having motor tax,' came a voice from the far side of a one-way mirror.

'But he's not in a car,' I said.

'Book him. You want to be a guard, don't you?' said the voice.

'I do, but … '

'No buts. Your allegiance to us must be complete. We have to know you will follow orders. Book him.'

So I did it. I booked him for no tax, and imposed an on-the-spot fine, and ordered that he present his fully up-to-date tax disc to a station of his choosing within ten days. As I left, I walked over and took the bag off the man's head. It was my father. Tough stuff!

Panic as woman accidentally likes nemesis's profile pic while stalking account

A County Waterford woman had to temporarily delete her Facebook account this afternoon after accidentally hitting the like button under her arch rival's profile picture while stalking her account.

Janet Deegan, who claims to be usually quite good at this sort of thing, had no other option but to deactivate her profile in a bid to pretend she was hacked.

'That bitch Tracey Maher put up a another selfie today and I must have clicked like without thinking,' Ms Deegan recalled, visibly panicked. 'I unliked it again, but Facebook already notified her so it was too late. I had no other option but to delete my account, and go on Twitter and Snapchat to tell everyone that my Facebook was probably hacked.'

The quick-thinking mother of none made sure to tell as many of her friends who were also close to her nemesis as possible, making sure to let them know that it was 'probably some perverted male hacker looking for an easy target'.

'Jesus, I hope they believe me, otherwise I'll look a right tit,' Deegan added, desperately refreshing her browser for any updates. 'Last thing I want is that tramp thinking I'm stalking her account, when in actual fact I was just looking to see how pathetic her stupid fat face is.'

Following several agonising hours without Facebook, Janet Clare Deegan caved in and reactivated her account with a brief status update, apologising to 'anyone' who may have been approached through her profile, concluding that the hacker seemed to be only interested in the Facebook accounts of 'slutty looking women'.

TECHNOLOGY

Local man doesn't answer private numbers

'IF you can't be bothered showing your number, I can't be bothered answering your call.'

These are the words of Kevin Dalton, a local school teacher who refuses to say yes to private numbers. *WWN* arranged to meet the 36-year-old at his home in Tramore, where he bravely spoke to us about his ongoing dilemma.

'I've fallen out with a few friends over it,' Dalton began, referring to an emergency situation involving one of his elderly neighbours who locked herself in a toilet for four days. 'Like, how was I supposed to know she was ringing 369 times for help? Turn off your private number if you want someone to answer you.'

Dalton claims that most private calls are debt collectors or scams anyway, and branded anyone hiding their number as a 'gobshite' who should have their phones taken from them for using the discreet option.

'I have Eir chasing me for Film4 channels I drunkenly subscribed to. I have the Provident loan guy pestering me for a €100 loan I got last year, which is now €14k with interest for some reason. And then you have all these phone scams that charge your phone a fortune,' added Dalton. 'Fuck answering that shit.'

However, during our interview, Dalton's phone began ringing.

'Ah for fuck sakes,' he barked, now holding up the phone in disgust. 'It's a private number. I bet it's the DHL guy delivering the Sports Direct stuff I ordered. They can never find my house.'

Following a tense stand-off between Dalton, the phone and this intrigued reporter, the grandson of four finally caved in and answered the phone, but without greeting the caller on the other end, just leaving them to speak first.

'Yeah, it was the DHL guy,' he later admitted, slightly embarrassed he answered, forcing an end to our interview. 'I'd rarely do that now. Hey, where are you going? Come back. Please don't write that I answered. Hey! Call me later?' before adding, 'Don't block the number though.'

'Fuck this, I'm switching to long ball,' confirms Guardiola

MANCHESTER City manager Pep Guardiola has sensationally revealed he intends to change his football philosophy after his side's 4-0 trouncing by Everton yesterday.

'Fuck this, I'm switching to long ball,' Guardiola confirmed in his post-match press conference before instructing the City hierarchy to do everything to sign Peter Crouch and Marouane Fellaini before the January transfer window shuts.

Guardiola ruled out a move for Andy Carroll, after the West Ham player displayed a hint of skill and technique in his performance against Crystal Palace at the weekend.

It is believed City approached Dion Dublin and Duncan Ferguson to sound the ex-pros out about a return to the game.

'I have been humbled,' the City manager added, his head now buried in his hands. 'I thought I could pass the ball, encourage crazy concepts like attractive football and something called "new ideas". I was wrong, yes? I see that now.'

'Does anyone know if Rory Delap can still do those long throws?' Guardiola added, appealing to the assembled journalists.

Leading footballing minds encouraged the public not to be too hard on Guardiola, with visionary football philosopher Paul Merson saying, 'It's not his fault he's foreign and soft. You don't win nothing in England with foreigners.'

Guardiola has, however, won renewed praise from football purists since confirming that City will still play out from the back. This tactic will now involve kicking the ball as long and as hard as possible at the head of a very tall striker.

FIVE-A-SIDE FOOTBALL

Five-a-side player faces two-match ban for being a prick

A key player for a Waterford five-a-side astro football team has been handed a two-match ban by his fellow players after repeated on-pitch offences such as blasting the ball too hard and just being a bit of a dickhead to everyone.

Kevin Meehan, named locally as a prick, togs out for astro football every Tuesday night with a rotating team of friends, neighbours, lads from school and the occasional Polish fella someone knows from work.

The 27-year-old, who had a trial for West Brom when he was 17 and takes his football very seriously, has been cautioned in the past by his fellow players. They had previously urged him to 'tone it the fuck down' during their weekly game, described by everyone except Meehan as 'just a bit of craic on a Tuesday'.

With offences mounting against the Tramore native, a two-match ban has been imposed by the rest of the lads and will be implemented by taking Meehan's name off the WhatsApp group for a fortnight.

'Yeah, we've kind of had it with him smashing the ball as hard as he can and shouldering everyone around the place,' said Seán Hanlon, sometimes midfield, sometimes in nets.

'Half of us aren't fit to run at all, we just tog out for the laugh and to get out of the house,' admitted Hanlon. 'But Meehan shows up like it's the Champions League final or something. We've warned him to cool it on several occasions. Now he can kick the ball as hard as he wants at home for the next fortnight.'

Meehan was said to be unflustered by the development as he is currently in talks to join an indoor five-a-side team that play on Thursdays in town.

Local darts player out of competition due to 'pint elbow'

WATERFORD city darts professional Damien 'The Double' Lyons has announced today that he will be out of the game for the next six months due to what doctors are calling 'pint elbow' – a condition in which the outer part of the elbow becomes sore and tender at the lateral epicondyle from the excessive downing of pints.

Lyons, who has won dozens of major Irish darts competitions over the past 24 years, first complained of a pain in his elbow last month at the Irish open, forcing him out of the competition during the early stages.

'It's not something you would imagine happening to you,' he opened up for the first time since bowing out. 'You'd hear stories about pint elbow, but never meet anyone who actually had it … until now.'

Following a series of tests, X-rays and MRIs, Lyons was finally told by doctors on Friday that he had full-scale pint elbow and that if he didn't rest his pint arm, he may never be able to play darts again.

'Darts is my life, and drinking pints goes hand-in-hand with playing; if I can't drink, I can't play,' the now emotional 38-year-old explained. 'The doctors suggested using a straw to drink from the pint glass, but can you imagine a darts player walking into a competition with a fecking straw in a pint? I'd be laughed off the stage and called a big pansy.'

Since contracting pint elbow, Lyons claims that his fellow dart peers have all but abandoned him over fears the condition may be contagious.

'There's a lot of stigma attached to pint elbow and I can understand how some of the lads may want to keep away from me,' he added, now caressing his box of darts on the table in a nostalgic manner. 'Players need to be educated about pint elbow and know how to prevent it from happening. It's not contagious, just very debilitating. More should be done in the sport to highlight the condition.'

Specialists believe 'The Double' Lyons may have to learn to use his other hand to drink pints, which could take several years to perfect, before he's allowed back into the darts league.

'It's like learning to walk again,' Lyons concluded.

THERE was massive transfer window news this afternoon as third declension side Gromflorth Rovers made a stunning club-record bid of sevemfty-three crillion British pounds for Frackelinesch Harskelliningtorp, the No. 8 pitch general for German side Massive Trucks FC.

Harskelliningtorp (21) has had the transfer market buzzing for months with speculation over which side he would sign with, resulting in huge amounts of chatter between sports fans around the globe and at least five news articles every day centred on the rumours as to where the ball-kicker would end up.

Although the news may sound like gobbledy-gook to non-sports fans, who can't understand why their co-worker just stood up at his desk and screamed, 'Nice one, we landed Harskelliningtorp!

Gromflorth Rovers make sevemfty-three crillion bid for Frackelinesch Harskelliningtorp

That'll really help us in our bid to become the Yankee Scented Candles division champions for the third year in the row', pundits are now calling the announcement the most important thing to happen to football since the invention of air.

'Sevemfty-three crillion is a lot for a side like Gromflorth to put up, but it'll be worth it when you see Frackelinesch Harskelliningtorp lining out in the ol' maroon and puce,' said Sir Dirk Fuckhead, owner of GRFC.

'He'll fit right in with the rest of the boys: Mark Lesion, Orc the

Conqueror, Lady Kneecap and Boris Clicktoreadmore. This is our year. Mark my words!'

The story of Harskelliningtorp's signing was accompanied by nine more equally exciting transfer window stories, each of which made as much sense to non-sports fans as this one.

Did you know?

100% of runners are mostly worn by people while they lie on couches watching people exercising in runners on TV.

Our expert gives you his tips for Day 3 of Punchestown

Punchestown is by far the biggest event in Ireland's horse-racing calendar, and who better to run you through today's races than 19-year-old professional gambler, Mossey Kennedy.

THIS is my fucking day, lads. I can feel it in me balls. Yours too if you stick with me. Fucking lost me stones yesterday and the day before, but luckily the gran left her pension in the usual spot this morning, so the first tip is to borrow a hape of money from someone, as they'll get it all back today ... definitely today.

Usually I'd use a betting app to put me money on, but me account is empty and the bank won't give me any more on me overdraft so I've to back the horses today in the old-fashioned way. But it's not all bad 'cause you pick up a few tips from the smelly auld lads in the bookies and they obviously know what they're talking about because they've been in there years, and even make enough money to sit in the pub all day. Lucky bastards have it sussed, they do. Someday, kid.

I seen one lad with a real packet of fags too: obviously one of the good gamblers. Wouldn't give me any tips though, but I did manage to catch his docket on the pass. Clever cunt put a tenner on all the second favourites – a man after me own heart.

Second tip is to stay clear of the favourites as there's fuck-all returns, unless you have wads of cash like that Chinese lad in the bookies earlier – the mad cunt put a grand on a horse. I'd never do that now, unless of course I'd won the grand on a previous horse,

then it's alright to back that kind of money, but only then. Free money sure.

Any horse with Ruby Walsh or Paul Townend on it is always worth an each-way gamble. I don't look at form or any of that shite, just see which horse has the second or third best price and stick a tenner on it. Grey horses always win too.

There's eight races on today, starting at twenty to four, so tip three is get your grub in early and line that stomach for winning pints tonight. Always keep enough money for the few pints of Tuborg while you watch the races in the local.

I also like to pre-roll a few Drum for the walk between the pub and the bookies, 'cause

sometimes there's no time to just roll. Remember: it's a big day today. Races are not over till eight tonight. You'll be in bits at that stage sure, all going to plan.

Now, the most important tip I'll give ya is never let the other lads in the pub know who you're backing, 'cause they'll be all over ya like a leech when you come back with the few euro. Best contain yourself sitting at the bar. Give naughtin' away. Stick to the €3 pints.

Last tip: always do a few practice runs on the virtual racing yoke in the bookies if there's a big event on, like Punchestown. From there you will see how your luck is going and you can place your bet amounts accordingly. I'd usually do this most days, you know, so I don't get rusty at betting. If you leave it a few days at all, you're back to square one and you'll lose your momentum.

Right, I'm off to the pub to watch this. If I see ya later this evening then you'll know it's been a good day for me. Hopefully I'll make it past *Home and Away*. Nothing worse than coming home drunk to that shite on telly and you after losin' your bollocks on a Willie Mullins nag.

HEARTWARMING!
Man looking for an excuse to drink just realised the rugby is on

IT'S Friday! It's the end of the week, and so many of us deserve that pint or 12; however, for some people out there it is becoming harder and harder to justify drinking from the early evening all the way into the wee small hours without being labelled an alcoholic. Enter Waterford man Anthony Foggins, who was faced with this dilemma earlier today until inspiration struck and he realised he had the perfect excuse for going on the lash.

'You doubt yourself sometimes, ya know,' explained the novice alcoholic. 'How can I hide my alcohol dependency on days when there's no compelling reason to drag someone to the pub with me? That's when I copped it. Just sitting on the toilet at work, doing my 11.30 a.m. Friday shit, like clockwork, and I remembered we're playing Wales tonight!' Foggins said, punching the air with delight.

It was joy unconfined for Foggins as he realised he wouldn't have to wait until Saturday or, God forbid, Sunday for some soccer match to provide the excuse for being on a bar stool, sipping pints. It's a cold heart that wouldn't join in Foggins's happiness in realising the rare Friday night fixture took the pressures off finding an excuse to drink his head clean off his shoulders.

'I feel about seven stone lighter after that. I won't have to badger anyone too hard to convince them to head out – some will want to watch the game at home by themselves considering the mess I made of myself last time out, but I'll give them the "watch it on big screen" bullshit routine and one or two of them will give in,' added Foggins.

'Couldn't give two fucks about the rugby myself but it makes it easier to get a few of the lads out,' explained the man who wasn't all that happy if he was being perfectly honest.

Wonderful World of Science

2017 was a record year for nightmares involving a naked Donald Trump.

Local man had trial for United but got injured

WATERFORD man Gary Begley confirmed that he would have signed a 10-year contract worth €100 million with Manchester United only for an unlucky injury, *WWN* can reveal.

The 36-year-old was relaying the story for the 1,245th time, prompted to do so by encountering someone in his local pub he had never seen or spoken to before.

'Richard Dunne was marking me that game, yeah *that* Richard Dunne. Well I say marking me, I was running rings round him,' Begley explained, careful not to give away enough information to give substantial merit to his story.

Begley confirmed that the Manchester United manager at the time, Alex Ferguson, never went to those sorts of youth matches himself normally, but he turned up that time especially to watch the Waterford native.

'I was sort of an Ineista-type player crossed with a Ronaldo and a Roy Keane, but before the footballing world had copped on to the fact that that sort of player was truly special and unique, ya know,' Begley continued. 'At half-time Fergie said he wanted me and I could have a trial – but he basically signed me on the spot.'

However, before the sales manager could sign the lucrative, one-of-a-kind contract, he suffered an injury that would end his career.

'Ah, Dunne got annoyed that I was making a fool of him – I'd scored seven goals – and he lashed out with a kick. He missed me completely, but in moving away from him I was struck down with a devastating stitch. I never recovered,' Begley explained, the full weight of the loss of a football career etched on his face.

FOOTBALL

Gareth Southgate named England's next scapegoat

OFFICIALLY unveiled as England's next excuse for losing, Gareth Southgate has signed a lucrative four-year deal in exchange for being the subject of endless ridicule and abuse, *WWN* can confirm.

The FA, taking time out from trying to manage PR around the emerging abuse scandal in football, confirmed that Southgate is to become Sam Allardyce's official successor in the role of chief scapegoat when England do an England and reveal the true extent of their shittiness.

'While obviously the role of manager and chief scapegoat is multifaceted and ever-evolving, one thing is for sure and that is this will all end in tears,' FA chief executive Martin Glenn shared with the media as he warmly embraced Southgate.

Southgate has already been heavily criticised for signing his England manager's contract with his left hand, completely disregarding 'the English way' of signing contracts with your right hand.

The media urged that expectations to remain grounded due to the fact that the England football team is not on the same level as leading international teams. They also pointed out that in the event of qualifying for Russia 2018, they will make the lives of the manager and his players a living hell.

'The key is not to shoot our outrage and indignation load, as it were, before we are approaching a major tournament,' explained *Daily Mail* scrawler of words Henry Finnan. 'By 2018 we should hopefully have a 16-year-old world beater that we'll pressure Southgate into picking, only to turn around and say it was a disgrace he was taken on the plane. God, I'm already getting goosebumps just thinking about it. It'll be so much fun.'

The FA confirmed there was an option in Southgate's contract to become a vilified scapegoat before the 2018 World Cup and that it could not rule out sacking him over something ridiculous by the end of the week.

McGregor's baby in heated stand-off during ultrasound

THERE were tense scenes at today's weigh-in for Conor McGregor's upcoming first child when the spirited foetus squared up to the doctor performing his ultrasound, reportedly telling him, 'Get that fuckin' thing out of my face.'

The Notorious Baby McGregor was getting a routine check-up at the time and took issue with what he termed 'aggro' from the other side of the uterine wall, as the doctor pressed the ultrasound wand on the belly of Dee Devlin, partner of UFC champion Conor.

Swimming in amniotic fluid with the same swagger and attitude as his father walking into a room, the utero-weight champion went on a rant that would make his dad proud. He stated in no uncertain terms that he wasn't there to be poked and prodded at by 'some prick who couldn't make it as a real doctor'.

'See you with the tube of jelly and the thing and the machine, yeah you, I'll fuckin' burst you when I get out of here,' burbled Baby McGregor, making a series of aggressive gestures with his pharyngeal arches.

'You think you can mess with the king? I may weigh the same as a tangerine at the minute, but by the time I get out I'll be at fighting weight and anyone that wants a dig can fuckin' get one.'

Dad-to-be Conor was said to be incredibly proud of his baby's outburst, and started flinging bottles of water at staff in the clinic just to help out.

12 MONTHS A GUARD *Month 11*

Everything for the last month has been building up to today, lottery day; the day when all trainee guards find out what division they're going to be assigned to. One by one, we were called up to the stage, in front of everyone, to spin a heavy wooden wheel and watch as a ping-pong ball danced round the wheel before settling on the division we will spend our lives in. The guy before me landed on 'Mountain Bike' and had to be dragged off the stage to stop him screaming that he 'didn't spin it properly and should get another go'. My turn came. I held my breath, closed my eyes, and spun. Just not Segway, just not Segway, I prayed. I opened my eyes. Traffic Corps. That'll do just nicely.

TRENDING 'What the fuck am I going to do with all these fidget spinners?' asks Santa

SAINT Nicholas doesn't make many mistakes, but the jovial old soul will be the first to admit that he has really fucked himself over by anticipating that the fidget spinner craze that swept the globe in spring and early summer would still be around for Christmas.

As such, Santa now finds himself with a gigantic warehouse filled with the fleetingly popular three-pronged toy, with massive amounts of every colour, size and weight of spinner in his inventory.

'It's not the elf-power that I put into having these fucking things made, it's the storage issue,' grumbled St Nick, absent-mindedly spinning a light-up deluxe spinner between thumb and middle finger.

'I coulda fitted a million PlayStations in this shed, instead of this crap. What am I going to do now? Wait for 20 years until the fidget spinner craze comes back? It's not even like I can repurpose them for anything, like when I melted down all those *Frozen* dolls to make Lego. I'm stuck with these, unless I can sharpen them up and sell them as ninja stars or something.'

Admitting defeat after he hadn't receive a single letter from a child looking for a fidget spinner for Christmas, Santa loaded the lot up into his sleigh in late November and dumped them over the ocean, raising the sea-level by six feet around the world and causing massive agricultural upheaval and the homelessness of millions.

'Ho! Ho! Ho!' he was heard to say. 'Bye, you spinny bastards.'

'MMA is useless in a real fight,' claims aikido black belt

A Dublin-based aikido black belt today slammed mixed martial artists over their outrage that the Irish Martial Arts Commission (IMAC) described MMA as 'pornographic, sadistic and voyeuristic to its core' in official documents that surfaced from the organisation online.

Kevin Reilly, who has been practising aikido for 10 injury-free years, said UFC fighters and the likes have 'very little skill' and he could probably throw them around the place with one hand given the chance.

'These MMA lads are brain-dead thugs who couldn't beat their way out of a wet paper bag,' Reilly stated, while wearing very silly pants. 'Real martial artists, like me, use ancient techniques, handed down from grandmaster to grandmaster, over thousands of years. There is a tradition behind it that makes aikido one of the most revered martial arts in the world. MMA is useless in a real fight.'

'You'll never see an aikido master fighting in MMA as they would keep winning all the time. So it would just get boring.'

Demonstrating his technique, Reilly urged a fellow student to attack him, before stepping aside lightly and pushing him out of the way, forcing the attacker to do a somersault onto the floor, for no apparent reason whatsoever.

'Did you see that?' the 46-year-old asked, as if this should impress this reporter somehow. 'Did you see the way I used his own force against him? You won't see moves like that in MMA.'

Asked whether his opponent slipped or something, he replied, 'No, that was my chi power disabling him.'

Unsure of his point, or indeed his defensive strategy, I asked whether aikido could be put into practice against an MMA fighter who would be coming at him with a flurry of kicks and punches.

'If I'm honest, I could probably take on three or four MMA fighters at the one time,' Reilly concluded. 'They would just have to learn how to roll to the ground first.'

⊗ TOP 4
Weather reports in Ireland 2017

4   Nuala Carey - RTÉ *Six One News* - Thursday 11 May. The pressure was on, remember that bit of decent weather we had in May? Nuala had to calmly inform the nation it'd be pissing rain again from the next week. She delivered it with reassuring authority. Magisterial.

3   Jean Byrne - RTÉ *Nine O'Clock News* - Tuesday 21 February. An impossibly boring and run-of-the-mill weather report, but that's never the case in Jean's capable hands. It was like hearing a weather report for the very first time again. She's a dream weaver.

2   Deric Hartigan - TV3 *3News at 5.30* - Saturday 29 April. While TV3 is known for its picture segment of the weather, if you had told us we would be enchanted by 47 photos from Joanne in Castlebar's back garden on a misty morning we would have called you liars. Deric knows his way around a photo, and he created a story about sunflowers that could bring a tear to the eye.

1   Caitlín Nic Aoidh - TG4 *Nuacht* - Monday 10 July. Doing the weather live outside can always present a problem. However, Caitlín, ever the pro, remained calm when a tiger kidnapping unfolded in the background of her weather report from Galway. Caitlín could have called the guards and helped the family, but she knew delivering the weather was more important and informed us all of the balmly 12-degree sunshine we had awaiting us the next day.

Did you know?
90% of people's declarations that they will go for a run in 2017 proved to be overambitious.

Local man dusting off 'I played against Johnny Sexton' story ahead of Six Nations

A Dublin man is planning to dust off an old story about that one time he played opposite Johnny Sexton in a junior match just in time for the start of this year's Six Nations championship.

Conor 'Con' Kelleher will be giving his story an airing in a number of pubs in the Ballsbridge area of the capital in the coming weeks, but he also admitted that the story is in need of some serious renovations.

'I haven't told it since the November test series, so it needs a drop of oil applied to the narrative hinges, if you follow me. Might just practice it in front of the mirror before making it available to the public again,' shared the 31-year-old.

While details of the story are subject to change depending on the number of drinks Kelleher has consumed or whether he is in the presence of someone who knows he never made it off the bench when playing for his school, the core aspects of that fateful afternoon remain intact.

'He was ball-hogging, trying to run the game, but I set my sights on him and went through him for a shortcut,' Kelleher shared, painting a visceral picture of the time his school faced off against St Mary's 17 years ago.

'They say he changed his style after that. The big hit I gave him shook him that much. So he wouldn't be the player he is today if it wasn't for me,' added the former rugby player of the incident that almost certainly never took place.

Concerned that the story may not be compelling enough, Kelleher is open to adding a bit about bumping into Sexton recently only for the Irish international to say, 'God, I can still feel that tackle, Con; I never properly recovered from it.'

FOREIGN STUFF

Patriots achieve stunning victory in who honestly gives a fuck

MILLIONS of people across the world are waking up today to the stunning news that the New England Patriots were successful in their bid to win the ... oh Jesus like who even fucking cares, honestly?

Social media feeds and news channels are awash with articles and opinion pieces about the victory over the Atlanta Falcons in last night's Super Bowl, all seemingly operating under the impression that anyone outside America gives a shit about this kind of thing.

Praise has been heaped upon Patriots player Tom Brady, who is a man of some sort, and his amazing ability to mean so much to some people and so very little to more or less every other person on the planet.

Although some people have made attempts to get excited about the final scoreline of the game, which featured a great comeback by the Patriots apparently, the overall boring nature of American Football combined with the general dislike for America at the moment has led to record amounts of so-fucking-whats this morning.

'Even the Lady Gaga performance was a bit meh,' said one man we interviewed, before leaving it at that and moving on to something more interesting than American football, such as literally anything else at all.

Pogba hits back at critics with yet another world-class haircut

FRESH from renewed criticisms about his insipid and error-strewn performance against Liverpool at the weekend, Paul Pogba has silenced the doubters with yet another display of haircut prowess.

Despite viewers of the 1-1 draw pointing out how poor Pogba's performance was in yet another big game for his club, there was little they could criticise about what many people are calling 'a well dank do'.

A complete and detailed replica of Caravaggio's 'The Taking of Christ' has been painstakingly etched into the side of Pogba's head, replacing his bright green 'PP' haircut, which drew universal praise and admiration.

'The boy hasn't been at the club long, but when you think about the number of standout hairdos he's had – to be fair, no one can compete with that,' Sky Sports pundit Jamie Redknapp shared,

effusive in his praise for Pogba's ability to pick up new Twitter followers.

'He's gone up another level, hasn't he?' added Gary Neville, while bringing up a highlight reel of Pogba's best haircuts of the season so far. 'If we just slow this one down ... that's magic. You're talking about your Ronaldos, your Beckhams, your David Luizs, your Nainggolans – they just aren't on Pogba's level.'

Pogba remains a commanding presence on social media, and displays deft technique when it comes to remaining active on multiple accounts, drawing praise from football experts after a return of six goals and 16 haircuts so far this season.

'Each selfie of Paul dabbing translates into shirt sales and you can't ask more of your players,' Jamieson Reigle, commercial director at Manchester United, confirmed.

McGregor V. Mayweather: Read the expert opinion of this lad who fixes our printer

THE long-awaited clash between Floyd 'Money' Mayweather and 'The Notorious' Conor McGregor, which took place in Las Vegas on Saturday night, was one of the most important moments in the history of Ireland, according to the young lad with the neck tattoo who comes around and fixes our printer when there's a particularly bad paper jam.

'Conor boxed the head off him. Sure Mayweather was cheating and turning his back on Conor through the whole thing,' said Cian Tremmell, a UFC fan who admits that Saturday night was the first time he'd watched an actual boxing match.

Tremmell (22) went on to give us a blow-by-blow account of every round while he dug around in our Canon printer for a sheet of paper that had gotten snarled up in the gears, and emphatically stated how the fight had been stopped 'way too early' by the referee.

'Do these boxing referees not even watch UFC?' wondered Cian, while vaping inside even though we have signs up.

'Conor was still on his feet when the ref called it. Sure normally in UFC you get to throw a few extra digs when the fucker is on the ground, not when he's just lying against the ropes a bit. If you ask me, the whole thing was fixed in favour of Mayweather. Another round and Conor would have battered the shite out of him. Anyways, it was good craic watching it in the gaff with the lads and a load of cans, streaming on a laptop from some Turkish station with no English commentary. Up McGregor!'

BREAKING NEWS

DISTURBING news emerging online in recent hours seems to suggest that football pundit Eamon Dunphy is still being listened to, *WWN* can confirm.

'We are not in the business of stoking fear and panic, but it's looking like people are listening to things he says and then trying to critically engage with it,' Ronan Philips, Head of Ireland's There's Better Ways To Spend Your Time Unit, explained.

The most vulnerable subgroup of people said to be affected by being aurally subjected to the thoughts, musings and predictably half-hearted rants of Dunphy are regular watchers of football games.

'If exposed to his utterances, it may cause football viewers significant distress and confusion,' Philips explained.

Shocking report claims Eamon Dunphy still being listened to

'Owing to the fact that they actually watched the players and teams that Dunphy claims are legless cavemen with the footballing acumen of an upturned tortoise, they are left with rising blood pressure and steam coming out of their ears when they should have just switched off the radio or TV the second he started,' Philips advised.

Gardaí have yet to make an official statement, and it is not their practice to comment on ongoing investigations, but it is believed that RTÉ will be charged with crimes against football for allowing Dunphy access to the country's ears via RTÉ 2 and 2FM.

Most recently Dunphy, speaking using his mouth, claimed that both Manchester clubs were the worst thing to happen to anyone since the Holocaust, while also describing ice cream, puppies, happiness and newborn babies as 'overrated'.

Dublin man spends €54k on cauliflower ears to look like hero Conor McGregor

FOR Dublin man Jeremy Casey, UFC champion Conor McGregor is more than a hero, he's a way of life.

'He's just deadly he is,' Casey began. 'From the moment I set eyes on him, I knew I wanted to be just like Conor. His movements. His style. He is everything I want to be in life.'

Last week, the 36-year-old underwent a 17-hour operation to cosmetically change the appearance of his ears to match his idol.

'I'm glad I got them done now,' he explained, gently caressing the tender skin around his right ear. 'It's sore an' all, but I think the doctors did a great job on them. You wouldn't even notice that the skin is from me hole. These cauliflower ears are worth every penny.'

So far Jeremy's surgery has cost him €54,000 – money he inherited from an uncle who passed away last year.

'It was either get the ears done or start up me own security business,' said the long-term unemployed man. 'The ears are a good investment I think. I've already got interviews lined up with Joe.ie, Goss.ie, Benchwarmers and there's talk of appearing on Joe Duffy. I'm going to be fucking minted after this. There's big money in impersonating celebs, you know.'

It is understood Casey has also secured 43 likes on a picture post of his ears on Facebook and three shares.

'All I've got to do now is sit back and watch the TV offers flow in,' he concluded.

UFC

Dana White out of UFC 202 weigh-in after testing positive for performance enhancers

PRESIDENT of the UFC, Dana White, has suspended himself from appearing in Las Vegas this weekend after testing positive for performance-enhancing drugs.

White, who routinely pairs off contenders before fight night, is expected to miss the UFC 202: Diaz v. McGregor 2 weigh-in because traces of a banned substance were found in his system after he requested a surprise blood test on himself.

'I needed juice for this one. Separating fighters at the weigh-in isn't as easy as it looks,' he tweeted shortly after being pulled from Friday's weigh-in. 'You have to have the strength to be able to separate contenders with just two arms. People underestimate my purpose

at these events. I'm there to maintain order.'

The rather buff White hinted that he may have to call the whole event off as he is unable to think of anyone strong enough to fill his place, and intimated that the entire UFC sport could be in jeopardy as a result.

'There is no one I trust or who is powerful enough to stand between Conor and Nate this

Friday,' White tweeted again, this time with a picture of himself flexing in a mirror. 'What if Conor pushes Nate and all hell breaks loose? Who's going to stop it? I've let everybody down here, including myself and my muscles.'

This is the first time the UFC president has suspended himself for performance-enhancing drugs.

More as we get it.

Performance-enhancing hurls: GAA's secret shame

'LADS come in all the time looking for the ash to be laced with nandrolone, or even some cocaine. The hurls on cocaine are easy to spot on TV, they're the ones that strike out at lads after the players square up.'

Cillian Corcoran doesn't even hide it, brazenly selling hurls laced with performance-enhancing drugs at a local under sevens camogie match. *WWN* wishes this was the most unpalatable element of our recent investigation into performance-enhancing hurls, but sadly this epidemic has the GAA rotting to the core.

'Ah, quit your moaning, everyone is doing it boy,' one of the camogie player's fathers tells me as he hands over a crisp €500 note for just one hurl, said to be absolutely caked with PEDs.

'Some lads douse their hurls in protein shakes, the fucking eejits. It makes next to no difference,' Corcoran tells me from behind his impressive pitch-side stall of hurls for sale.

'Fellas will feel the hurl is lacking in some way and then they'll come to me to sort it out. The GAA is years behind in terms of testing for drugs in hurls so there's no fear of getting caught,' Corcoran explained, handing me what looked like a normal hurl.

'G'wan there and take her for a spin,' he encouraged, and before I knew what was what I had entered the field of play at the St Jude's v. Ballyfinn Finn Gaels under sevens camogie match. I absolutely slaughtered the field, scoring 7-7. Ignoring the fact I am an able-bodied 35-year-old man for a moment, the drugged-up hurl's contribution cannot be overstated. But what are the side-effects?

'Ah, now ash is a resistant wood. Don't you come round here peddling lies about it being bad for the wood now, for the hurls love it,' Corcoran spat at me, rising to an anger that was intimidating.

WWN pressed Corcoran to reveal the identities of the hurlers who came to him, seeking to give their hurls the advantage.

'Sure, I wouldn't know them from Adam. I couldn't pick them out in a police line-up even if I wanted to. Sure any time I see hurlers in action they've their helmets on.'

It's the perfect crime. Selling to men who take to the field in helmets, making them unrecognisable, leaves Corcoran free from the risk of implicating anyone should the gardaí come knocking on his door.

The GAA refused to provide comment for this story, but it seems that the presence of hurls on enough steroids to hit a point from 90 yards out is set to continue.

Local fan still hasn't a fucking clue what's going on in rugby

A passionate and rabid rugby fan, eagerly awaiting Ireland's clash with France in the Six Nations this Saturday, has admitted that, try as he might, he hasn't the faintest idea as to what is going on in rugby games.

'I shout "go on" a lot, which seems to disguise most of my lack of knowledge,' explained Dubliner Cormac Sheehan. 'Oh, and I go absolutely fuckin' nuts when one of our lads smashes someone in a tackle.'

Sheehan admitted to adopting a reactionary style to the action on pub TV screens, drawing on other people present in his local pub in an attempt to appear knowledgeable.

'When something is kicking off in the game, I keep an ear out for what the auld lads do be saying and I quickly sort of say the same thing just in a slightly different way, a few seconds later,' Sheehan added.

'I get this nod from a few of them as if to say "yeah buddy, you know your fucking rugby", but I've been at this 10 years and it's still a mystery to me. Like the offside is different to the offside in soccer, but I don't exactly know how,' the imposter confirmed.

Sheehan added that despite his lack of understanding of the most basic facets of the game, he was looking forward to relying on old and redundant stereotypes about French people when shouting during this weekend's match.

Brian Cody now part of Waterford after Ferrybank land grab

THE fallout from a decision to transfer 15,000 acres of Ferrybank land in Kilkenny to Waterford continues as it can now be reported that Brian Cody has become the property of County Waterford, *WWN* has learned.

At the time of the decision regarding the 15,000 acres being made official, Kilkenny senior hurling manager Brian Cody was travelling in his car in the Ferrybank area, thus the redrawing of the county boundary had the unintended consequence of transferring the medal-laden man to Waterford.

'He's ours now,' confirmed a spokesperson from Waterford, struggling to hide her broad smile. Cody was permitted to coach Kilkenny to a loss to Waterford in the Allianz Hurling League at the weekend, with a formal handing-over ceremony expected later this week.

The completely uncontroversial decision to transfer 15,000 acres and its 5,000 inhabitants to Waterford has been roundly praised by absolutely everyone, with Cody's move to the county just the latest good news story for all involved.

Waterford GAA officials denied orchestrating Cody's need to drive to Ferrybank at the very moment a decision was issued, confirming that it had nothing to do with an anonymous call to Cody from a man claiming to be Henry Shefflin who had expressed interest in returning to inter-county hurling on the condition that Cody immediately drive to Ferrybank.

'Look, we don't know what you're talking about, but now that he's here in Ferrybank, Waterford, we say why not pop down to hurling training, Brian, we'd love to have you,' added a member of the Waterford GAA.

TRENDING Idiot jockey-less horse thinks it won race

STEWARDS at Punchestown racecourse have labelled a jockey-less horse an 'idiot' today after it mistakenly thought it won the 3.45.

Swing Both Ways, trained by Ruby Mullins, spent several hours being debriefed by stablehands, who desperately tried to explain to the horse that it didn't actually win the race because it threw jockey Peter Roche off at fence two.

'Sure God love him, the poor eejit just kept on running like a little trooper,' the horse's minder Jeremy Power told *WWN*. 'Of course he passed the whole field, but little did he know he needs a jockey on his back to actually win the race.'

Swing Both Ways was seen prancing around after passing the finish line, embarrassing both the unseated rider and his trainer.

'It's heartbreaking to see the long face on him in the stable,' trainer Mullins explained. 'He finished a good 30 seconds before the rest of the pack, but he did also cut a few corners and skip a few fences along the way. He'll get the hang of it eventually – if not, it's curtains, one behind the ear, dog food.'

★ TOP 6
Most-used emojis in Ireland 2017

6 Peach (as a substitute for a bum)

5 Corn on the cob (as a substitute for a penis)

4 Breadstick (as a substitute for a penis)

3 Water (as a substitute for an ejaculate)

2 Courgette (as a substitute for a penis)

1 Winky face (sent after sending any of the above)

12 MONTHS A GUARD
Month 12

Have you ever gotten everything you ever wanted, only to realise that it isn't what you thought it would be? That's how I felt walking away from my graduation ceremony as a fully fledged member of An Garda Síochána. Last year I thought that I'd graduate, forgo any celebrations and head out immediately to clean this country up. Instead, I'm looking at 10 to 20 years of doing lads for going 65 in a 60 zone. But I still firmly believe that I'm doing good; the money I collect from booking people goes right back into the economy; it filters through the budget straight into the force, paying for better equipment, more guards, more vehicles, better training … well, after everyone at the top of the ladder takes their cut. Man, it's pretty sweet up there. Maybe I'll try and climb the ladder myself … although I wish I'd thought of it six months ago when the 'Shoulder-rubbing' and 'Knowing the right people' modules were signing people up! Ah, well, at least I'm a guard. I might not be sliding over the bonnets of cars like I thought I'd be doing when I was a child, but I'm still doing good. You people would miss me if I wasn't here. And if not, what the fuck do I care? Last night I got in free to a nightclub just by showing them my identification. Fucking nice one! Some lad on the door called me up on it so I took note of his nametag. I've a funny feeling his car will be found to be speeding later this week. LOL.

FOOTBALL

'Who do you think allowed women to play football in the first place?' defends FAI

'FIRST off, calm down love, we can't make out what you're saying with that shrill voice of yours. Secondly, we've yet to receive a thank you for letting you play football in the first place.'

The FAI was in a combative mood as it responded to low-born womenfolk and their claims that they are not being treated with even a pretence of respect by Irish football's governing body.

Ashen-faced and visibly upset, an FAI spokesman countered claims that the FAI could invest more money in the women's national team so that they no longer have to get changed in airport toilets before away matches and don't have to hand back tracksuits because they are being shared with underage teams.

'We're genuinely offended and heartbroken that these women have lost all perspective,' the spokesman said, his hands shaking as he read from a pre-prepared statement. 'We haven't even received a thank you for letting girls play a man's sport. Not a hint of gratitude. And we know you lot aren't known for your rational thinking, but take a breath and think of how much you've hurt us with your press conference nonsense yesterday.'

Several outrageous demands made by the women's team included having access to a nutritionist and a €300 match-day fee as well as compensation for loss of earnings for players who are away from work when representing Ireland.

'It's just sickening to think these girls have it in their heads that we have stacks of money to hand out. I really fear if pressure grows on us, we're going to have to get the money from somewhere, and it's a horrible thought that someone like John Delaney could possibly have to take a pay cut on his modest salary,' concluded the FAI spokesman, before adding, 'This is nothing only feminist financial terrorism.'

Irish tennis player disqualified from Wimbledon after using hurl

THE Irish tennis fraternity is in mourning this afternoon after news broke of World No. 1,239 Conor Creally's disqualification from Wimbledon after he resorted to smashing serves with a hurl, *WWN* can confirm.

There were bizarre scenes on court 16 as the Kilkenny tennis star battled against his opponent John Isner in a gruelling five-set match, which came to a sudden end when Creally produced a hurl and proceeded to play Isner off the court.

After breaking several rackets in frustration while screaming, 'Why are you so fuckin' shite?' Creally grew tired of using the unreliable but traditional striking apparatus of the game of tennis.

'Ah, I'm fairly shite now in fairness. Just never got used to the racket. I blast the tennis ball for fun, though, with a hurl. Sure you saw me absolutely bating him out of it. But the umpires just can't hack it. I'd be World No. 1 if they just relaxed the fucking rules,' an irritated Creally told *WWN* in the aftermath of his disqualification.

Creally had successfully served out the match in the final game, striking four aces with the aid of his trusted hurl. Once the umpire questioned what Creally was doing, the end of his tournament was brought about by disqualification.

'I just thought, "Say nothing" and I was all, like, "What are ya on about? 'Tis a tennis racket. Go away, you're seeing things. Don't worry about it." But I suppose when I served using a sliotar I really gave things away,' Creally conceded.

BREAKING NEWS

McGregor injures jaw in chewing-gum-related incident

THERE was fresh drama in the ongoing build up to the Conor McGregor–Floyd Mayweather faceoff today after the Irish UFC star was rushed to hospital with a suspected broken jaw, which sources confirm came from a chewing-gum-related incident during 'trash-talking training'.

McGregor, who has been spotted chewing huge wads of gum at high speeds during every pre-fight press conference so far, was admitted to hospital early yesterday morning before being released later in the day with his entire face in a sling.

Fight analysts have taken to social media to discuss the implications of this injury in the lead up to the August bout between the two fighters, with concerns mounting that McGregor may not be able to yell as many insults at Mayweather at the 27 press conferences yet to be held.

'Conor appears to have snapped his jaw during a trash-talk sparring session,' said the source. 'The gum is to ensure soft cushioning between insults, but something went wrong during his borderline-racist routine and he just fell to the ground in agony as he said, "Dance for me, boy", a phrase he has been practising for years.'

'Fight-wise he should be fine, but Dana White has been freaking out because McGregor won't be able to trash talk his way through the remaining press conferences, which is really what he was there to do to begin with.' The source concluded, 'There's no concern about his jaw when he actually faces Mayweather, as we expect it will be the first thing to get broken in the opening round anyway.'

The Undertaker struggles to find work in non-tombstone-piledriver-related jobs market

FORMER undertaker The Undertaker has admitted that he is finding it hard to hold down a steady job in the non-tombstone-piledriving, non-chokeslamming sector after leaving his high-profile position at the top of the wrestling world.

The Undertaker, who hung up his boots and bid an emotional farewell to the wrestling world at Sunday's Wrestlemania event, spoke exclusively to *WWN* about the difficulties faced by a 52-year-old man with limited experience in anything except being an occasional bike-gang member and full-time dead person who beats the crap out of scantily clad men on a frequent basis.

Following his retirement from wrestling, The Undertaker uploaded his CV to countless job websites and although he has had probationary periods as everything from a florist to a Zamboni driver, he has come up short at tasks and schedules that do not involve making people rest in peace.

'It's hard out there for a zombie biker high priest,' said Under, waiting to be called for an interview at his local Subway.

'It's like these places don't even take into account my 23-2 Wrestlemania win-loss record or my ability to lick the underside of my own chin. I'd like to find work that involves giving someone the odd tombstone, as I was always very good at that, but unfortunately it doesn't seem to be a very transferable skill.'

Meanwhile, wrestling fans around the world have stressed that if Mr Taker would like to come back to the WWE and fight for another few years, then they're perfectly okay with that.

IRON MAN

Tony Stark wins 50th consecutive Iron Man competition

FOLLOWING his 50th consecutive first-place finish, playboy Tony Stark was banned from competing in any further Iron Man competitions after athletes claimed that his biomechanical suits of armour give him an unfair advantage in the gruelling feat of endurance.

Consisting of a 2.4-mile swim, a 112-mile bicycle ride and a full marathon, an Iron Man race is usually undertaken by athletes at the absolute peak of human fitness.

However, renowned party-goer Stark, who sometimes moonlights as part of the world-saving combat troop the Avengers, has been described as being 'of average or below-par fitness' and instead uses his homemade single-pilot flight suits to zip around the course ahead of everyone else.

'I trained for years to take part in this race, and I come second to a lad watching Netflix in his helmet while his rocket boots do all the work,' moaned one wannabe-Iron Man we spoke to.

'How is that fair? It's enough to make you want to join Hydra, if I'm honest.'

Meanwhile, Captain America has come under fire for falsely claiming that he was robbed at gunpoint in an attempt to cover up the fact that he simply got drunk and smashed up his hotel room.

Local man still wearing flared jeans from 2004

A County Waterford man is still wearing a pair of faded blue jean flares he bought in 2004 like it's no one's fucking business, it has been revealed by friends and family members earlier today.

The jeans, which are frayed around the heel and prone to soaking up ground moisture on wet days, have been out of fashion for over a decade now despite owner James Power's lack of fucks given for that fact.

'He's been dressed like that as long as I've known him,' friend Tony Graham recalled. 'I think he sleeps with them on. And don't forget his runners, those awful skate shoe runners. He's caught in a time warp and doesn't seem to care.'

Now 38 years of age and working from home as an Apple technical support agent, Power admits his fashion style is 'a little behind', but he knows that life goes full circle and so his favourite cut of jeans will soon enough become *á la mode* again.

'The way I see it, flares became popular in the '70s, fizzled off for a couple of decades and came back into fashion again in the naughties,' he said. 'So if my calculations are correct, they'll be back in fashion again in another 10 to 15 years. And when that day comes, I'll be the coolest cat in town.'

'I wasn't a finger-up-my-hole-type of guy until I met my new girlfriend'

In the latest instalment of WWN's Voices series, we give a platform to someone we really shouldn't. Today is the turn of Dave Killeen, who was firmly against the firm placement of a finger up his bum until he met his new girlfriend.

LOVE makes us do crazy things. A finger up the bum, at just the right time, makes us do even crazier things. This is something I can attest to. Which is gas really, 'cause like, if you asked lads I went to school or college with they'd be like 'ah, no way is Dave a finger-bum combo man' and, you know, I would have agreed with them for the longest time.

Enter Clare. In a literal and figurative sense. Clare entered my heart with her gorgeous smile and easy-going charm long before she entered my anus with her finger, but looking back now, it was inevitable really.

I'd call it a yelp – the sound I make when she launches Operation Finger Insertion. I used to be more of a grunter when it came to the bedroom, but with Clare, I've no say in what sounds I utter.

It's a liberating feeling, and I'd encourage any stick-in-the-mud whose far too concerned with preserving his masculinity to embrace it and give the finger a go. I cried the first time Clare did it, not because it hurt, but because it unlocked something in me. Something long dormant. Something I had forgotten was present in me.

My head was wired a completely different way before I met Clare. My bum was strictly for number twos and the occasional machine-gun-like fire of farts, done for the sole purpose of my own amusement. But the more myself and Clare got to know one another, the more I realised my bum wasn't just for me. I was being selfish keeping it to myself.

It's been a whirlwind two months for us and there's still so much more to learn about one another. One thing I can say I know about Clare though is that with a few glasses of wine in her she will more than likely instinctively place an index or middle finger up my arsehole while we're getting down to business.

I can only hope other men are lucky enough to find a woman like Clare, who was brave enough, daring enough to guide me by her finger to a new plane of sexual pleasure. Men, women, humanity: be brave like Clare, dare like Clare.

Four hunting holidays to compensate for your incredibly small penis

SMALL penis? Erectile dysfunction? Craving some kind of alpha-male-type adventure to compensate? Well, we have got just the holiday for you. Every year, thousands of people spend large sums of money for arranged hunting packages in a bid to get back at life while also filling the deep-seated void within. Here are four of the best hunting holidays to compensate you for your horridly sized penis.

Fox hunting in Ireland

This is the perfect low-budget murderfest for those of you pussies who hate flying or spending too much money on your sadistic tendencies. Nothing says pencil-dick like following a bunch of half-starving dogs on a horse with a group of strangely dressed men and women sculling whiskey.

Spend the entire day prancing about over ditches while your entourage of psychos chases down a 14 kg wild dog, probably out searching for food for its cubs. Watch on with your half-erect penis as men with shovels dig out the frightened animal and brutally kill it in spectacular fashion. The best thing about this is that it's totally free and legal.

Blowing a giraffe's brains out

Giraffes are stupid with their big silly eyelashes and floppy necks, right? These animals don't even kill other animals. They eat sissy leaves and spend most of their waking time embracing one another like the Brady fucking Bunch. These animals deserve to be shot, even if it's just to see the stupid look on their face.

South African hunting tours range anywhere between $10,000 and $100,000 a head, which is cheap considering the absolute joy you'll get from cracking one off over a dead giraffe's body, you big strong alpha, you. Curl that fucker's head around, and take a picture of yourself standing on it like the hero you are. Post it on your social media channels, but don't make them public – you know how those animal rights hippies are.

Tusk hunting

This one is our favourite hunting holiday here at *WWN*. Mainly because it's illegal in most countries and we love a good challenge. Tusk hunting is popular in those parts of Africa that turn a blind eye to poaching animals for their horns, which, let's face it, is a good majority of the continent. Not only will tusk hunting give you a horn, you'll actually have your own horn to take away forever. The best thing about this trip though is the guns. They're fucking massive and the bullets leave a nice chunky hole in whatever you're shooting, whether it be an endangered elephant or a poor man's triceratops, the rhino. Although we found the rhinos a lot scarier and harder to shoot than the elephants.

Pokémon hunting

Sometimes a line is crossed in the hunting world and we here at *WWN* are not afraid to call a spade a spade. Pokémon hunting is one such thing we do not condone. How anyone can capture these cute innocent creatures is beyond us. You should be ashamed of yourself for even suggesting such a thing. Did you know that some Pokémon hunters are actually encouraging others to catch them all? What will the planet look like when the last Pokémon is captured? Unarousing to say the least.

Wonderful World of Science

Can a man covered in fur successfully pose as a lion? We simply don't know as the intern we sneaked into the lion enclosure at Dublin Zoo two months ago hasn't gotten back to us yet.

Tips for keeping yourself busy in rural Ireland if you're a young fella

LIVING in a virtual ghost town in rural Ireland can be tough if you're a so-called 'young fella'. How in God's name can you pass the time if there is nothing doing? *WWN* is on hand to help you wile away those hours until the rest of Irish society remembers they've completely forgotten you.

With youth unemployment in the country around 16%, we'll just skip ahead and rule out getting a job, because if there's none up in the big smoke for young fellas, there certainly won't be any going down the town. What to do?

Do one of them courses – you know the ones, they solve everything.

Government cut that course out your way? Have you considered developing a substance abuse problem like your da and his mates? If you're already well on your way, it may be an idea to start driving home from the pub; sure it's miles away and you can't be walking home in the dark – that's crazy unsafe.

Not a fan of the drink but love a good drive? Your prayers have been answered, there's loads of roads out your way and you can cover them all double-quick if you drive as fast as you can. Ask a mate along to see if he can keep up with you.

Do you have a strange feeling in the pit of your stomach that you can't quite explain? Have you presented yourself to your local GP and asked for help? If so, chances are the doctor has done all he/she can and you've been added to a waiting list for a specialist to see you in about five years.

But did you know there is a much easier option? Just start drinking more, and when you start feeling feelings, hit the nearest lad to you and keep hitting him until someone pulls you off him.

If punching faces isn't for you, there's loads of things around the place you could be smashing up instead. Don't be afraid to think outside the box.

EXCLUSIVE

Martin Luther King Jr's guide to spotting fake news

'I have a dream, that someday people on the Internet will be able to tell the difference between genuine current affairs and wild speculation/outright lies,' began Dr Martin Luther King Jr, speaking exclusively to *WWN* via a magical basin that allows people in our time to look into 1967 by just filling it with water and sticking their face in it.

Outraged at the volume of potentially harmful 'fake news' stories buzzing around on social media, the legendary civil rights figure gave a few key pointers that today's Internet users can employ to determine what is fact and what is made up.

'Take a long, hard look at what it is you're reading,' said King, speaking to the ghostly liquid-metalesque image of the *WWN* reporter who had appeared in his bedroom mirror out of nowhere.

'If it seems that the writer of the piece is trying too hard to push one side of the story instead of presenting both sides equally, then you're dealing with someone with an agenda. And a journalist with an agenda is never going to be impartial to both sides of the argument.'

Dr King paused to eat an entire pineapple, skin and all, before continuing with his lesson.

'Fake news is a powerful thing; it can be used to sway the public in a direction that they would not otherwise lean towards if they had the full facts of the matter.'

'There are people who stand to gain a great deal by clouding the facts and by making sure that news outlets play along with what they want to present as truth.'

'So, simply put, never blindly take anything you read from a media outlet as gospel. Use it as a starting-off point for your own research on the matter. Come to your own conclusions instead of the conclusion that someone else wants you to come to.'

Before we had a chance to tell him that 6:01 p.m. on 4 April 1968 would be a really good time to tie his shoelace, Dr King engaged his rocket-booster backpack and blasted out the window of his room, severing the time-travel link between our worlds.

Peek inside this amazing house you'll never be able to afford, you broke fuck

LOOK at you there, God love ya, scrolling down through your social network newsfeed after a long hard day at work, desperately trying to distract yourself from that spiralling debt and crippling anxiety that has been plaguing you since you left third-level education. What you need right now is some house porn to distract your mind and a nice daydream about winning money on the lottery to help fill that bottomless void in your optimistic little heart.

This south Dublin home, whose current owners are rich enough to advertise in this premium publication, is on the market for €975,000 and is way out of your price league, but you knew that already.

D4 Manor has got everything a young wealthy family could need, including: a tennis court for those couple of weeks in summer when Wimbledon is on; a heated swimming pool, which, let's be honest, you couldn't afford to heat even if you did manage to scrape together the money for the house; a cinema; multilevel parking; its

own Subway outlet; a fully fitted gym you'll never use; sparkling water fountains; and, of course, 97 acres of mature gardens that you'd probably let grow to shit now that we think about it.

For vendors, Sir Kevin Casey II and his wife, Theresa, the Duchess of Dundrum, it has been the perfect place for their five perfect children to grow up in. The couple insist that their now all-grown-up children are all professionals who are better than you. In fact, if you were to ring the intercom at the gate of D4 Manor, they'd look at their 4,000 security cameras and not even answer. So, yeah, lovely gaff, but ...

The two-storey-over-basement house is approached along a gravelled avenue, and leads right

up to ... seriously, do you even own a car? Like, you couldn't park any old banger outside this gaff; nothing less than the latest Merc will do. So, moving on ...

The grand drawing room overlooks the garden and has an elegant original fireplace and ornate plasterwork ceiling, a beautifully lit room to place all your utility and credit card bills ... before fucking them into the fire in the hope they all go away.

Why not hide out in the basement from the Provident loan guy, or just simply sulk on the balcony as bailiffs change the locks on the doors and wait for the gardaí to remove your weeping ass?

Sure it's nice to pretend, isn't it?

CAN swear words be improved by simply adding the word 'bag' to the end of them? This is a question no one has thought to answer. Until now. *WWN*'s investigative team pored minutes of research and work into finding out the answer for our dear readers. When given the chance to dedicate our enviable resources to something more important, we immediately declined. We had the greater good to consider. The astonishing results have huge implications for future swear word use in Ireland and beyond. Here are a few examples.

'What would you know, you massive dickbag?'
This one is all about intent and tone. In the wrong hands, it rates just 2 childish chuckles out of 5. Said by an elderly woman or a toddler, it's a solid 5 out of 5.

'I'm fucking sick of you, you fucking fuckbag.'
We rate this one 3 childish chuckles out of 5 and would consider using it again in the future. Best deployed when blindingly enraged by some complete fuckbag.

'Oh well if it isn't John, Waterford's resident bollockbag.'
This one is factual as a bollock does come in a bag of sorts, but it just leaves us cold for some reason, unlike a bollockbag itself, which helps keeps a testicle at the optimum temperature.

Despite it being a strict 0 childish chuckles out of 5, after further research we found a variant of the swear word earned at least a 3.

'Oh well if it isn't John, Waterford's chief practitioner of bollockbaggery.'
Extending bag to baggery breathes new life into the swear word.

Can swear words be improved by adding 'bag' to the end of them?

WWN INVESTIGATES

Although not strictly within the rules of adding 'bag' to swear words, we can't ignore its potent allure.

'Stop it Aisling, you're such a little bitchbag sometimes.'
Initially, it seemed like a no-brainer 5 childish chuckles out of 5. After our team used it repeatedly in conversation, however, it became clear that there is a huge risk that 'bitchbag' will be appropriated by middle-class teenage girls up in Dublin, the bitchbags, and could tragically become the next 'lol' or 'soz'. The risk is too great. Never use 'bitchbag' in public for fear it is a phrase that you could come to loathe immensely over a short period of time.

'Yeah, well, you tell that cuntbag I'll see him down the pub on Friday and we'll straighten things out then.'
Effortless. A joy that sits upon your lips before swan-diving off into a pool of aural satisfaction. It's the kind of swear word modification you dreamed of as a kid. Swear word perfection.

It was hard not to get emotional as the team worked round the clock shouting swear words at one another, after all we were witnessing a giant leap for swear word usage in the 21st century. Although our analysis requires peer review, the investigative team here at *WWN* is confident that yes, swear words are definitely improved with the addition of 'bag'.

Choosing bridesmaids who won't outshine you in photos

AMONGST the toughest tasks in life, next to giving birth and pretending to be interested in seeing photos from your elderly aunt's holiday in Greece, is choosing the right sort of bridesmaid. Someone who won't outshine you in your wedding photos.

How can you tactically ask someone to be your bridesmaid who you aren't all that great friends with but who is a lot less attractive than your Victoria's Secret model of a best friend? How can you avoid asking that stunning friend, whom you have known since the first day of junior infants, to be in your wedding party?

These are the hardest and most delicate operations any bride-to-be can become engaged in, and many women confess to failing in their attempts to ensure that they come out of their wedding day and wedding photos looking head and shoulders above everyone else.

WWN is on hand to provide you with all the essential information.

Wonderful World of Science

Has it gone too far? Again? How many times is that now?

Did you know?

100% of break-ups are caused by cheating pricks, isn't that right, Richard? ISN'T IT?

Preparation is key

Wait, you're not even engaged yet? In fact, you don't even have a boyfriend? Perfect. We've caught you at the ideal moment. Now is the time to put in the preparation for your wedding-day photos. If and when you meet a guy in a bar, or match someone on Tinder, you must begin the slow phasing out of your closest, your most loyal and best friend, in favour of bumping up someone who doesn't catch the eye to the position of your new BFF.

Pick horrible bridesmaid dresses

Obviously. This isn't fucking amateur hour.

Never warn your friend when she is in danger

Is she about to step out in front of oncoming traffic? Well, look, it could result in some horrible disfiguration for her, and that would be no bad thing for your photos.

Cull, cull, cull

If you are unfortunate enough to have several very attractive female friends, we feel your pain. You must act now and act fast. Repeat the phasing-out method with every single one of them. Decline brunch invites. Stop sending them GIFs of cats playing the piano. Be ruthless. This is your big hypothetical day and you can't have anyone outshining you.

Easy ways to get Irish people to love you if you're famous

ARE you famous and seeking to ingratiate yourself with the Irish people without putting in any effort? If so, you'll love this list! *WWN* has carefully compiled some easy and straightforward ways to get Irish people to irrationally worship you, mainly down to the fact you're already famous and are acknowledging the existence of our little-known island.

Wear a tricolour

If you have touched down on Irish soil and have a pressing business engagement, e.g. a concert, a press tour or are receiving one of the 43,000 honorary doctorates we hand out every week, simply make sure you are pictured with a tricolour draped around yourself. What's a tricolour? Don't worry about it. You are now loved unconditionally.

Say 'Hello Ireland'

Owing to our fragile sense of self and our struggle to simply believe in our abilities without first receiving praise from someone we perceive to be superior to ourselves, we Irish people will respond to the utterance 'Hello Ireland' with a wild and pathetic enthusiasm. Just be careful not to say 'I can't hear you' directly after Irish people respond – ceilings have collapsed in the past as a result.

Be pictured with a pint of Guinness

By doing so, you will become an honorary Irish person whose citizenship can never be revoked. Sadly, large numbers of citizens fail to comprehend that simply tasting a beer doesn't carry with it any great significance, but you're famous so don't worry about it. If you also sample a pack of Tayto crisps, there is an unwritten rule that all Irish people will now be willing to offer up to you any and all sexual favours.

Say something, anything, in bastardised Irish

'An mac maith grá Celtic is liomsa.' What the fuck did you just say? Don't worry, we don't know either, you absolute legend! We can barely contain our delight that someone from a big country, with a profile ranging from the highly prominent to someone once in an episode of *Home and Away*, was able to do that for little old us. We love you, famous person!

Say 'Fuck the Brits'

A classic line that some feel is losing its relevance here in Ireland. We have moved on since those days of nursing our post-colonial wounds, and yet this phrase is guaranteed to elicit such an enthusiastic response from Irish people that they will happily hand over their vital organs to you, no questions asked.

TRENDING
Suicide bomber's family totally called it ages ago

THE family of the young man who perpetrated a suicide-bomb attack that left dozens injured admitted yesterday that they saw it coming a mile away.

As is customary on such dreadful occasions, all eyes turned to the al Shaquairi family in the aftermath of their son Abdel's attack, seeking answers as to how they could have let their son commit such an awful act.

But whereas most families in this situation state that they had no idea how their son or other relative could have perpetrated such a heinous crime, the al Shaquairi family instead stated that 19-year-old Abdel 'had suicide bomber written all over him'.

'Ah yeah, he never stopped going on about how he was going to blow himself up and take as many people with him as he could,' said Abdel's dad, in a tone that sounded pretty sarcastic.

'Just like all young boys his age, he told his parents everything. And we just said yep, good man Abdel, you work away, just make sure you're careful.'

'So there you go, there's your story for your newspaper or whatever. I don't want to take up too much of your time, I'm sure you've got the parents of some kid who stole a car and killed a pedestrian, or one who stabbed someone outside a nightclub to interview. Ask them why they raised a monster. On you go.'

Can you be a feminist AND have a boyfriend?

WWN INVESTIGATES

IN the first of a new series we answer some questions from our readers. Today Sarah from Bray writes:

My friends are a bit feministy, and seem to have an issue with the fact I have a boyfriend, but I'm a feminist too. Can I be a feminist and have a boyfriend? Thanks, Sarah.

In today's brave new world of asserting yourself in the face of the patriarchy, it can be hard to determine if you can irrationally hate men AND date one of them.

For the unfamiliar, all feminists are required to hate all men without exception and showing any affection for a male can result in excommunication. But, on a purely ideological level, Feminazi Party rules aside, can you be a feminist AND have a boyfriend? Can you really want equality for all if you are in a healthy and functioning relationship with, of all things, a fucking man?

Sarah's friends would say it's a big fat NO, but they'd probably murder all men given half the chance. We pressed Sarah for more information in order to find a definitive answer and help her out of this quagmire.

I can't remember the last time he quoted some Simone de Beauvoir or Judith Butler to me.

Sure, he says he's all for equality, but your feminist friends don't allow for any half-assing it – it even says so in the handbook you received when you joined the Feminazi Party. But we'd say cut him some slack. Has he shared a *Broad City* GIF recently, or had a 4,000-word op-ed defending Lena Dunham published on TheJournal.ie? We're sure he's trying. I think we can chalk this one down as a rush to judge your boyfriend by your friends.

Shouldn't he strictly be called my manfriend? He's 27 for Christ's sake. After checking out his online habits, it seems he's calling you his 'side bitch' on 4chan, so boyfriend is fine.

He doesn't have the best fashion sense.

Bold black uniform with a red patch on his arm, he's just being fashion-forward, relax.

He's started learning German on Duolingo.

He has ambitions to better himself, and probably wants the same for you.

I'm not all that sure we share the same beliefs. He opened up a sham abortion advice clinic in the centre of Dublin, which tells women they'll go to hell if they have an abortion.

So? He's enterprising and set up a business. It's good that the two of you are driven. And hey, every couple has their minor disagreements.

He has a tattoo of Pepe the Frog on the tip of his penis.

Honestly, it sounds to us like your friends are just jealous they don't have a boyfriend, and fear becoming those old and embittered feminist types who criticise people (men) for no reason.

I caught him masturbating to a video of Milo Yiannopoulos.

Shit, okay …

He screams 'Heil Hitler!' when he climaxes.

Sarah, you've got a keeper and best of all your belief in equality for everyone isn't compromised in the slightest.

Only in Ireland! Things that happen absolutely every-fucking-where!

WE here at *WWN* Towers absolutely love Ireland. If Ireland was a food it'd be a food that everyone absolutely loves. If it was a TV show it would be one of those TV shows everyone agrees is very, very good. If it was any piece of pop culture ephemera it'd be the type that doesn't offend anyone and that would entice you to click. God, we ruddy love Ireland so we do!

And what would Ireland be without things that can make up lists? So, without further attempts to reach the minimum word count my editor has told me I have to ~~reach, here are some things that~~

In tractors! You just couldn't make it up. Granted Argentina, Canada, China, India, France, Brazil, UK, Australia and America to name but a few other countries dwarf us when it comes to agricultural output, but there's no way that between them their lads in tractors look as farmery and shit as our lads in tractors.. It's uniquely Irish.

A particular lad with a pint in a pub

Classic! Only. In. Ireland. Only in Ireland would there be a man named Danny Kelly, born on 5 July 1971, drinking a pint in The ~~Street right this moment~~

Ireland but don't fucking ruin this on me, seriously!

Words, phrases and experiences

Aw stop, that is too Irish! Where else would you find a broad array of things, places, activities and shared experiences that could be celebrated en masse by a nation other than in Ireland!

Bad things

Hang on, we said we wouldn't talk about this. And look, stop trying to fucking ruin this. There's loads of bad things that happen in Ireland that happen elsewhere, we're not unique in that respect.

Failure of all manner of societal structures to protect children

You've some neck bringing that up in a list that was supposed to be about good things.

Loads more bad things

Ah ye can fuck off now, you've ~~already tried to ruin my word~~

***** BREAKING NEWS *****

WE interrupt this book to bring you the unfortunate news that some country has launched a nuclear weapon. Probably because one country said something about another country, which forced some country to step in and act the Billy the Big Bollocks (no prizes for guessing which one). Phone your loved ones, hold them tight, tell them you love them or hate them, whichever works best for you.

Seriously. That's it. Strange way to go all the same. Some overweight man from some country fucking it up for the rest of us. Never even met the guy, but yeah, sound, blow us all up.

Remember, this is a print edition, so who knows how long you're reading this after the time the news officially broke, you could have next to no time left.

And no, don't ring the guy or girl you've always had a thing for but never said anything to. Where's that going to lead you? We're all about to get eviscerated by a nuclear holocaust, hardly the best time to try to get the ride. No, best just ring someone and tell them how much you hate them – that'll feel much better.

Sorry to be the bearer of bad news, but look it, if you didn't hear it from us, someone else was going to tell you the world was about to end. Don't shoot the messenger!